for AQA

Psychology A Level Year 1 and AS

Revision Guide

Mike Cardwell

Rachel Moody

OXFORD
UNIVERSITY PRESS

OXFORD
UNIVERSITY PRESS

Great Clarendon Street, Oxford, OX2 6DP, United Kingdom

Oxford University Press is a department of the University of Oxford. It furthers the University's objective of excellence in research, scholarship, and education by publishing worldwide. Oxford is a registered trade mark of Oxford University Press in the UK and in certain other countries

British Library Cataloguing in Publication Data
Data available

ISBN 978–019–844489–3

10 9 8 7 6 5 4 3 2 1

MIX
Paper from
responsible sources
FSC® C007785

Paper used in the production of this book is a natural, recyclable product made from wood grown in sustainable forests. The manufacturing process conforms to the environmental regulations of the country of origin.

Printed in Great Britain by Bell and Bain Ltd. Glasgow

Acknowledgements

Cover: Shutterstock

Artworks: Oscar at KJ Artists, Kamae Design

Photos: p9: PAUL ELLIS/Getty Images; **p29:** Ros Drinkwater/Alamy Stock Photo; **p45:** ZSSD/Minden Pictures/Getty Images; All other photos are from Shutterstock.

How to use this book

The Complete Companions for AQA Psychology Revision Guides offer you condensed versions of the bestselling Student Books by Mike Cardwell and Cara Flanagan along with the structured revision approach of Recap, Apply and Review to prepare you for exam success. Although this Revision Guide draws solely on the material in *The Complete Companions Year 1 Student Book*, it is a standalone resource and so will be invaluable for all students taking Papers 1 and 2 of the AQA AS and A Level Psychology exam.

RECAP Each 'Recap' section provides you with easy-to-digest bullets for the AO1 (description) you need to know for the exam. The material is stripped down to make it straightforward to revise from without sacrificing the detail necessary for full marks. This makes it easier to reproduce in an exam. The AO3 (evaluation) material is also condensed down to the right amount necessary for elaborated discussion/evaluation points in the exam. We have split each AO3 point into Point, Elaboration/Evidence and Conclusion/Link back format that makes each point clearer and more focused. The **AO3 PLUS** material on most spreads offers an extra AO3 point for those seeking the very highest grades.

APPLY These 'Apply it' sections give you some essential practice for the AO2 (application) questions for each topic area. On each topic spread we have provided you with a worked example of an application question relating to that topic as well as a second application question for you to try yourself. We also provide sample AO2 (research methods) questions in the context of each topic for you to try. You can then compare your own answers with the answers we have provided on pages 152—160. A unique feature of this book is the 'How do I answer… questions?'. We show you how to structure responses to all the most common forms of question you are likely to encounter in your exams.

REVIEW Throughout each chapter you can review and reflect on the work you have done, and find advice on how to further refresh your knowledge and prepare for your exams.

Issues/Debates
You will also find some 'Issues and Debates' points scattered through the book. You will find these examples useful when you eventually take Paper 3 of the AQA A Level Psychology exam.

Contents

| | RECAP | APPLY | REVIEW |

RECAP

AO1 Description

- **Compliance** is when individuals go along with the group to gain its approval or avoid disapproval.
  - > This does not result in any change in underlying attitudes, only in the views and behaviours that person expresses in public.
- **Internalisation** is when individuals go along with the group because of an acceptance of its views.
  - > This can lead to acceptance of the group's point of view both publicly *and* privately.
- **Identification** is when individuals accept influence because they want to be associated with the group.
  - > The individual accepts the views of the group as correct (internalisation), but does this to be accepted as a member of the group (compliance).
- **Normative social influence** occurs when individuals go along with the majority because of a desire to be liked rather than an acceptance of the majority's point of view.
  - > It is based on a need for social companionship and a fear of rejection.
  - > Individuals must believe their behaviour is being monitored by the group.
  - > They conform to the majority position in public but not in private.

- **Informational social influence** occurs when individuals accept the majority viewpoint because it is most likely to be right.
  - > If objective tests against reality are not possible, individuals rely on the opinions of others.
  - > More likely in ambiguous situations and where others are seen as experts.
  - > Individuals change their behaviour to fit in with the group position.

They must be right because they know more than I do

I should go along with them and I should change my attitude

I don't have to accept their views

I want to fit in and be liked

I suppose I could conform in action alone

It's ok. I'm complying, not internalising

AO3 Evaluation/Discussion

It is difficult to distinguish between compliance and internalisation…

The distinction between them is complicated because of difficulties in knowing when each is actually taking place.

If someone agrees with the majority view in public but disagrees with it in private it is assumed that they are showing compliance. However, it is possible that the group's views were originally internalised but the person has subsequently changed their mind after receiving new information.

This demonstrates the difficulty in determining what is, and what is not, simple compliance rather than internalisation.

Research supports the concept of normative influence…

Normative beliefs have an important role in shaping behaviours such as smoking and energy conservation.

Linkenbach and Perkins (2003) found that adolescents exposed to the message that the majority of their peers did not smoke were less likely to take up smoking themselves.

This supports the claim that people shape their behaviour out of a desire to fit in with their reference group.

Research supports the concept of informational influence…

Exposure to other people's beliefs and opinions can shape many aspects of social behaviour and beliefs.

Wittenbrink and Henley (1996) found that individuals exposed to a negative viewpoint (about African-Americans), represented as the view of the majority, later reported the same negative attitudes themselves.

This shows the importance of informational social influence in shaping our attitudes and behaviour.

Normative influence may not be detected…

It is possible that individuals do not recognise the behaviour of others as a causal factor in their own behaviour.

Nolan *et al.* (2008) found that people judged the behaviour of neighbours as having the least effect on their own energy conservation. However, results showed that this had the strongest effect.

This suggests that people rely on beliefs about what should motivate their behaviour and so under-detect the impact of normative influence.

AO3 PLUS

 APPLY: Exam skills

AO2: An example

SCENARIO Andy has just started his first job, working as a picker in a large distribution warehouse. He wants to do well so he can progress into management. He watches the other workers carefully, taking his cue from them in how he collects and delivers the goods to the transport bay. At one point in the morning a klaxon sounds and the other workers stop what they are doing and leave the building. Andy follows them without hesitation.

What type of conformity is Andy displaying and why does he conform to the behaviour of the other workers? **(3 marks)**

ANSWER *Andy is displaying internalisation. He conforms to the behaviour of the other workers because of informational social influence. Because he is new to the job, he accepts that the way the other workers behave must be the appropriate way of carrying out the role of picker. When the klaxon sounds, the situation is ambiguous so he follows the other workers because they are more 'expert' than he is.*

AO2: Research methods

A researcher was interested in the beneficial effects of normative influence. She arranged for Year 10 pupils at a comprehensive school in Southport to receive information that the majority of 14–18-year-olds in Southport did not smoke. A second school, with the same catchment area, did not receive this information so was used for comparison. Six months later the researcher returned to calculate the percentage of Year 10 pupils at each school that had taken up smoking.

a. **Identify the experimental design used in this study. (2 marks)**

b. **Briefly explain one advantage and one limitation of using this experimental design in this study. (2 marks + 2 marks)**

c. **Identify an appropriate sampling method that could have been used in this study and briefly explain why this would have been the best way of getting a representative sample from each school. (3 marks)**

AO2: One for you to try

Dave and his friends were walking home from school. One of his friends picked up a stone and threw it at the window of an abandoned building. Dave's other friends did exactly the same, and then all looked at Dave. He didn't want to throw a stone, but he thought that if he didn't his friends wouldn't let him walk home with them any more. He threw the stone.

What type of conformity was Dave displaying and why did he conform to the behaviour of his friends? (3 marks)

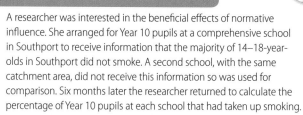 **How do I answer... selection (multiple choice) questions?**

Which **one** of the following is describing normative social influence? (1 mark)

A Going along with a majority because we believe them to be correct.

B Going along with a majority because we want to be accepted by them.

C Going along with a majority to because they offer an alternative point of view.

D Going along with a majority because we believe them to be experts.

Sometimes these questions require you to pick out the **one** statement that is correct, or that matches or defines a concept or idea. They may also ask you to pick out the **one** statement that is *false* or does *not* match or define a concept or idea.

Although these are generally worth only 1 mark, getting them correct is still important because that 1 mark can be the difference between one grade and another. So, some general advice on answering these:

- Read the question very carefully. Is it asking you to pick the statement that matches or the 'odd one out' that doesn't match?
- Cross out any that are obviously *not* going to be the correct answer given the specific demands of the question.
- Applying this to the question above we cross out **A** and **D** because they are about informational influence and **C** because that is describing minority influence being exposed to an alternative point of view. That leaves **B**, so that is the correct answer.

 REVIEW

Knowing what is and what is not compliance, internalisation and identification, and the difference between normative social influence and informational social influence, is vital for all the questions you are likely to face on this topic. There are a few things that you can do to help you with this.

1 Can you come up with a couple of *examples* for each of compliance, internalisation and identification?

2 Can you highlight the *differences* between compliance and internalisation, compliance and identification, internalisation and identification, normative and informational influence?

3 Try writing a few of your own selection (multiple choice) questions to consolidate this understanding.

Variables affecting conformity

AO1 Description

- **Group size** Asch (1956) found very little conformity with a majority of one or two, but above this, conformity rates rose to 30 per cent.
  - > Group size is more significant in the absence of an objectively correct answer and when the individual is concerned about fitting in.
  - > It is less significant when there *is* a correct response and the individual is concerned about being correct.
- **The unanimity of the majority** When a confederate (an individual who pretends to be a participant but who is actually working for the experimenter) gave correct answers, conformity rates dropped to 5.5 per cent.
  - > Even when a confederate went against the majority, giving a different wrong answer, conformity rates dropped to 9 per cent.
  - > This suggests that breaking the unanimity of the majority was the key factor in reducing conformity rates.
- **The difficulty of the task** When task difficulty was increased (smaller differences between line lengths), conformity levels also increased.
  - > The relationship between task difficulty and conformity is moderated by self-efficacy (confidence in one's own ability).
  - > In situations where individuals have high self-efficacy, they are more likely to remain independent, regardless of the difficulty of the task.

Asch (1956)

- **PROCEDURE** Individual participants were seated round a table with confederates and asked to judge lines of different lengths and match one of these to a 'standard' line.
  - > On 12 of 18 trials, confederates were instructed to give the same wrong answer. Asch was interested in whether real participants went along with (conformed with) the majority.
- **FINDINGS** On these 'critical' trials, the average conformity rate was 33 per cent. One quarter of participants never conformed and one in 20 conformed on all 12 critical trials.
  - > The majority of those who conformed admitted to only changing their public behaviour to avoid disapproval from other group members.

AO3 Evaluation/ Discussion

Asch's research may be a 'child of its time'...

Asch's findings may be unique because the study took place in a period of US history where conformity was more important.

Perrin and Spencer (1980) repeated Asch's study with UK students but obtained virtually no conformity. However, in a subsequent study, with youths on probation as participants and probation officers as confederates, they found similar levels of conformity found by Asch in the 1950s.

This confirmed that conformity is more likely if the perceived costs of not conforming are high, as with the McCarthy era (a period of widespread suspicion of alleged communist sympathisers in the US).

There are problems with determining the effect of group size...

Bond (2005) suggests a limitation of research in conformity is that studies have used only a limited range of majority sizes.

Bond points out that no studies other than Asch have used a majority size greater than nine, and the range of majority sizes used is much narrower, typically between two and four.

This, suggests Bond, means we know very little about the effect of larger majority sizes on conformity levels.

Asch's study showed independent behaviour rather than conformity...

In Asch's study, only one third of the critical trials produced a conforming response.

On two thirds of these trials the participants stuck to their original judgement despite being faced with an overwhelming majority expressing a totally different view.

Asch believed that, because participants tended to stick to what they believed to be correct, this was evidence of independent behaviour more than conformity.

There are cultural differences in conformity...

We are likely to find different levels of conformity depending on the culture in which a study takes place.

Smith *et al.* (2006) analysed the results of conformity studies across a number of different cultures. The average conformity rate for individualist cultures was about 25 per cent, whereas for collectivist cultures it was 37 per cent.

Markus and Kitayama (1991) suggest the reason that conformity rates are higher in collectivist cultures is because conforming is viewed more favourably in these cultures.

APPLY: Exam skills

AO2: An example

SCENARIO Sabrina has just finished studying conformity and would like to use what she has learned to demonstrate to her younger brother just how easy it is for people to go along with the crowd in group situations. Sabrina worries about him being too impressionable and feels this will be a valuable lesson for him. She wants to use an Asch-type task with a group of four friends who will act as the majority.

Using your knowledge of variables affecting conformity, explain how Sabrina could increase the likelihood of her brother conforming on the task. **(4 marks)**

ANSWER *Asch found that group size influenced conformity, therefore Sabrina's four friends would represent a suitable majority size to make conformity more likely. Unanimity is also important in determining conformity so Sabrina would have to brief her friends that on the trials where they gave the wrong answer, they must all give the same wrong answer. Finally, as Asch found that conformity levels were higher with difficult as opposed to easy tasks, she could make the size discrepancy between the comparison lines and the standard lines smaller, so her brother would be more likely to conform to the judgement of the majority.*

AO2: Research methods

Asch's research on the effects of group size on conformity was a laboratory experiment in that there was an independent variable and a dependent variable, participants were randomly allocated to the different conditions and it took place in an artificial environment with a high level of control (the laboratory).

a. **In this particular study, what would have been the independent and dependent variables? (2 marks)**

b. **Write an appropriate directional hypothesis for this particular study. (2 marks)**

Asch's results for this study are in the table below.

Number of confederates	1	2	3	4	6	7	9	15
Percentage of errors	3.6	13.6	31.8	35.1	35.2	37.1	35.1	31.2

c. **Draw an appropriate, fully labelled graph using this data. (4 marks)**

d. **What conclusion can you draw from this graph? (2 marks)**

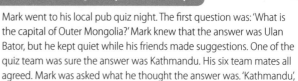

AO2: Two for you to try

Mark went to his local pub quiz night. The first question was: 'What is the capital of Outer Mongolia?' Mark knew that the answer was Ulan Bator, but he kept quiet while his friends made suggestions. One of the quiz team was sure the answer was Kathmandu. His six team mates all agreed. Mark was asked what he thought the answer was. 'Kathmandu', he replied.

a. **Explain Mark's behaviour in terms of one of the variables that affects conformity. (3 marks)**

Just as the team captain was about to write down the answer, a team member who had only just arrived said, 'Kathmandu? Are you mad, it's Ulan Bator!' The rest of the team said they had never heard of Ulan Bator. Mark said, 'He's right you know. You need to write down Ulan Bator.'

b. **Explain the change in Mark's behaviour in terms of one of the variables that affects conformity. (3 marks)**

How do I answer... description only (AO1) questions?

Q1: Briefly explain the effect of group size on conformity. **(2 marks)**

Q2: Explain how the unanimity of the majority affects conformity. **(3 marks)**

Q3: Briefly outline the effect of group size and task difficulty on conformity. **(4 marks)**

Q4: Outline the effect of task difficulty and the unanimity of the majority on conformity. **(6 marks)**

There is a fairly simple formula in answering description only questions. For 2 marks, say two things, for 3 marks say three things and so on.

Work through the sample questions above, using the following advice. The AO1 material for these questions is on the opposite page.

Q1: Use the first **two** 'Group size' points (Asch found very…, Group size is…).

Q2: Use all **three** 'The unanimity of the majority' points.

Q3: Use the first **two** 'Group size' points and the first **two** 'The difficulty of the task' points.

Q4: Use all **three** points for 'The difficulty of the task' and all **three** points for 'The unanimity of the majority'.

This approach adds an appropriate level of detail to each answer and gives the examiner a useful way of discriminating between your answer and one that would be worth fewer than the maximum marks for that question.

REVIEW

Being able to describe something concisely, while maintaining accuracy, is not as easy as it sounds. On the opposite page, we have stripped down the descriptive detail you will find in the main Student Book to give you some guidance about how to do just that. Let's play around with that content to make it a bit more familiar.

1 Try answering the four questions above using the advice given. How long did it take you and would you be able to reproduce this in exam conditions? (Note: you should be aiming for about one minute per mark.)

2 If the answer is 'no', then read over the material again and see how much you can reproduce just from memory.

3 Repeat Step 2 frequently over the coming weeks until the whole process becomes second nature.

Conformity to social roles

Stanford Prison Study (Haney, Banks and Zimbardo, 1973)

- **PROCEDURES** A mock prison was set up at Stanford University. Male students were randomly assigned to play the role of 'prisoner' or 'guard'.
  - > Prisoners wore a smock uniform and were assigned an ID number, by which they were referred to for the duration of the study.
  - > Guards were given uniforms, clubs and whistles and wore reflective sunglasses. The study was planned to last two weeks.
- **FINDINGS** The guards grew increasingly tyrannical and abusive towards the prisoners and made them carry out various degrading activities.
  - > Despite the fact that this was a study, prisoners and guards conformed to their roles, even when they were unaware of being watched.
  - > Five prisoners were released early because of their extreme reactions and the study was ended after six days following the intervention of Christina Maslach.

AOI Description

The BBC Prison Study (Reicher and Haslam, 2006)

- **Procedure** Male participants were randomly assigned to roles of guard or prisoner in a mock 'prison'.
  - > Participants were divided into groups of three, with each person closely matched with the other two. One was assigned the role of guard, the other two prisoners.
- **Findings** Participants did not conform to their assigned roles. Prisoners worked collectively to challenge the authority of the guards.
  - > Guards were reluctant to impose their authority on the prisoners, which led to a collapse of the prisoner-guard system.

Issues/Debates
Free will versus determinism. Reicher and Haslam argue that conformity to social roles is not automatic (i.e. determined) but is a matter of personal choice (i.e. free will).

AO3 Evaluation/Discussion

Conformity to roles is not automatic...

Haslam and Reicher (2012) challenged Zimbardo's belief that the guards' behaviour was simply a consequence of them embracing their role.	They pointed out that, although some of the guards behaved sadistically towards the prisoners, others were 'good guards' who did not degrade or harass the prisoners.	*They argue that this shows that the guards chose how to behave, rather than blindly conforming to their social role as suggested by Zimbardo.*

The study suffered from the problem of demand characteristics...

Banuazizi and Movahedi (1975) claimed that participants acted the way they did because they guessed how the researcher wanted them to behave.	They presented details of the study to a large sample of students. The vast majority guessed the true purpose of the study and predicted that guards would act in a hostile, domineering way and prisoners in a passive way.	*This suggests that the behaviour of Zimbardo's guards was less to do with conformity to social roles and more to do with the demand characteristics of the artificial situation.*

Zimbardo's study could still be regarded as unethical...

Despite the fact that Zimbardo followed the Stanford University ethical guidelines, it is clear participants still suffered distress.	Zimbardo acknowledged that the study should have been stopped even earlier. However, debriefing sessions over several years found no lasting negative effects due to participation.	*Reicher and Haslam reacted to this issue, and took greater steps to minimise any potential harm for their participants. As a result, the BBC study was testing, but not harmful.*

The Stanford prison study can help explain events at Abu Ghraib...

Zimbardo argues that the conformity to social role effect can explain the abuse of Iraqi prisoners by US military personnel at Abu Ghraib prison in Iraq.	Zimbardo believes that the guards who committed these abuses were victims of situational factors that were present in his study and at Abu Ghraib. These included lack of training or accountability to higher authority.	*He concludes that these factors, combined with an opportunity to misuse the power associated with their role, led the guards to abuse their prisoners in both situations.*

AO3 PLUS

APPLY: Exam skills

AO2: An example

SCENARIO Rob's dad has just come back from a business meeting in Scotland. He flew there and back and is complaining about how he was treated during the security screening at his local airport. He describes the staff as 'rude' and 'power crazed' and wonders if they only employ rude and aggressive people.

Using your knowledge of research into conformity to social roles, explain why the security staff might be behaving in the way described by Rob's dad. **(3 marks)**

ANSWER *Zimbardo's Stanford prison study found that male student volunteers quickly conformed to the role they associated with a prison guard. As they settled into their role the guards grew increasingly tyrannical and abusive towards the prisoners. Therefore it is possible that the people employed on security at the airport might have done the same, which would explain the 'rude and aggressive' behaviour shown by the security staff.*

AO2: Research methods

Researchers wanted to see if awareness of what happened in Zimbardo's study would change the way prison officers treated prisoners in British prisons. The researchers showed a film of Zimbardo's study to six newly qualified prison officers. A second group of six were shown a documentary on the history of the prison service. They were then placed in two different prisons where CCTV recorded their interactions with prisoners over the next month.

a. **What was the aim of this study? (2 marks)**

b. **Write a non-directional hypothesis for this study. (2 marks)**

c. **Identify the IV and DV in this study. (2 marks)**

d. **Identify one possible extraneous variable in this study. Explain how this extraneous variable could have affected the results of the study. (1 mark + 3 marks)**

REVIEW

On this spread we have concentrated on a special type of conformity: conformity to social roles. In order to feel comfortable with this topic you should practise using the material in all the different ways that might be assessed in your exam.

1 Try constructing 3-mark, 4- mark and 6-mark descriptions of Zimbardo's study.

2 Using the material on this spread, write an essay plan showing how you might answer 8- mark, 10- mark and 16-mark extended writing questions.

3 Write out one of these AO3 points onto a card and carry it round with you for the day, reading it several times during the day. Test yourself until you feel confident that you can explain it to someone else in an appropriate amount of detail.

4 Once you have given this treatment to all four AO3 points, write down just the headings for these four points. Get someone to test you – can you remember the expansion for each of these points in an appropriate amount of detail?

AO2: One for you to try

Mike successfully applied for a job at Liverpool's Anfield football stadium. His job was to ensure that people watching the game were safe and well behaved. On his first match day, Mike was stewarding the supporters in the Kop end of the ground. He was given a bright orange high-visibility jacket with 'LFC Steward' on the back. Because it was a hot sunny day, Mike wore his 'Aviator' sunglasses. Five minutes into the game, a young boy in the front row stood up and shouted at one of the players. Mike shouted at the boy to sit down. From that point on, every time the boy stood up or shouted, Mike told him off. The boy spent the second half of the match sitting very quietly, avoiding eye contact with Mike.

Explain Mike's behaviour and the boy's behaviour in terms of conformity to social roles. (4 marks)

How do I answer... application (AO2) questions?

Let's look again at the scenario of Mike in **AO2: One for you to try** above.

One way of answering questions such as this is to remember the 'Say one thing for 1 mark' and 'Say four things for 4 marks' strategy.

1 **Find a bit of appropriate psychology** (e.g. 'Zimbardo's prison study found that prisoners and guards conformed to their social roles, even when they were unaware of being watched.').

2 **Use this to explain some aspect of the scenario** (e.g. 'Mike was behaving in an authoritarian way towards the boy because he believed his role at Anfield gave him power over members of the crowd. The boy did as he was told because he too was conforming to a role of crowd member.').

3 **Find a second bit of psychology** (e.g. 'Zimbardo's guards wore reflective sunglasses to make them more anonymous. Other research has shown that people are more likely to behave aggressively under conditions of anonymity.').

4 **Use this to explain the scenario** (e.g. 'Because Mike was wearing his 'aviator' sunglasses, this increased his feeling of anonymity, and so made him less concerned about personal evaluation of his actions in shouting at the boy.').

Situational variables affecting obedience

AO1 Description

Situational factors in obedience

- **Proximity** With the learner in the same room, levels of obedience dropped to 40 per cent.
  - > When the teacher had to force the learner's hand onto a shock plate (touch proximity condition), levels dropped further to 30 per cent.
  - > When the authority figure left the room (experimenter absent condition), obedience levels dropped to just 21 per cent.
- **Location** Because the studies were conducted at Yale University, participants reported that this gave them confidence in the integrity of the study.
  - > As a result, this made them more likely to obey.
  - > When the study was moved to run-down offices with no affiliation to Yale, obedience levels dropped to 48 per cent.
- **The power of uniform** Uniforms influence obedience because they are easily recognisable and convey power and authority.
  - > Bushman (1988) found people were more likely to obey a researcher in a police-style uniform than dressed as a business executive.

Milgram (1963)

- **PROCEDURE** The study involved a series of different conditions, each varying some aspect of the situation. Participants always acted as the 'teacher' while a confederate acted as 'learner'.
  - > The teacher tested the learner's ability to remember word pairs, administering (bogus) shocks for any errors. These increased in 15-volt increments.
  - > In the 'voice-feedback' condition, the learner was in another room and stopped responding at 315 volts. The experimenter used 'prods' to try and keep the teacher delivering the shocks.
- **FINDINGS** Milgram asked various groups to predict how far participants would go before refusing to continue. Predictions were that very few would go beyond 150 volts.
  - > However, all participants went to at least 300 volts with only 12.5 per cent stopping there.
  - > Contrary to predictions, 65 per cent delivered the maximum shock level at 450 volts.

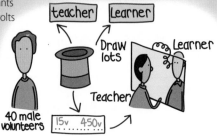

AO3 Evaluation/Discussion

Milgram's study

Milgram's study suffered from a lack of realism...

Orne and Holland (1968) claimed that participants have learned to distrust experimenters as the real purpose of a study is often disguised.	Perry (2012) discovered that many of Milgram's participants were skeptical about whether the shocks were real. Those who believed the shocks *were* real were less likely to obey the experimenter.	*This challenges the validity of Milgram's study, suggesting that in real life people would be more likely to disobey a destructive authority figure.*

Milgram's study has been found to have historical validity...

This study might be dismissed as having no relevance to modern life because it was carried out over 50 years ago.	However, Blass (1999), in an analysis of obedience studies carried out between 1961 and 1985, found no relationship between the year of publication and levels of obedience.	*This suggests that Milgram's studies are still as relevant today as they were in the 1960s, i.e. they have 'historical validity'.*

Situational variables

Proximity: Increasing proximity does not always lead to decreased obedience...

Mandel (1998) claims that Milgram's findings about the influence of proximity on obedience are not borne out by real-life events.	A study of Reserve Police Battalion 101 found that close physical proximity to their Jewish victims did not make these men less obedient.	*Mandel concludes that using 'obedience' as an explanation for these atrocities masks the real reasons behind such behaviours.*

Location: High levels of obedience were not surprising...

Fromm (1973) claims that as Milgram's participants knew they were part of a scientific experiment, this made them more likely to obey.	Because the experimenter represents a prestigious institution (science), and the experimenter is a representative of science, Fromm suggests that the 65 per cent obedience was less surprising than the 35 per cent disobedience.	*As a result, we should not generalise from Milgram's laboratory to events such as the behaviour of perpetrators in genocides such as the Holocaust.*

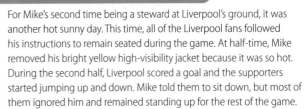

APPLY: Exam skills

AO2: An example

SCENARIO Zak has recently moved from a prestigious public school to a local comprehensive. In his public school, he was taught in small classes, so there was much more one-to-one contact with the teacher. In the comprehensive the classes are much larger, with very little one-to-one contact. His former teachers wore academic gowns; his new teachers dress more casually. Zak doesn't feel the same need to do as he is told in the new school, and for the first time in his school life he is in trouble for discipline problems.

Use your knowledge of the situational factors involved in obedience to explain why Zak is less obedient in his new school. **(4 marks)**

ANSWER *Milgram obtained higher rates of obedience within the prestigious setting of Yale University compared to the less prestigious setting in Bridgport. This would explain why Zak does not feel the same need to obey in his new comprehensive school, which is less prestigious than his former public school. Research has shown that obedience rates are high when the authority is in uniform. In Zak's former school the teachers wore the 'uniform' of academic robes whereas in his new school the teachers are more casually dressed, so that is why Zak is less obedient in his new school.*

AO2: Research methods

The graph below shows findings from Milgram's study.

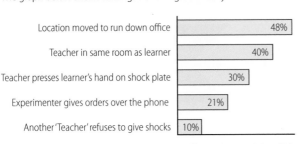

Location moved to run down office	48%
Teacher in same room as learner	40%
Teacher presses learner's hand on shock plate	30%
Experimenter gives orders over the phone	21%
Another 'Teacher' refuses to give shocks	10%

% of participants giving 450v

State two findings and for each one draw a conclusion (state what the finding shows).

Finding 1:

Conclusion 1: This shows that…

Finding 2:

Conclusion 2: This shows that…

AO2: One for you to try

For Mike's second time being a steward at Liverpool's ground, it was another hot sunny day. This time, all of the Liverpool fans followed his instructions to remain seated during the game. At half-time, Mike removed his bright yellow high-visibility jacket because it was so hot. During the second half, Liverpool scored a goal and the supporters started jumping up and down. Mike told them to sit down, but most of them ignored him and remained standing up for the rest of the game.

In terms of research into situational variables affecting obedience, explain the Liverpool fans' behaviour. (3 marks)

How do I answer... description and evaluation (AO1 + AO3) questions?

Q1: Briefly outline and evaluate the influence of proximity in obedience to authority. (4 marks)

Q2: Outline and evaluate the power of uniform in obedience to authority. (6 marks)

Q3: Outline and discuss Milgram's study of obedience to authority. (6 marks)

- **Step 1** in answering these mixed AO1 + AO3 questions is recognising that this is actually what you are being asked to do! Having two different command words, e.g. 'Outline' (an AO1 term) and 'Evaluate' (an AO3 term) is usually a good clue.
- **Step 2** is planning how much you should write for each. In mixed AO1 + AO3 questions up to 6 marks, the division is half and half (it is different with mark totals higher than this as we will see on p.17).
- **Step 3** is deciding *what* to write. If you have followed the advice in the previous spreads, this should be easy to work out. For **Q1**, this would mean using all the AO1 material associated with proximity on the opposite page.
- Although 'Discuss' is more commonly used to indicate that both AO1 *and* AO3 are required, in **Q3** it is being used just as an AO3 term. You have a number of ways to answer this, but there should be about 75–90 words of AO1 and 75–90 words of AO3. You should pick the three AO1 points about Milgram's study that you think best serve to 'outline' it. These could be the first two points from **Procedure** and the last one from **Findings**, or the first one from **Procedure** and the last two from **Findings** or even all three from **Findings**. For the AO3 content you might use one complete AO3 point from **Milgram's study** opposite, or the first two columns from both of the AO3 points for this study.

REVIEW

You should be ready to address different aspects of this topic in an exam. You could try making a list of things that could be assessed in exam questions on 'obedience'. When you feel you have mastered an individual topic, you have earned a tick in the **Got it!** column. This list might include:

TOPIC	Got it!		Got it!
The procedure of Milgram's study (A01)		Outline of the role of uniform in obedience (A01)	
The findings of Milgram's study (A01)		One evaluative point about location and obedience (A03)	

Agentic state and legitimacy of authority

 **RECAP**

AO1 Description

The agentic state

- In this state, a person does not see themselves as responsible for their actions, but attributes responsibility to someone else, particularly an authority figure.

- Under certain circumstances, a person may shift from an autonomous state, where they feel responsible for their own actions, to an agentic state.

- One explanation is the need to maintain a positive self-image. By shifting responsibility onto the authority figure, the person does not feel guilty about their actions.

- When in the agentic state, the individual is kept in it by 'binding factors', e.g. the fear of appearing rude by refusing to obey the authority figure's commands.

Legitimacy of authority

- The power of a legitimate authority figure stems from their perceived position in a social situation rather than any personal characteristics.

- In Milgram's experiment, participants had the expectation that someone 'would be in charge', and the experimenter fulfilled this expectation by having an 'air of authority'.

- People tend to accept definitions of a situation that are provided by a legitimate authority figure. In Milgram's experiment, participants unquestioningly accepted the experimenter's reassurances about the learner.

- For an authority to be perceived as legitimate, they must represent a respected institution. This was the case because the experimenter was in a scientific laboratory within a prestigious university.

AO3 Evaluation/Discussion

The agentic state

The agentic state explanation does not explain real-life obedience…

Lifton (1986) argues that Milgram's claim that people shift back and forth between an autonomous and agentic state does not explain the behaviour of German doctors at Auschwitz.	These doctors changed gradually and irreversibly from medical professionals concerned with the welfare of patients into people capable of horrific experiments on prisoners.	*Staub (1989) suggested it was the experience of carrying out these actions over a long time that changed the way doctors thought and behaved rather than agentic shift.*

Milgram's obedient participants might just have been cruel…

Milgram did concede that there could be other possibilities that would explain participants' behaviour.	The possibility that obedient participants used the situation to satisfy sadistic impulses was given substance by Zimbardo's finding that guards were willing to inflict cruelty on prisoners without being ordered to do so.	*This suggests that, although obedience may be due to being in an agentic state for some people, for others it is the desire to inflict harm on another person.*

Legitimacy of authority

The legitimate authority explanation can account for some acts of destructive obedience…

Despite having many positive consequences, legitimacy of authority can also serve as a justification for causing harm to others.	If people are willing to let authority figures make judgements about what is acceptable conduct, then they no longer feel their own moral values are relevant to how they behave.	*A consequence of this is that people may readily engage in unquestioning obedience to authority, no matter how destructive or immoral these actions.*

Obedience in the cockpit provides a test of the legitimate authority explanation…

AO3 PLUS

Tarnow (2000) provided support for the importance of obedience to legitimate authority in a study of aviation accidents.	As with Milgram's study, Tarnow found that excessive dependence on the captain's authority ('lack of monitoring' errors) was a contributory factor in a large proportion of the accidents investigated.	*This provides a real-life demonstration of the power of legitimate authority figures to enforce obedience in those around them.*

You sure this is right?

Yes, it's fine

APPLY: Exam skills

AO2: An example

SCENARIO Whilst watching a TV news broadcast about UK airstrikes against Syria, Myles wondered what enables a pilot to release missiles and bombs in the knowledge that they cause such devastation to humans. He doesn't think he could obey such an order. Jean, his mother, who teaches psychology, explains about the agentic state and the legitimacy of authority, and why these would contribute to the pilot's decision.

Describe how Jean would explain the pilot's obedience using the agentic state and legitimate authority explanations. **(6 marks)**

ANSWER As the pilot has received orders from someone else in the chain of command, he is in an agentic state. His actions are therefore virtually guilt-free, however harmful the consequences. Refusing to follow his commands would mean the pilot would be breaking the commitment that he made when he joined the British Armed Services Force, i.e. to do his duty. For a person to shift to the agentic state they must perceive the orders as coming from a legitimate authority. In this case it would be his commanding officer who fulfils that role and who has given the orders to fire. If an authority figure's commands are of a potentially harmful or destructive form, as would be the case when dropping bombs, then for them to be perceived as legitimate they must occur within some sort of institutional structure (i.e. the British Armed Forces).

How do I answer... evaluation (AO3) questions?

Evaluation questions come in all sorts of shapes and sizes. Terms like 'Evaluate', 'Discuss', 'Explain', 'Criticism', 'Strength' and 'Limitation' all indicate that AO3 is required. Some examples are below.

These questions differ not just in terms of the content they require, but also the amount of elaboration necessary for the marks on offer.

To make it easier for you to answer this type of question, we have split up our AO3 points into discrete 'chunks'. Putting these 'chunks' together to match the marks available should be a straightforward task.

Q1: Give one limitation of the agentic state explanation of obedience. **(2 marks)**

Q2: Briefly evaluate the legitimacy of authority explanation of obedience. **(3 marks)**

Q3: Evaluate the agentic state explanation of obedience. **(4 marks)**

Q4: Evaluate the agentic state and legitimacy of authority explanations of obedience. **(6 marks)**

Q1: Use the lead-in phrase plus material from the first two columns of **one** AO3 point on the agentic state explanation. Alternatively you could produce a summary of all three columns, aiming for around 50 words or so.

Q2: Use **one** complete AO3 point on the legitimacy of authority explanation.

Q3: Use the first two columns of **both** the AO3 points for the agentic state explanation.

Q4: Choose **one** AO3 point for the agentic state explanation and **one** for the legitimacy of authority explanation.

AO2: One for you to try

Susan, the head of sixth form, was told by the head teacher to announce to the sixth form that they would have to wear uniform starting next term. Susan made the announcement at the next assembly. The students booed and hissed when Susan gave them the news. 'Don't blame me, I'm only the messenger,' she said.

Explain Susan's reaction in terms of Milgram's agentic state theory. (4 marks)

AO2: Research methods

The table below lists the main methods that might be used to select participants for a hypothetical obedience study.

Underneath the table are descriptions of these sampling methods. Place the letters A–D next to the sampling method that matches the description. Finally, give a strength and a limitation of each of the four sampling methods in the table.

Hint: Questions that ask you to do this tend to be worth 2 marks each, so a little elaboration of each would push them up to 2 marks' worth. One way of doing this would be to link to the sample material, showing why the use of that particular sampling method would be a strength or limitation in *this* study.

Sampling method	Matching description	Strength	Limitation
Volunteer			
Random			
Systematic			
Stratified			

A Participants for an obedience study are selected by using computer-generated numbers to pick 20 names from a list of students enrolled on a social psychology course.

B As females make up the majority of the 100 students (70%) taking the social psychology course, the researcher selects 14 females and 6 males for his sample.

C A colleague suggests that the best way to get his sample of 20 participants is simply to get the computer to select every fifth student on the course.

D The researcher decides that might be a little problematic, so instead he advertises for participants by putting a notice on the department noticeboard.

REVIEW

To enhance your practical expertise in questions on this topic over and above selecting material to answer AO3 questions and completing the research methods exercise above, there are a couple of other useful things you can do, including:

1 Write 2-, 3-, 4- and 5-mark descriptions of the agentic state explanation and the legitimacy of authority explanation.

2 Using the format of bullet-pointed material (for AO1) and AO3 points, write a plan for a 12-mark and a 16-mark essay question, 'Discuss the agentic state and legitimacy of authority explanations of obedience'.

The Authoritarian Personality

 **RECAP**

A01 Description

The Authoritarian Personality

- The identification of a specific Authoritarian Personality type provides a possible explanation as to why some individuals require very little pressure in order to obey.
- Adorno *et al.* (1950) developed the F scale to measure the different components that made up the Authoritarian Personality.
- Agreeing with statements on this scale such as 'Obedience and respect for authority are the most important virtues children should learn' was indicative of an Authoritarian Personality.
- Adorno *et al.* found that people who scored high on the F scale tended to have grown up in a particularly authoritarian family with a strong emphasis on obedience.
- Altemeyer (1981) refined the concept of the Authoritarian Personality by identifying a cluster of three of the original personality variables that he referred to as right-wing authoritarianism (RWA).
- High RWA individuals possess these personality characteristics (conventionalism, authoritarian aggression and authoritarian submission) that predispose them to obedience.

Elms and Milgram (1966)

- **PROCEDURE** A follow-up study using 20 'obedient' and 20 'disobedient' participants from Milgram's study.
    - > Each participant completed a personality scale (the Minnesota Multiphasic Personality Inventory or MMPI) and the authoritarianism scale (F scale).
    - > They were also asked questions about their upbringing and their attitude to the experimenter and the learner in Milgram's study.
- **FINDINGS** Little difference between obedient and disobedient participants on MMPI scores.
    - > Higher levels of authoritarianism among obedient participants than disobedient participants.
    - > Obedient participants reported being less close to their fathers during childhood and saw the authority figure as more admirable than the learner.

A03 Evaluation / Discussion

There is research evidence for the authoritarianism/obedience link…

Although several studies have found that authoritarian participants are more obedient, there has been considerable suspicion about whether participants really believed they were giving electric shocks.	Dambrun and Vatiné (2010) used an 'immersive virtual environment', yet participants still responded as if the situation was real, with a significant correlation between RWA scores and the maximum voltage shock level.	As participants who displayed higher levels of RWA were the ones who obeyed the most, this confirms the link between authoritarianism and obedience.

The social context is more important…

Milgram did not believe that the evidence for a dispositional basis to obedience was particularly strong.	Milgram showed that variations in the social context of the study (e.g. proximity of the victim) were the primary cause of differences in participants' levels of obedience, not variations in personality.	Relying on an explanation of obedience based purely on authoritarianism lacks the flexibility to account for these variations (Milgram, 1974).

> **Issues/Debates**
> Nature versus nurture. Milgram claimed that the social context (nurture) was more important than personality (nature) in determining obedience.

There are differences between authoritarian and obedient participants…

Elms and Milgram's research found important differences in the characteristics of the Authoritarian Personality and the characteristics of obedient participants.	For example, obedient participants reported having a good relationship with their parents, rather than having grown up in the overly strict family environment associated with the Authoritarian Personality.	Given the large number of participants who were fully obedient in Milgram's study, it is implausible that the majority would have grown up in a harsh parental environment.

Any causal relationship between authoritarianism and obedience may be more illusory than real…

Research suggests that education may determine both authoritarianism *and* obedience.	Research (e.g. Middendorp and Meloen, 1990) has found that less-educated people are consistently more authoritarian than the well educated. Milgram also found that participants with lower levels of education tended to be more obedient than those with higher levels.	This suggests that instead of authoritarianism causing obedience, lack of education could be responsible for both authoritarianism and obedience.

A03 PLUS

APPLY: Exam skills

AO2: An example

SCENARIO

Having recently moved to the UK from a country where absolute obedience was demanded by the ruling regime, Amer and Raghda are concerned that their children should not grow up to be overly obedient. After reading about the Authoritarian Personality, they try to ensure that this does not develop in their own children.

Suggest two changes Amer and Raghda might make to their approach to child-rearing that would reduce the chance of their children developing an Authoritarian Personality. **(2 marks)**

ANSWER

As the Authoritarian Personality is associated with an authoritarian parenting style, Amer and Raghda could adopt a more child-centred style. Children acquire an Authoritarian Personality through learning and imitation, so Amer and Raghda must make sure they do not model uncritical obedience in their own behaviour.

AO2: Research methods

A student asked 24 members of her class to complete two questionnaires. One of these was the California F Scale. The higher the score is on the F scale, the more authoritarian the person is. The other asked people to state the likelihood of them obeying in various situations. The higher the score, the more obedient the person is. The scores on these two questionnaires were plotted in a scattergram, which is shown below:

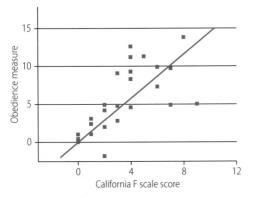

a. **What kind of correlation does the scattergram show? (1 mark)**

b. **What conclusion would be drawn about the relationship shown in the scattergram? (2 marks)**

c. **In terms of the two variables measured, what is the main limitation of correlational analysis? (2 marks)**

d. **Why was it important for the order of presentation of the two questionnaires to be counterbalanced? (1 mark)**

AO2: One for you to try

Tony and Guy are very different characters. One night they watched a film. It was about the trial of a police officer who had been physically abusive to prisoners supposedly in his care. As the judge was about to give the verdict, Tony said: 'The prosecution has a good case against him. I think he's guilty.' Guy replied: 'How can he be guilty? He was just doing what he'd been told to do.'

Using your knowledge of the Authoritarian Personality, explain how the fact that Tony and Guy are 'very different characters' might lead to their differences of opinion. (3 marks)

How do I answer... research methods questions?

Research methods questions probably cause more anxiety than any other type of question, but they can be a source of fairly easy marks if tackled properly. The most basic distinction between different types of question is whether they are embedded within a specific context or not. Although some questions have no specific context (e.g. 'What is an independent variable?' or 'Give **one** limitation of correlational analysis'), the majority of questions *do* have a context that must form a part of your answer.

Below are two different forms of the 'limitation of correlational analysis' question and how we would answer them differently.

> Give **one** limitation of correlational analysis. **(2 marks)**

A limitation of correlational analysis is that, although it shows two variables are related in some way, it does not show a causal relationship between these variables, i.e. that one has caused a change in the other.

> In terms of the two variables measured, what is the main limitation of correlational analysis? **(2 marks)**

The main limitation of correlational analysis is that, although it shows that there is some relationship between F scale scores and obedience, it does not show a causal relationship between the two, i.e. it does not show that authoritarianism, as measured by the F scale, has caused a change in obedience.

REVIEW

Being able to answer questions with different mark allocations concisely yet keeping enough detail to explain the concept clearly is a skill. Practise answering AO1 questions on the Authoritarian Personality explanation of obedience worth 2, 3, 4 and 6 marks. You should spend about 1 ¼ minutes per mark, so for a 2-mark question you have 2 ½ minutes and for a 4-mark question you have 5 minutes. Make sure you allow time to plan your answers, to make sure you write them in a logical way.

1. Practise recalling the bullet points (a friend could help you with this).

2. Practise writing the full answer, setting a timer to make sure you use the time available.

3. Check your answer is clear and logical, and has relevant key terms in each point.

Resistance to social influence

A01 Description

- **Social support** is the perception that a person has assistance available from other people within the group.
  - > This makes them better able to remain independent in situations where they would be expected to conform or obey.
  - > It enables individuals to resist pressures to conform because it breaks the unanimity of the majority.
  - > Disobedient peers act as role models on which a person can base their own behaviour, e.g. resisting an order from an authority figure.

- **Locus of control** (LOC) is a person's perception of personal control of their own behaviour.
  - > People with a strong *internal* LOC believe what happens to them is a result of their own ability and effort rather than the influence of others.
  - > Because internals are less likely to rely on the opinions of others, this makes them less vulnerable to social influence.
  - > People with a strong *external* LOC believe what happens to them is determined by external factors, such as the influence of others or luck and so are less likely to display independent behaviour.

A03 Evaluation/Discussion

Social support

Response order is important in social support…

Allen and Levine (1969) believed that the response position of someone providing social support made a difference to its effect.	Support was significantly more effective when confederates gave the correct answer (with other confederates all giving the same wrong answer) first rather than fourth (just before the real participant responded).	*A correct first answer, because it confirms the participant's own judgement, produces an initial commitment to the correct response that endures even though other group members disagree.*

Research supports the importance of social support in resisting social influence…

Rees and Wallace (2015) showed that social support provided by friends helped adolescents resist conformity pressures from the majority.	They found that individuals who had a majority of friends who drank alcohol were able to resist pressures to drink when they had a friend or two who also resisted.	*This shows that the social support offered by non-drinking friends can decrease the likelihood of a non-drinker deciding to consume alcohol even when faced with a drinking majority.*

Locus of control

Locus of control does not always help us to resist pressures to conform…

In a study of undergraduates, Spector (1983) found that differences in locus of control only predicted their ability to resist *some* types of social influence.	He found that internals were more likely to resist normative social influence than externals, but found that locus of control did not appear to be a significant factor in resisting informational social influence.	*This suggests that a high degree of internality only helps individuals to resist pressures to conform where their main motivation is to gain approval.*

People are more external than they used to be and so less able to resist social influence…

Research has found a historical trend in locus of control, with young people becoming increasingly external.	A meta-analysis by Twenge *et al.* (2004) found that locus of control scores in US students had become substantially more external between 1960 and 2002.	*Twenge suggests this is due to an increasing belief among young people that their fate was determined more by luck and powerful others rather than their own actions.*

The importance of social support in resisting authority has been demonstrated in real life…

The Rosenstrasse protest in Nazi-controlled Berlin in 1943 was a stark illustration of Milgram's research in real life.	German women protested against the arrest of their Jewish husbands. Despite threats that they would be fired upon, the women collectively refused orders to disperse and their husbands were eventually set free.	*The Rosenstrasse protest mirrors Milgram's finding that the presence of disobedient peers gives an individual the confidence and courage to resist the authority's orders.*

A03 PLUS

APPLY: Exam skills

AO2: An example

SCENARIO Parveen is just starting a course at an FE college in the Midlands, having attended a very strict all-girls school up until now. Her parents are concerned because she is easily influenced by those around her. They fear she will stray from the straight and narrow and will lose the strict values they have strived to instil in her. Parveen's best friend Hayat is also starting at the college at the same time.

Using your knowledge of the importance of social support, explain why Parveen will be better able to resist social influence with Hayat's presence.
(4 marks)

ANSWER *Asch's research on conformity found that the presence of social support made it easier for an individual to resist conformity pressure from the majority. For example, Parveen may find herself in a situation with her new peer group where she is pressured to drink alcohol, as 'everybody else is drinking'. Having social support in the form of Hayat breaks the unanimous position of the group because Hayat also declines to drink. This makes Parveen feel more confident and better able to stand up to the majority.*

AO2: Research methods

A researcher was interested in seeing if locus of control (LOC) was an important variable in resistance to social influence. She measured LOC in a large sample of students, and then classified them according to whether they were 'strong internals' or 'strong externals'. She then asked the school's caretaker to act as a confederate. He was asked to inform the students that they couldn't park their cars, even though the car park was obviously empty, without giving them a reason. Other students were told they couldn't use the car park because it was going to be resurfaced. The caretaker recorded which students asked him why they couldn't park their cars and which did not. The results are shown in the table below:

	Percentage of internals questioning caretaker	Percentage of externals questioning caretaker
No reason given	89	14
Reason given	15	14

State two findings and for each one draw a conclusion (state what the finding shows).

Finding 1:

Conclusion 1: This shows that…

Finding 2:

Conclusion 2: This shows that…

AO2: One for you to try

Liz and Jane are sisters who are very different in their approach to life. Liz is hardworking and successful and has no time for people who 'don't try to help themselves'. Jane, on the other hand, failed to get into university, blaming her teachers for her poor A Level results. She infuriates Liz because she seems to have no opinions of her own and, now that she is married, she relies on her husband to make all her decisions for her.

Using the information above, explain how the two sisters differ in terms of their locus of control, and how this would influence their ability to resist social influence. (4 marks)

How do I answer... extended answer (8-mark) questions?

Q1: Outline and evaluate the role of social support in resisting social influence. (8 marks)

Q2: A researcher wanted to study the link between locus of control and resistance to social influence. A sample of 40 16-year-old students from a school in Truro completed a locus of control scale and were then put into an Asch-type conformity situation, where they were required to estimate line lengths with a majority of confederates who all gave the same wrong answers.

Discuss the role of locus of control in resisting social influence. Refer to the likely findings of the study above in your answer. (8 marks)

Not all extended writing questions follow the 12-mark or 16-mark format. Some have a slightly lower tariff. Of these lower tariff extended writing questions, the 8-marker is the most common. It does help to know what you are dealing with, however, as they are not always straightforward.

For example, **Q1:**, if it were on an AS paper, would be worth 4 marks for AO1 (4 points) and 4 marks for AO3 (first two columns of two AO3 points or two complete AO3 points using material from all three columns but abridged to 50 words each). In fact, it is simply two thirds of a 12-mark question, so two thirds of the marks for each skill. However, it is *half* of a 16-mark question at A Level, so that would lead to a different mark division of 3 marks for AO1 and 5 marks for AO3. So, your division of content would depend on whether you are taking an AS or an A Level paper.

Q2: includes a scenario and that is referred back to in the question. This is an indication that there is an additional AO2 requirement in the question. AO2 marks tend to be 'stolen' from the AO3 allocation, so this question would be 3 marks of AO1 (first three points), 3 marks of AO3 (one complete AO3 point) *and* 2 marks' worth of AO2. This would be for correctly identifying the likely findings (those with an internal locus of control would be least likely to conform) and a brief explanation of *why* this would be the case.

REVIEW

Craik and Lockhart (1972) proposed a theory of memory called the 'level of processing model'. This model claimed that the more information is elaborated, the more likely we will be able to access that information later on.

So… that means that just *reading* material doesn't make it particularly memorable. There are various ways of elaborating the material on this spread to make it more memorable.

For example, try these steps to revise the content on this spread:

1 Write out the key points

2 Explain them to someone else in as much detail as you can

3 Construct a visual mind-map of all the information on this topic.

Try it and trust in psychology!

Minority influence

A01 Description

- A form of social influence where members of the majority group change their beliefs or behaviours as a result of their exposure to a persuasive minority.
- Successful minorities are consistent, committed and flexible in their arguments.
- **Consistency** If the minority is consistent in its arguments, others consider the issue more carefully as there must be a reason why the minority is sufficiently confident to maintain this position over time.
  - > Wood *et al.*'s (1994) meta-analysis found that minorities who were consistent in their position were particularly influential.
- **Commitment** A minority that adopts commitment to its position suggests certainty and confidence in the face of a hostile majority.
  - > Greater commitment may then persuade majority group members to take them seriously, or even convert to the minority position.
- **Flexibility** is more effective at changing majority opinion than rigidity of arguments because minorities must negotiate their position rather than try to enforce it.
  - > A rigid minority that refuses to compromise is perceived as dogmatic. One that is too prepared to compromise is seen as inconsistent. Neither approach is effective.

A03 Evaluation/ Discussion

There is research support for flexibility…

Nemeth and Brilmayer (1987) provided support for the role of flexibility in a simulated jury situation.	A group discussed compensation to be paid to someone involved in an accident. A confederate who adopted an inflexible position had no effect on other group members. A confederate who compromised late in negotiations (showing flexibility) did exert an influence, but one who compromised earlier did not (perceived as having 'caved in').	*This suggests that flexibility is only effective at changing majority opinion in certain circumstances.*

The real 'value' of minority influence is that it 'opens the mind'…

Nemeth (2010) argues that exposure to a minority position causes people to make better decisions.	As a result of this minority influence, people search for information, consider more options, make better decisions, and show evidence of more creative thought processes.	*This view is supported in a study of the role of dissent in work groups (Van Dyne and Saavedra, 1996). When exposed to a minority perspective, groups showed improved decision quality.*

The majority rather than the minority creates greater message processing…

Mackie (1987) argues that the views of the minority do not lead to greater processing, but it is the majority who create greater message processing.	We believe that the majority shares similar beliefs to ours. If it expresses a different view, we consider it carefully to understand why this is the case.	*By contrast, people tend not to waste time trying to process why a minority's message is different, therefore it tends to be less, rather than more, influential.*

Minority influence exists in name only…

Nemeth (2010) claims it is still difficult to convince people of the value of minority influence and dissent.	People accept the principle only on the surface, and quickly become irritated by a dissenting view that persists. They may also fear that welcoming dissent would create a lack of harmony within the group, and fear repercussions.	*As a consequence, the majority view persists and the opportunities for innovative thinking associated with minority influence are lost.*

A03 PLUS

APPLY: Exam skills

AO2: An example

SCENARIO Rachel and Joe are touched by the news stories about migrants from the Middle East fleeing war and oppression and looking for a new life in Europe. They try to convince people in their town to welcome migrants into their community, and to help financially in converting a row of disused terrace houses into homes for migrant families.

Using your knowledge of minority influence, explain how Rachel and Joe could try to convince members of their community to accept migrants and contribute to the renovation of the houses for their use. **(4 marks)**

ANSWER Rachel and Joe must put together their reasons why people in their town should help the migrants and they must then present these arguments consistently. If they express their arguments in a consistent manner, people are likely to consider the issues more carefully. Consistency also suggests commitment to a cause. By showing they are willing to give up their time and energy to help migrants, even in the face of hostility from some members of the community, Rachel and Joe will be able to persuade others to take them seriously and to share their concern for the migrants. As others begin to accept their views, then a snowball effect occurs until these views become established within the whole community.

AO2: Research methods

Moscovici *et al.* (1969) found that when a numerical minority expressed their views consistently, they were able to influence a numerical majority around 8 per cent of the time. However, when the minority expressed their views inconsistently, the majority were influenced only about 1 per cent of the time. Moscovici *et al.* also included a control condition in their study.

a. **Briefly explain what is meant by a 'control condition' in an experiment. (2 marks)**

b. **Briefly explain the difference between an independent and a dependent variable. (2 marks)**

c. **Identify the operationalised independent and dependent variable in this study. (2 marks + 2 marks)**

d. **Identify one possible extraneous variable that Moscovici might have had to control in this study. (1 mark)**

e. **Briefly explain the difference between extraneous and confounding variables. (2 marks)**

AO2: One for you to try

Sylvia told her friends that she ate nothing but sushi, which her friends thought was a little bit strange. Every day Sylvia told them of the benefits of eating raw fish, which she said increased her intelligence and made her feel extremely fit. Sylvia seemed so convinced of the benefits of sushi that her friends decided to buy some and try it. On their way to the supermarket they passed the burger restaurant. There was Sylvia eating a super deluxe beef burger. Later, Sylvia asked her friends if they were going to become sushi eaters. 'NO!', they all replied.

Using your knowledge of research into minority influence, explain why Sylvia was unsuccessful in changing her friends' eating behaviour. (3 marks)

How do I answer... 'Distinguish between' questions?

There are some fairly simple rules for answering this sort of question. If you are asked to 'Distinguish between…', 'Compare…' or 'Explain the difference between…', then these rules apply:

1 Don't just *describe* the two things you are being asked to distinguish between.

2 Pick a characteristic that applies to both but which is different for each and point that out (e.g. each is due to some form of social influence).

3 Use words like 'whereas', 'however' and 'on the other hand' to point out this difference.

4 Don't be over-ambitious; one point of difference is usually enough.

So… how might we distinguish between, for example, 'minority influence' and 'conformity'?

Conformity is usually due to normative social influence, leading to public compliance rather than internalisation, *whereas* minority influence is usually due to informational social influence, leading to internalisation of the minority's view.

REVIEW

Before leaving this topic, ensure you can do the following:

1 Write 2-mark and 3-mark AO1 answers on the role of *consistency*, *commitment* and *flexibility* in minority influence.

2 Construct 4-mark and 6-mark AO1 answers on minority influence.

3 Write one fully elaborated AO3 point (for 3 marks) and two slightly less elaborated AO3 points (or one fully elaborated and one less elaborated point) for a 4-mark answer.

4 Write three fully elaborated AO3 points (for a 12-mark essay) or four fully elaborated points (for a 16-mark essay).

The more confident you are with the material, and the more practised you are at reproducing these different types and tariffs of answers within the appropriate time, the better prepared you will be for whatever question on minority influence you might face in the exam.

Social influence processes in social change

AO1 Description

Social change through minority influence

1. **Drawing attention to an issue** A minority can bring about social change by drawing attention to an issue (e.g. suffragettes and the lack of votes for women).

2. **Cognitive conflict** A minority creates a conflict in the minds of the majority between what is currently believed and what the minority believes (e.g. only men being allowed to vote).

3. **Consistency** Social change is more likely when the minority is consistent in its position (e.g. suffragettes were consistent in their views regardless of other people's attitudes).

4. **Augmentation principle** If a minority suffers for its views, it is taken more seriously (e.g. suffragettes risked imprisonment or even death).

5. **Snowball effect** Minority influence initially has a small effect, but this spreads more widely until it eventually leads to large-scale social change (e.g. after the suffragettes' actions, the idea finally spread to the majority).

Social change through majority influence

- Young adults misperceive the frequency with which a behaviour (e.g. binge drinking) occurs among their peers.

- Social norms interventions communicate to a target population the actual norm concerning such behaviour, in the hope that recipients will change their behaviour to bring it in line with the norm.

- In Montana, the correction of misperceptions about the norm of 'drink driving' led to a reduction in the frequency of this behaviour.

AO3 Evaluation / Discussion

Social change happens only gradually through minority influence...

The role played by minority influence may be limited since minorities rarely bring about social change quickly.	Because there is a tendency for human beings to conform to the majority position, people are more likely to maintain the status quo rather than engage in social change.	*This suggests that the influence of a minority creates the potential for change rather than bringing about actual social change.*

Being perceived as 'deviant' limits the influence of minorities...

The potential for minorities to influence social change is often limited because they are seen as 'deviant' by the majority.	This means that members of the majority may avoid aligning themselves with the minority position because they do not want to be seen as deviant themselves.	*Minorities therefore face the double challenge of avoiding being portrayed as deviants and also persuading people to embrace their position.*

The social norms approach doesn't always work...

While social norms interventions have shown positive results in a number of settings, they have their limitations.	DeJong *et al.* (2009) tested the effectiveness of social norms campaigns to reduce alcohol use among students. Despite receiving normative information that corrected their misperceptions of drinking norms, students did not report lower alcohol consumption as a result of the campaign.	*It appears, therefore, that not all social norms interventions are able to produce social change.*

Attempting social change through the social norms approach can have a 'boomerang effect'...

Social norms interventions are aimed at individuals whose behaviour is less desirable than the norm, but those whose behaviour is more desirable also receive the message.	For those who already engage in the constructive behaviour being advocated, a normative message can cause them to behave more in line with the norm.	*Schultz calls this the boomerang effect. For example, a social norms campaign concerning energy usage caused those who used less than the norm to increase their usage.*

AO3 PLUS

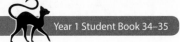

APPLY: Exam skills

AO2: An example

SCENARIO The mayor of a city in the South West is determined to persuade people to use their cars less and public transport more. He intends to set up a congestion charge for cars coming into the city centre and limit the parking to make people use public transport instead. He knows this will be an unpopular message to the people of the city so seeks advice on how he can achieve this social change.

Using your knowledge of the social influence processes in social change, explain how the mayor can bring about this social change. **(4 marks)**

ANSWER *He could use techniques based on minority influence. For example, he could draw attention to the issues (congestion, pollution, etc.), which would produce a conflict in the minds of those who want to drive, but don't want congestion or pollution and do want a cleaner city. If the mayor set an example by not using his own car, his arguments would be taken more seriously (augmentation principle). He could also change the current reliance on cars by using a social norms intervention, e.g. by informing citizens that the majority of people who live in the city expressed a willingness to make more use of public transport and use their cars less.*

AO2: Research methods

a. **In order to carry out the study aiming to decrease city-centre car usage (in the 'Scenario' above), researchers decided to use a stratified sample of car users in the region. Briefly explain what is meant by a stratified sample, and why it might be appropriate for this study. (4 marks)**

b. **Researchers also decide to carry out a pilot study. Briefly explain what is meant by a pilot study, and the reasons for carrying one out in this study. (4 marks)**

c. **Explain in what ways this study might have implications for the economy. (3 marks)**

AO2: One for you to try

At the end of every football match, Mike the steward had to pick up litter the supporters had thrown away. It was a job he hated, so he wished he could find a way to change the supporters' behaviour so that they put their litter in the litter bins provided.

Using your knowledge of social influence processes in social change, explain how Mike could change the behaviour of those supporters who don't put their litter in bins. (4 marks)

How do I answer... longer (12-mark or 16-mark) questions?

Q1: Outline and evaluate the role of social influence processes in social change. (12 marks)

Q2: Outline and evaluate the role of social influence processes in social change. (16 marks)

Q3: Discuss the role of social influence processes in social change. (16 marks)

The first thing you need to do is work out how much AO1 and how much AO3 you should write. For a 12-mark question (usually found at AS Level), this is a straightforward half and half, so half your content should be AO1 (outlining) and half AO3 (evaluating). For the 16-mark questions (found at A Level), AO1 is worth 6 marks and AO3 10 marks, so you would write a little less than double the amount of AO3 compared to AO1.

The second thing is to decide *what* to write. It will always be 6 marks' worth of AO1, so we have provided you with the right amount of AO1 on the page opposite. Practise writing this AO1 material (legibly) to see if you can do it in 7 ½ minutes. Then you have the choice of what to write for either 6 marks' worth of AO3 (in a 12-mark question) or 10 marks' worth of AO3 (in a 16-mark question). We have aimed to make each AO3 point around 60–75 words, so that would be 3 for a 12-mark question and 4 for a 16-mark question.

One last point regards the use of the command word 'Discuss', which still has the same AO1 requirement, but requires AO3 that is a bit more 'discursive', e.g. looking at applications, implications, counter-evidence etc. We have tried to make our AO3 points 'discursive' to accommodate this.

REVIEW

A useful exercise to make you more comfortable with the topic of social change is to look for evidence of the different processes (e.g. drawing attention to an issue; augmentation etc.) operating in real-life examples of social change. It will make you more familiar with the different processes, you can use your example as an AO3 application point and, because you are elaborating the material, it becomes more memorable. You could look at well-known examples such as recycling and healthy eating or be a bit more adventurous and look at the birth of the Polish Trade Union 'Solidarity', or even the spread of Communism in Russia in the late nineteenth and early twentieth century.

RECAP

A01 Description

- **Capacity** concerns how much data can be held in a memory store. Short-term memory (STM) is a limited capacity store whereas long-term memory (LTM) has a potentially infinite capacity.
  - The capacity of STM can be assessed using digit span tests. Miller (1956) reviewed several studies and concluded that STM capacity was 7 +/- 2 items.
  - For example, when dots were flashed on a screen, participants were reasonably accurate with their recall when there were seven dots but very inaccurate with 15 dots.
  - Miller also found people can recall five *words* as well as they can recall five *letters*. They do this by chunking – grouping sets of digits or letters into meaningful units.

- **Duration** is the measure of how long a memory lasts before it is lost. STM has a duration of less than 18 seconds unless items are rehearsed. LTM potentially lasts forever.
  - Peterson and Peterson (1959) found that participants were 90 per cent correct in their recall of consonant syllables after 3 seconds, but only 2 per cent correct after 18 seconds.
  - Bahrick *et al.* (1975) found that in a photo-recognition test, participants could remember the names of former classmates with 90 per cent accuracy within 15 years of graduation, but this figure declined to 70 per cent after 48 years.
  - Bahrick also found that free recall was about 60 per cent accurate after 15 years, dropping to 30 per cent after 48 years.

- **Coding** refers to the way in which information is changed so that it can be stored in memory. STM is largely encoded acoustically (in the form of sounds).
  - LTM is largely encoded semantically (in the form of meaning). Semantic coding produces more durable memory traces in LTM.
  - Baddeley (1966) had four groups learn different word lists: A – acoustically similar; B – acoustically dissimilar; C – semantically similar and D – semantically dissimilar.
  - When STM was tested, group A (acoustically similar words) had the worst recall. When LTM was tested 20 minutes later, group C (semantically similar words) had the worst recall.

Capacity

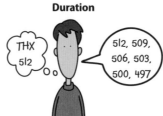

Duration

Coding

Acoustically similar | Acoustically dissimilar | Semantically similar | Semantically dissimilar

A03 Evaluation/Discussion

Capacity

The capacity of STM may be even more limited…

| A criticism of research into STM is that Miller's findings have not been replicated. | Cowan reviewed studies on the capacity of STM and concluded that STM is probably limited to four rather than seven 'chunks'. | *This suggests that STM is not as extensive as the 7+/-2 items claimed by Miller.* |

The size of the chunk matters…

| Research has shown that the size of the chunk affects the number of chunks that can be remembered. | Simon (1974) found that people have a smaller memory span for larger chunks (e.g. multi-syllable words, which take longer to rehearse, compared to single syllable words). | *This supports the view that the STM has a limited capacity, despite the benefits of chunking.* |

Duration

Testing STM is artificial…

| A criticism of STM research is that it tends to take place in artificial situations. | Much of the research has involved trying to remember meaningless consonant syllables. This does not reflect how we use memory in real life, where information tends to be more meaningful. | *However, we do also try to remember some essentially meaningless material (e.g. postcodes), so the research does have some relevance to everyday life.* |

STM results may be due to displacement…

| A criticism of Peterson and Peterson's research is that it did not measure what it set out to measure. | Counting back in numbers may have 'displaced' the syllables to be remembered. Reitman used auditory tones rather than numbers and found duration of STM was much longer. | *This suggests that forgetting in Peterson and Peterson's study was due to displacement rather than decay.* |

Coding

STM may not be exclusively acoustic…

Some studies have found that visual codes are also used in STM.

Brandimote *et al.* (1992) found that participants used visual coding in STM when they were given pictures to remember and prevented from verbally rehearsing.

This suggests there might be multiple types of coding in STM and that STM is not exclusively acoustic.

LTM may not be exclusively semantic…

In general, LTM appears to be semantic, but this is not always the case.

Frost (1972) showed that long-term recall was related to visual as well as semantic categories. Furthermore, Nelson and Rothbart (1972) found evidence for acoustic coding in LTM.

This suggests LTM is encoded using acoustic, visual and semantic information, depending on the type of information being remembered.

APPLY: Exam skills

AO2: An example

SCENARIO Petra is making a cake. On reading the recipe she finds that she does not have many of the ingredients in her cupboard. She drives 20 minutes to her local supermarket but on arrival realises she cannot remember what ingredients she needed to buy.

Using your knowledge of STM, explain why Petra can't remember the ingredients she needs to buy. **(3 marks)**

ANSWER *The list of ingredients for the cake was held in her STM. However, when driving 20 minutes to the supermarket she did not rehearse the items and so the memory decayed as STM has a very limited duration. Furthermore, as she needed to remember a lot of ingredients this may be more than the capacity of STM (less than 7 items) and so all the items could not be recalled unless she found a way to chunk items together.*

AO2: One for you to try

Yasmin is 18 years old. She can vividly remember a holiday she took to Disneyland when she was 5 years old, however she can't remember her new mobile phone number which is 11 digits long.

Using your knowledge of short- and long-term memory, explain why Yasmin can remember her holiday to Disneyland but not her new mobile number. (4 marks)

AO2: Research methods

A researcher wanted to test the hypothesis that there is an age-related decline in the capacity of short-term memory. To do this she assessed the digit-span of ten participants ranging in age from 16 to 80. The results of this assessment are detailed below.

Participant number	1	2	3	4	5	6	7	8	9	10
Participant age	16	18	24	27	35	44	58	67	74	80
Digit-span	10	8	9	7	8	7	6	5	4	5

a. **Write a suitable directional hypothesis for this study. (2 marks)**
b. **Draw a suitable graphical display to represent the data in this table. Label your graph appropriately. (4 marks)**
c. **Estimate the correlation coefficient most likely to result from analysis of the data in the table. Shade one box only. (1 mark)**
  + 0.25 ☐   -0.42 ☐   +0.60 ☐   -0.82 ☐

How do I answer... selection (multiple choice) questions?

Which one of the following statements about coding in short-term and long-term memory is correct? (1 mark)

A STM uses semantic coding and LTM uses acoustic coding.

B Both STM and LTM use acoustic coding.

C STM uses acoustic coding and LTM uses semantic coding.

D Both STM and LTM use semantic coding.

Although these are generally worth only 1 mark, getting them correct is still important because that 1 mark can be the difference between one grade and another. So, some general advice on answering these:

- Read the question very carefully. Is it asking you to pick the statement that is correct or the 'odd one out' that is false? In this example we are looking for the correct statement.
- Make life easier by crossing out any that are obviously *not* going to be the correct answer, given the specific demands of the question.
- If you know that they don't use the same type of coding (after all, you did study two *different* types of coding), then you can start by crossing out **B** and **D**.
- That leaves **A** or **C** as the right answer. If you don't know yet, check the text and have another go.

REVIEW

You should be ready to address different aspects of this topic in an exam. You could try making a list of things that *could* be assessed in exam questions on the topic of 'short- and long-term memory'. When you feel you have mastered an individual part of this topic, you have earned a tick in the **Got it!** column. This list might include:

TOPIC	Got it!		Got it!
Capacity of STM and LTM (AO1)		Evaluation/discussion of capacity (AO3)	
Duration of STM and LTM (AO1)		Evaluation/discussion of duration (AO3)	
Coding in STM and LTM (AO1)		Evaluation/discussion of coding (AO3)	

The multi-store model of memory

AO1 Description

- **The multi-store model (MSM)** is an explanation of memory based on three separate memory stores, and how information is transferred between these stores.
  It comprises:
  1 **Sensory memory**
  2 **STM**, a short-term store which stores a limited amount of information for a short time
  3 **LTM**, a long-term store which is potentially unlimited in capacity and duration.

- Information in the sensory memory register is held at each of the five senses. The capacity of these registers is very large but the duration is very limited (milliseconds).

- Most of the information is lost as it receives no attention. If attention is focused on one of the sensory stores, information is passed to STM.

- Information held in STM is used for immediate tasks such as working on a maths problem or remembering a telephone number before writing it down.

- STM has a limited duration of approximately 18 seconds and decays rapidly unless rehearsed. It has limited capacity, and new information entering STM pushes out (displaces) current information.

- Eventually rehearsal can lead to information being transferred from STM to LTM. LTM is potentially unlimited in duration and capacity.

- Information that is stored in LTM can be returned to the STM by the process of retrieval, where it becomes available for use.

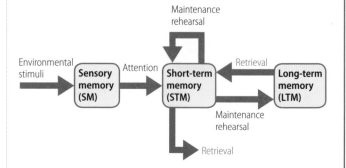

AO3 Evaluation/Discussion

There is supporting evidence for the MSM model…

Controlled lab experiments (e.g. Peterson and Peterson, 1959) support the existence of separate short- and long-term stores.	Studies using brain scanning techniques have demonstrated a difference between STM and LTM. Beardsley (1997) found that the prefrontal cortex is active during STM but not LTM tasks. Squire et al. (1992) found that the hippocampus is active on LTM tasks but not STM tasks.	*This supports the idea of separate short- and long-term memory stores, which is the basis of the multi-store model.*

Support from case studies…

Studies of brain-damaged individuals show that different brain areas are involved in STM and LTM.	HM's brain damage was caused by an operation to remove both hippocampi. He could not form new LTMs, although he could remember things from before the surgery (Scoville and Milner, 1957).	*This provides support for the MSM as HM was unable to transfer information from his STM to LTM, but was able to retrieve memories from before his surgery.*

The MSM is overly simplistic…

The MSM proposes that the STM and LTM are single stores but evidence does not support this.	The working memory model (Baddeley and Hitch, 1974) suggests that STM is divided into a number of qualitatively different stores. Research has also found different types of LTM, for example episodic, procedural and semantic memory.	*This suggests that the MSM provides a simplistic model of memory and does not take into account the different types of STM and LTM.*

Long-term memory involves more than maintenance rehearsal…

The MSM has been criticised for its emphasis on maintenance rehearsal as the reason why information is transferred to LTM.	Craik and Lockhart (1972) suggest that long-term memories are created by the level of processing that information is subjected to and not its rehearsal. Deeper processing leads to more enduring memory traces than more shallow processing.	*This suggests that the process of rehearsal does not fully explain the process of remembering information in LTM.*

AO3 PLUS

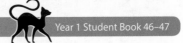

APPLY: Exam skills

AO2: An example

SCENARIO Sam suffered a serious head injury after falling from his bicycle. On recovering it quickly became clear his memory ability had been damaged. STM duration was greatly reduced. For example, he could not recall information his doctor had just told him or remember what he had had for lunch as soon as he had eaten. His LTM showed some damage too, in that he could not remember his experiences at university but could recall factual knowledge such as capital cities.

To what extent does the case study of Sam support the multi-store model of memory? **(4 marks)**

ANSWER *Sam's STM duration is much shorter than other adults and it seems he is unable to rehearse information to keep it in STM. This suggests he cannot form LTMs (he quickly forgets what he ate for lunch or advice from his doctor), supporting the multi-store model's claim that information moves from STM to LTM. However, as Sam can remember some types of LTM (semantic – facts) but not others (episodic – university life) it suggests the model's view of LTM is too simplistic. If LTM was a single store, Sam shouldn't be able to access any LTMs.*

AO2: Research methods

A researcher used a lab experiment to test whether using mind-maps helped to consolidate memory for new material in long-term memory. Thirty students read a 5000-word article about the Caribbean island of St Lucia and then read it once more. A second class of 30 students also read the article but, instead of reading it a second time, they were asked to make a visual mind-map of the main points of the article. Both groups then gave back the article, and the second group returned their mind-maps, to the researcher. One week later, all participants returned to the lab and took a test comprising 20 questions on the information in the article they had read the week before.

a. **What is the aim of this study? (2 marks)**

b. **Identify the independent variable and the dependent variable in this study. (1 mark + 1 mark)**

c. **Write an appropriate hypothesis for this study. (2 marks)**

d. **Is your hypothesis directional or non-directional? (1 mark)**

e. **Identify one possible extraneous variable in this study. Explain how this extraneous variable could have affected the results of this experiment. (1 mark + 3 marks)**

f. **With reference to this study, explain one strength and one limitation of lab experiments. (3 marks + 3 marks)**

AO2: One for you to try

Radha is concerned about her grandfather. She has noticed that his memory is not as good as it used to be. Although he can easily recall things that happened years ago, he struggles to remember recent events and finds it hard to follow conversations or plot lines when watching TV.

Explain how Radha's grandfather's condition might be seen as supporting the multi-store model of memory. (4 marks)

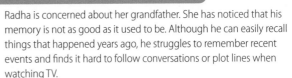 How do I answer... description and evaluation (AO1 + AO3) questions?

In mixed AO1 + AO3 questions up to 6 marks, the division is half and half (it is different with mark totals higher than this as we will see on p.33).

Q1: Briefly explain what is meant by the multi-store model of memory and give one criticism of this model. (4 marks)

For this question you would use the content of the first AO1 bullet point opposite together with the first two columns of one of the AO3 points on the opposite page. You would be aiming for about 100 words in total.

Q2: Outline and evaluate the multi-store model of memory. (6 marks)

In **Q2:**, the word 'briefly' disappears and the mark tariff is raised to 6 marks. Consequently, you would use AO1 points 3, 4 and 6 as these outline the three stores without unnecessary elaboration and also offer an appropriate overview for 3 marks' worth of AO3. One complete AO3 point should be enough, although you could also offer one complete point and a second, slightly less well-developed point.

Q3: Outline and discuss the multi-store model of memory. (6 marks)

Although 'Discuss' is more commonly used as an AO1 + AO3 term in its own right, in **Q3:** it is being used purely as an AO3 term, inviting you to go beyond merely stating strengths or limitations of the model. You have a number of ways to answer this, but whichever route you take, there should be about 75–90 words of AO1 and 75–90 words of AO3.

 REVIEW

Being able to describe something concisely, while maintaining accuracy, is not as easy as it sounds. On the opposite page, we have stripped down the descriptive detail you will find in the main Student Book to give you some guidance about how to do just that. Follow the tips to the right to make the content a bit more familiar.

1 Try answering the four questions above using the advice given. How long did it take you and would you be able to reproduce this in exam conditions?

2 If the answer is 'no', then read over the material again and see how much you can reproduce just from memory.

3 Repeat Step 2 frequently over the coming weeks until the whole process becomes second nature.

The working memory model

AO1 Description

- Baddeley and Hitch (1974) proposed the working memory model (WMM) because they felt that the STM was not just one store, but multiple stores. WMM is an explanation of the memory used when working on a task.

- The WMM suggests one store for visual processing and a separate store for processing sounds.

- **Central executive** directs attention to particular tasks by allocating the brain's resources to one of the three slave systems.

- **Phonological loop** deals with auditory information and preserves the order of information. It is divided into the phonological store, which holds the words heard, and the articulatory process, which allows for maintenance rehearsal of acoustic information.

- **Visuo-spatial sketchpad** is used for the planning of spatial tasks and temporary storage of visual and/or spatial information. It contains the visual cache, which stores information about visual items, and the inner scribe, which stores the arrangements of objects in the visual field.

- **Episodic buffer** is a general store for both visual and acoustic information. It integrates information from the central executive, phonological loop and the visuo-spatial sketchpad. It also sends information to LTM.

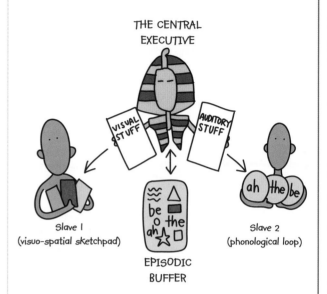

AO3 Evaluation/Discussion

The problem of dual task performance...

A strength of the WMM is its ability to explain dual task performance, i.e. the ability to perform two tasks simultaneously.

Hitch and Baddeley (1976) found that participants were slower in a dual task study that involved both the central executive and the articulatory loop, in comparison to a task that required just the articulatory loop.

This demonstrates the dual task performance effect and shows that the central executive is separate from the articulatory loop.

Evidence from brain-damaged patients...

Case studies of individuals with brain damage support the WMM.

Shallice and Warrington (1970) studied KF, whose short-term forgetting of auditory information was much greater than his forgetting of visual information. His brain damage appeared to be restricted to his phonological loop and did not affect his visuo-spatial sketchpad.

This supports the idea of separate components for auditory and visual information, as suggested by the WMM.

Problems with using case studies...

There are problems with using evidence from individuals with brain damage.

Some supporting evidence for the WMM comes from case studies of individuals (such as KF) with serious brain damage. However, such individuals may have difficulty in paying attention and so simply underperform on certain tasks.

This is an important issue because the results of case studies are difficult, if not impossible, to generalise to the general population.

A problem with the central executive...

The concept of the central executive has been criticised as being too vague and lacking in explanatory power.

Eslinger and Damasio (1985) studied EVR, who had a cerebral tumour removed. Although he performed well on some tests requiring reasoning, he had poor decision-making skills and had difficulties making simple decisions.

The case of EVR suggests that the central executive is more complex than in the original model and that there are possibly several different components within the central executive.

APPLY: Exam skills

AO2: An example

SCENARIO Mariam enjoys singing along to music while completing a still-life drawing for her art homework. However, she finds the same songs distracting when she is trying to listen to her friend explain events in a novel they are studying in English.

Use your understanding of the working memory model to explain Mariam's dual task performance. **(4 marks)**

ANSWER *To complete her art homework Mariam is using her visuo-spatial sketchpad to consider the colour and form of objects (visual cache) and the relationships between the objects in the still-life composition (inner scribe). She is able to do this while singing to music as a different store, the phonological loop, is attending to this auditory information. However, the phonological store has a limited capacity so is unable to successfully perform two auditory tasks simultaneously (singing and listening to her friend explain events in the novel).*

AO2: Research methods

A researcher wanted to test the hypothesis that there is an age-related decline in working memory. She used a group of volunteers drawn from her undergraduate students (aged 18–25) and a second group drawn from the local community (aged 60–75). To test their working memory, she showed participants items on a computer screen. Items were shown one at a time for one second, with the number of items shown in a sequence gradually increasing. After each sequence of items, participants were shown a group of eight items and asked to remember which of these they had just seen. From this test, the researcher was able to calculate a score for each participant's working memory.

a. **The researcher might have used a pilot study prior to the main study. What would have been the purpose of a pilot study for this research? (2 marks)**

b. **Construct a suitable directional hypothesis for this study. (2 marks)**

c. **Why would the researcher have chosen to use a directional hypothesis rather than a non-directional hypothesis for this study? (2 marks)**

d. **Identify and explain one limitation with using a volunteer sample in this study. (3 marks)**

e. **Other than the use of a volunteer sample, identify and briefly explain one other design problem with this study. (3 marks)**

AO2: One for you to try

Carly was busy talking to her mother on the phone while idly flicking through the latest Internet deals on her laptop. Her son was trying to talk to her although she wasn't really following what he was asking her. After a while she just said, 'Yes, fine' to get rid of him. When she came off the phone she was aghast to find that the kitchen looked like a complete mess, and her son was standing in the middle of it all, covered in chocolate and cereal. 'But you *said* I could make chocolate crispy cakes!', he protested.

Use your knowledge of the working memory model to explain why Carly was able to talk to her mother and browse on her laptop but could not talk to her mother and follow her son's verbal request at the same time. (4 marks)

How do I answer... evaluation only (AO3) questions?

Like the description only questions on p.31, evaluation questions come in all sorts of shapes and sizes. Terms like 'Evaluate', 'Discuss', 'Explain', 'Criticism', 'Strength' and 'Limitation' all indicate that AO3 is required. Let's look at some examples:

Q1: Briefly explain one limitation of the working memory model. (2 marks)

Using one of the AO3 points opposite as your material, you would use the first two columns (the main critical claim and its expansion). Alternatively, you could summarise the content in all three columns into about 50 words (i.e. including the 'link-back' conclusion).

Q2: Explain **one** limitation of the working memory model. (3 marks)

This simply requires a little more elaboration, so you would add in the material in the third column to access the third mark on offer.

Q3: Evaluate the working memory model. (6 marks)

Take the same approach as with **Q2:**, but this time using **two** of the AO3 points on the opposite page. Don't try to use more than two, it would make your answer look too superficial.

Issues/Debates
Holism and reductionism. Models such as the WMM are an example of experimental reductionism because complex behaviour is reduced to operationalised variables that can be manipulated and measured to determine causal relationships.

REVIEW

From time to time in this book we suggest various techniques for elaborating the material you have just covered in order to make it more memorable. Here is one really useful technique:

Take a large sheet of paper (A3 works well here) and construct a mind-map so that all your material on the multi-store model of memory is linked together in a wonderfully visual way for you. This serves several purposes:

1. It *elaborates* the material, making it more memorable.

2. The act of constructing the mind-map counts as *revision*, again making it more likely you can recall it in an exam.

3. You have a *visual* image of the material, which, for many people, is a much easier way of remembering complex material.

Tip: There is a wealth of useful revision videos on the Internet – take a look for some on mind-map construction.

Types of long-term memory

AO1 Description

- **Episodic memory** is concerned with personal experience and is an individual's unique memory of a specific event or events in which they were involved.
  - > Episodic memories have three elements: details of the event, the context and the emotions felt at the time. Examples would include memories from childhood, a night out or a traumatic event.
- **Semantic memories** are memories related to knowledge about the world. These are shared by everyone, rather than being a personal 'episodic' experience.
  - > Semantic memories are related to things, such as the function of objects, or what behaviour is appropriate in a particular situation. They may also be related to abstract concepts such as mathematics and language.

- **Procedural memory** is concerned with skills, such as knowing how to tie a shoelace or how to carry out a mathematical calculation. It is remembering *how* to do something, rather than knowing *what* to do.
  - > Procedural memories are typically acquired through repetition and practice. We are less aware of these memories as they have become automatic.

DECLARATIVE

$e=mc^2$

EPISODIC

PROCEDURAL

AO3 Evaluation/Discussion

Evidence from brain scans...

The distinction between these three types of LTM is supported by brain scans.	Different areas of the brain appear to be active when using different types of LTM. Episodic memory is associated with the hippocampus and temporal lobe, semantic memory also relies on the temporal lobe, and procedural memory is associated with the cerebellum.	*This suggests that these types of long-term memory are separate and are found in different areas of the brain.*

Distinguishing procedural and declarative memories...

Evidence from case studies offers further support for different types of LTM.	The case of patient HM highlights the distinction between procedural (knowing *how*) and episodic/semantic (knowing *what*) memories. After surgery, HM could still form new procedural memories but he was unable to form episodic/semantic memories.	*This supports the distinction between procedural and episodic/semantic memories, highlighting the existence of multiple types of long-term memory.*

Problems with evidence from patients with brain damage...

A criticism of research in this area is the reliance on patients with brain damage.	It is difficult to conclude from patients such as HM the exact parts of the brain that are affected until after the patient has died. Also, damage to a particular area of the brain does not mean that this area is responsible for a particular behaviour.	*This means that we cannot establish a causal relationship between a particular brain region and type of LTM.*

There may be a fourth type of LTM...

Research has shown that implicit memories also influence the response a person makes.	Priming refers to the influence of implicit (automatic and unconscious memories) on our responses. Priming is controlled by a brain system separate from the temporal system that supports explicit (semantic and episodic) memories.	*This suggests that the original theory of LTM is too simplistic and other types of LTM may exist.*

AO3 PLUS

APPLY: Exam skills

AO2: An example

SCENARIO A teacher interviewed her A Level class about their studies and school life. Emily said, 'I remember how stressed I felt when revising for my mock exams. I was moody at home and seemed to constantly argue with my parents.' Zac reported, 'I feel confident in my knowledge of different biological processes.' Katie responded saying 'I just hope we don't have to do any mathematical calculations. I have real problems remembering which steps to take'.

Identify the different types of LTM each student is discussing. **(3 marks)**

ANSWER *Emily's comment is an example of episodic memory as she is recalling her own personal experience of sitting mock exams because she remembers being moody at home. Zac is focusing on his semantic memory of facts because he remembers material on biological processes. Katie is discussing her procedural memory for mathematical calculations, mentioning that she has problems remembering the steps she needs to take.*

AO2: Research methods

A neuropsychologist working with Alzheimer's Disease (AD) patients was interested in whether the memory deficits commonly associated with this disease are caused by damage in specific brain areas. He was particularly interested in the role of the hippocampus in episodic memory and had published extensively on the role of this brain region in LTM prior to his work with Alzheimer's patients. As part of this research, he intended to assess episodic memory in AD patients compared to normal controls without AD.

a. **Briefly explain what is meant by 'investigator effects'? (2 marks)**

b. **Explain why investigator effects might have been a problem in this particular study. (2 marks)**

c. **Outline what the researcher might have done to have overcome these investigator effects. (2 marks)**

d. **Identify one ethical issue in this study and explain how this might have been dealt with. (3 marks)**

e. **If this researcher wanted to publish his research, it must first go through the process of 'peer review'. Explain why this is an important part of the scientific process. (3 marks)**

AO2: One for you to try

Clive Wearing is a British musician who contracted a virus in 1985 that caused severe amnesia. Since then, he has been unable to form new long-term memories. For example, he would not remember visiting his daughter in Australia. However, he does remember how to play the piano and sing.

Use your knowledge of long-term memory to explain which type(s) of long-term memory remain intact for Clive and which type(s) is/are no longer intact. (4 marks)

Issues/Debates
Idiographic and nomothetic approaches. Case studies of LTM are examples of the idiographic approach because of their focus on individuals and the unique insights they offer.

How do I answer... 'Distinguish between' questions?

There are some fairly simple rules for answering this sort of question. If you are asked to 'Distinguish between...', 'Compare...' or 'Explain the difference between...', then these rules apply:

1 Don't just *describe* the two things you are being asked to distinguish between.

2 Pick some characteristics that apply to both but are different for each and point that out (e.g. what type of thing each is a memory of or about). For example, episodic memories are *about* personal events, semantic memories are *about* shared knowledge).

3 Use words like 'whereas', 'however', and 'on the other hand' to point out this difference. For example, 'episodic memories are about personal events *whereas* semantic memories are about shared knowledge'.

4 Don't be over-ambitious; one point of difference is usually enough.

REVIEW

Knowing what is and what is not episodic memory, semantic memory and procedural memory, and the difference between them, is vital for all the questions you are likely to face on this topic. There are a few things that you can do to help you with this.

1 Can you come up with a couple of examples for each of these?

2 Can you highlight the differences between episodic memory and semantic memory, semantic memory and procedural memory, episodic memory and procedural memory?

3 Try writing a few of your own selection (multiple choice) questions to consolidate this understanding.

Explanations for forgetting – Interference

 RECAP

A01 Description

- **Retroactive interference** (RI) refers to the observation that learning something new interferes with previously learned material, leading to that material being forgotten.
    - > Müller and Pilzecker (1900) first identified RI in a study where participants given an intervening task in between learning nonsense syllables and recalling them performed less well than those without the intervening task.
    - > McGeoch and McDonald (1931) showed that forgetting of original material is greater if the intervening items presented prior to recall are more similar to the original, something that only RI rather than decay can explain.

- **Proactive interference** (PI) refers to the observation that previously learned material interferes with current attempts to learn something, leading to forgetting of current material.
    - > Underwood (1957) analysed findings from a number of studies and found that participants were less able to learn word lists presented later in a sequence, in comparison to those presented earlier on, showing evidence of PI.
    - > PI results from response competition between current and previously learned information at recall. The finding that the PI effect was greater in later lists is attributed to the increasing competition of multiple associations at recall.

A03 Evaluation/Discussion

Research is artificial…

One issue with evidence for interference explanations concerns the artificial nature of the methodology.

Most of the research studies that have investigated interference tend to be laboratory-based and use artificial lists of words and/or nonsense syllables. As a result, participants may lack the motivation to remember such lists and so the interference effects appear stronger than they actually are.

This suggests that the research lacks ecological validity and may not apply to everyday examples of memory.

Interference only explains some instances of forgetting…

A criticism is that, although interference effects do occur in everyday life, they do not occur that often.

For example, rather special conditions are required for interference to lead to forgetting, as the two memories need to be quite similar. Therefore, interference is considered a relatively unimportant explanation of everyday forgetting.

This means that other explanations are needed for a complete understanding of forgetting.

Interference may explain accessibility rather than availability…

Interference may not cause a memory trace to disappear but just make it temporarily inaccessible.

Ceraso (1967) found that if memory was tested again 24 hours later after an interference effect, recognition (accessibility) showed considerable spontaneous recovery, whereas recall (availability) remained the same. This shows that interference effects do not cause memories to disappear and the effects are only temporary.

This suggests that interference only occurs because memories are temporarily not accessible rather than lost (unavailable).

Real-world application to advertising…

There are interference effects when people are exposed to advertisements from competing brands.

Danaher *et al.* (2008) found that both recall and recognition of an advertiser's message were impaired when participants were exposed to two adverts for competing brands in the same week. This interference effect was minimised by running multiple exposures to an advert on one day rather than spread over a week.

This suggests that insights from interference research can enhance the effectiveness of advertising campaigns.

A03 PLUS

APPLY: Exam skills

AO2: An example

SCENARIO Baddeley and Hitch (1977) investigated rugby players' memory for teams they had played against during the rugby season. Some players played every game of the season while others, due to injury, missed some games. Players who participated in every game of the season showed poorer recall of opposing teams than injured players who had played fewer games.

Use your understanding of interference to explain the forgetting shown by the rugby players. **(4 marks)**

ANSWER *The time interval for all players was the same (from the start to the end of the rugby season). If forgetting occurred because of decay then all players should have shown similar levels of forgetting. However, as the players who played more games forgot more teams, it suggests interference was the cause of forgetting because the more items (teams) they learned the poorer their recall. Memories of teams played later in the season may disrupt memory for teams played at the start of the season (retroactive interference) or memories for teams played at the start of the season hindered learning of new teams played as the season progressed (proactive interference).*

AO2: Research methods

An experiment was carried out to test the effect of learning similar and dissimilar information.

In part 1 of the experiment, both groups (A and B) were given a list of 20 male names to remember. In part 2 of the experiment, Group A was given another list of 20 male names and Group B was given a list of 20 different types of fruit.

Both groups (A and B) were then asked to recall as many of the 20 male names from part 1 of the experiment as they could. The results from the two groups are shown below.

Group A	Group B
5	11
6	15
8	12
7	13
4	19
5	11
6	12
10	15
4	16
5	16
Mean =	Mean =
SD = 1.79	SD = 2.5

a. **Calculate the mean scores for Group A and Group B. Show your calculations for both groups. (4 marks)**

b. **The psychologist calculated the standard deviation for both groups. Why are the standard deviation scores useful for the experimenter? (2 marks)**

AO2: One for you to try

Vanessa is the daughter of a diplomat and so has lived in many different countries. She spent the first ten years of her life living in Germany and then the next eight years in Spanish-speaking Venezuela before moving to the UK, where she has now lived for six years. Despite speaking fluent German until she was ten, she now struggles with the language, often mixing words up with their Spanish equivalent. Likewise, since moving to the UK, she finds she has trouble remembering some Spanish words and so will, on occasion, resort to using English when speaking to Spanish visitors.

Using what you know about the interference explanation of forgetting, explain why Vanessa is experiencing these language difficulties. (3 marks)

How do I answer... description only (AO1) questions?

There is a fairly simple formula for answering description only questions. For two marks, say two things, for three marks say three things and so on. Work through the sample questions below, using the material under the AO1 heading on the opposite page.

Q1: Briefly explain retroactive interference as an explanation for forgetting. (2 marks)

Use the first **two** 'Retroactive interference' points.

Q2: Explain proactive interference as an explanation for forgetting. (3 marks)

Use all **three** 'Proactive interference' points.

Q3: Briefly outline proactive and retroactive interference as explanations for forgetting. (4 marks)

Use the first **two** 'Proactive interference' points and the first **two** 'Retroactive interference' points.

Q4: Outline the interference explanation of forgetting. (6 marks)

Use all **three** 'Proactive interference' points and all **three** 'Retroactive interference' points.

This approach adds an appropriate level of detail to each answer and gives the examiner a useful way of discriminating between your answer and one that would be worth fewer than the maximum marks for that question.

REVIEW

On this spread we have looked at two explanations of forgetting: retroactive interference and proactive interference.

To enhance your practical expertise in questions on this topic over and above selecting material to answer AO3 questions and completing the research methods exercise above, there are a couple of other useful things you can do:

1️⃣ Write 2-mark, 3-mark, 4-mark and 6-mark outlines of retroactive interference and proactive interference.

2️⃣ Write a bullet-pointed answer plan (including both AO1 and AO3 material) for the 12-mark and a 16-mark essay question: Discuss retroactive interference and proactive interference explanations of forgetting.

RECAP

A01 Description

- Memory is most effective if information that was present at encoding is also available at time of retrieval. The closer the **cue** to the original, the more useful it is (Tulving and Thomson, 1973).

- Forgetting in LTM is mainly due to **retrieval failure** – the failure to find an item of information because of insufficient cues during retrieval.

Context-dependent forgetting

- Recall of knowledge or episodes is greater when the context present during learning and retrieval are the same. When the context is different, it is more difficult to retrieve information.

  > Divers learned a word list on land or underwater and were then tested on land or underwater. The highest recall was when the initial context matched the recall environment (Godden and Baddeley, 1975).

State-dependent forgetting

- Recall is greater when an individual's physical or psychological state is similar at encoding and retrieval. When these states are different, it is more difficult to retrieve information.

  > Goodwin *et al.* (1969) asked participants to remember a list of words when either drunk or sober and then recall the list after 24 hours when either drunk or sober. Recall was best when in the same state at both times.

A03 Evaluation/Discussion

There is research support for the importance of cues...

Students often struggle to recall information in exams, experiencing a 'retrieval failure' of learned information.	Gallagher (2017) tested whether including information from class lectures in test items as retrieval cues enhanced student performance on tests. Performance on identical test items with and without these cues showed that the 'included cues' group recalled significantly more than the 'no cues' group.	*These results suggest that the selective use of retrieval cues on tests can help students overcome retrieval failure.*

Real-world applications...

Coveney *et al.* (2013) tested whether changing the recall context from the learning context affected recall.	Medical students were given audio lists of 30 words in two learning environments: a tutorial room while sitting around a table, and an operating theatre while around an operating table. There was no significant difference in subsequent recall when this was in the same or a different context.	*These findings have implications for medical education, as there was no significant difference in recall between classroom and clinical contexts.*

Retrieval cues do not always work...

Although there is evidence to suggest that retrieval cues prevent forgetting, this is not always the case.	In most of the research on retrieval cues, participants must learn word lists. However, everyday learning is far more complex. For example, learning about the working memory model requires complex associations that are not easily triggered by a single cue.	*This suggests that retrieval cues are unable to explain all types of learning and forgetting.*

Retrieval is a more important explanation than interference...

A03 PLUS

Tulving and Psotka (1971) demonstrated that apparent interference effects are actually due to the absence of cues.	When participants were asked to learn word lists, the effects of interference disappeared if category names were included as cues during recall. With these cues, participants remembered 70 per cent of the words regardless of how many lists they had been given.	*This shows that information is there (i.e. it is available) but cannot be retrieved due to interference. Retrieval cues overcome this problem.*

APPLY: Exam skills

AO2: An example

SCENARIO Psychology students asked participants to learn lists of words in either a classroom where lavender scented candles were burning or the same classroom where no additional smell was added. The next day all participants were asked to recall the word in the same classroom while lavender-scented candles were burning. Participants who learned the lists in the presence of the lavender scent showed greater recall than those who learned the lists without smelling lavender.

How might the psychology students explain their findings in relation to retrieval failure? **(3 marks)**

ANSWER *The lavender smell acted as a context-dependent cue for the participants who were initially exposed to the scent while learning the word lists – they encoded the cue at the time of learning the words. Participants who were not exposed to lavender when learning the word lists would not find lavender a useful cue in the retrieval phase as it was not present at the time of learning and so would not help them access those memories.*

AO2: One for you to try

Emmanuel spends hours revising at home for a psychology test. Despite his revision, when he enters the psychology room, his mind goes blank and he is unable to remember anything! His teacher suggests that he should revise in the classroom where he will take the exam.

Using your knowledge of psychological research, suggest why his teacher's advice might improve his memory. (4 marks)

AO2: Research methods

A researcher randomly allocated students to one of two groups. Both groups were given a one-hour lesson on research methods in their usual psychology classroom. The next day, Group 1 was tested on the contents of the lesson in the same classroom and Group 2 tested in a different classroom.

a. **Identify the type of experimental design used in this study. (1 mark)**

b. **What other type of design might the researcher have used in this study? Why might this have been a more suitable design than the one used? (3 marks)**

c. **What would be the most likely results of this study? (2 marks)**

d. **In what way would these results support the role of retrieval failure as an explanation of forgetting? (3 marks)**

How do I answer... extended writing (8-mark) questions?

Not all extended writing questions follow the 12-mark or 16-mark format. Some have a slightly lower tariff. Of these lower tariff extended writing questions, the 8-marker is the most common. It does help to know what you are dealing with, however, as they are not always straightforward.

> **Outline and evaluate retrieval failure as an explanation for forgetting. (8 marks)**

If this was on an AS paper, it would be worth 4 marks for AO1 (4 points) and 4 marks for AO3 (first two columns of two AO3 points). In fact, it is simply two thirds of a 12-mark question, so two thirds of the marks for each skill. However, it is *half* of a 16-mark question at A Level, so the mark division is 3 marks for AO1 and 5 marks for AO3. So, your division of content would depend on whether you are taking an AS or an A Level paper.

> **A researcher randomly allocated students to one of two groups. Both groups were given a one-hour lesson on research methods in their usual psychology classroom. The next day, Group 1 was tested on the contents of the lesson in the same classroom and Group 2 tested in a different classroom.**
>
> **Discuss the role of retrieval failure in forgetting. Refer to the likely findings of the study above in your answer. (8 marks)**

This question includes a scenario and makes reference to that scenario in the question. This is an indication that there is an additional AO2 requirement in the question. AO2 marks tend to be 'stolen' from the AO3 allocation, so this question would be 3 marks of AO1 (first three points), 3 marks of AO3 (one complete AO3 point) *and* 2 marks' worth of AO2. This would be for correctly identifying the likely findings (those with an internal locus of control would be least likely to conform) and a brief explanation of *why* this would be the case.

REVIEW

To prepare yourself for possible questions on this topic, make sure you can use the material on the opposite page effectively.

1. Write a 6-mark description of retrieval failure as an explanation for forgetting.

2. Write a 4-mark description of retrieval failure as an explanation for forgetting.

3. Come up with three elaborated AO3 points (if you are doing psychology at AS) or four points (if you are following the A Level course).

4. Construct an essay plan for an 8-mark essay on retrieval failure (remembering the rule outlined above concerning AS and A Level versions).

5. Construct an essay plan for a 12-mark (if you are doing AS Level) or a 16-mark (if you are doing A Level) essay on retrieval failure.

RECAP

AO1 Description

Leading questions

Loftus and Palmer (1974)

- **EXPERIMENT 1: PROCEDURE** The researchers showed 45 students seven films of different traffic accidents. After each film, participants were given a questionnaire with a critical question containing one of five verbs: 'How fast were the cars going when they [contacted / hit / bumped / collided / smashed] each other?'
- **FINDINGS** Participants given the verb 'smashed' reported an average speed of 40.8 mph, in comparison to participants given the verb 'contacted' who reported an average speed of 31.8 mph.
- **EXPERIMENT 2: PROCEDURE** Participants were divided into three groups and shown a film of a car accident and again asked questions about speed. One week later they were asked a series of questions about the accident, including the question, 'Did you see any broken glass?' (There was no broken glass in the film.)
- **FINDINGS** The leading question did change the actual memory some participants had for the event with 32 per cent of participants given the verb 'smashed' reporting broken glass compared with 14 per cent of those given the verb 'hit'.

Post-event discussion

- **Conformity effect** refers to how a person's memory of an event may be altered as a result of discussing it with others and/or being questioned multiple times.
  - > Gabbert *et al.* (2003) showed pairs of participants a different video of the same event, so that each participant viewed unique items. Pairs were encouraged to discuss the event before individually recalling what they had witnessed. Seventy-one per cent of these participants went on to mistakenly recall items acquired during their discussion.
- **Repeat interviewing** Each time an eyewitness is interviewed there is a possibility that the comments from the interviewer will become incorporated into their own recollection of the events.
- An interviewer may use **leading questions** and so alter the individual's memory for events. This is especially the case when children are being interviewed about a crime (LaRooy *et al.*, 2005).

AO3 Evaluation/Discussion

Social support

There is plenty of research evidence...

| Research has shown that misleading information can create false memories. | Braun *et al.* (2002) used misleading advertising material for Disneyland containing information about Bugs Bunny (a Warner character, not Disney). Participants incorporated it into their original memories and remembered meeting Bugs Bunny during their visit to Disneyland. | *This shows how powerful misleading information can be in creating false memories.* |

Eyewitness testimony (EWT) in real life may be different...

| Loftus' research has been criticised for lacking ecological validity. | It is argued that laboratory experiments in EWT do not represent real-life crimes/accidents because participants may not take the questions in an experiment seriously as they would in a real crime/accident. | *This suggests that misleading information may have less influence on real-life EWT than Loftus' research suggests.* |

There are real-world applications...

| EWT research has important implications for the criminal justice system, which relies on eyewitness identification for prosecution. | Recent DNA exoneration cases have shown that mistaken eyewitness identification was the largest single factor contributing to the conviction of innocent people (Wells and Olson, 2003). | *This suggests that research can help ensure that innocent people are not convicted of crimes on the basis of faulty eyewitness evidence.* |

Response bias may be responsible...

| The results of research on misleading information may be a result of response bias. | Bekerian and Bowers (1983) replicated one of Loftus' studies and found that participants were not susceptible to misleading information if questions were presented in the same order as the original information (Loftus had presented them in random order). | *This suggests the results of Loftus and Palmer's research may be due to a response bias and highlights the importance of question order in police interviews.* |

AO3 PLUS

APPLY: Exam skills

AO2: An example

SCENARIO Walking home from school, Dan witnessed a car crash. When he got home he told his parents about the accident. They asked whether anyone was injured, how fast the cars were travelling when they smashed into each other and the extent of the damage to the cars. Next day at school Dan discussed the incident with other students who had witnessed the accident. His friend Tom saw the crash from the other side of the road. Tom said one of the drivers had cuts on his face and guessed he must have hit his head on the steering wheel.

Why should the police treat Dan's eyewitness testimony with caution?
(3 marks)

ANSWER *Dan has engaged in post-event discussion with his parents and friends, which may have exposed him to misleading information. For example, Tom's comments may distort Dan's memory so he believes he too could see the driver's injuries (even though this may not be possible from where Dan was standing). Dan's parents' use of the verb 'smashed' might lead him to estimate a higher speed as well as more damage to the cars as 'smashed' suggests a more dramatic event than the actual incident.*

AO2: Research methods

A group of psychology students were keen to repeat one of the lab experiments on misleading information that they had read about in their textbook. They decided they were going to use students from the GCSE psychology class as their sample.

a. **Identify one lab experiment on misleading information. (1 mark)**

b. **Identify the independent and dependent variables in this experiment. (2 marks)**

c. **(i) Explain what is meant by 'operationalisation'. (2 marks)**
   (ii) Write a suitable, fully operationalised directional hypothesis for this study. (2 marks)

d. **Identify one possible extraneous variable in this study and say how this might be controlled. (3 marks)**

e. **Briefly outline how the students might ensure that their sample were able to give their 'informed consent'. (2 marks)**

AO2: One for you to try

On 28 January 1986, the Space Shuttle *Challenger* exploded 73 seconds into its flight, leading to the deaths of seven crew members. Many people off the coast of Florida witnessed the accident first hand and discussed the accident immediately afterwards, and then watched news reports detailing the tragic accident later that day. Psychologists later examined eyewitness accounts.

Using your knowledge of psychological research, explain why the eyewitness accounts may have been inaccurate. (4 marks)

How do I answer... research methods questions?

Questions requiring research methods knowledge can appear in any section of any paper in the AS or A Level exams. They could include any aspect of research methods, data analysis or ethical issues. Doing well in research methods questions is as much a case of thinking clearly and using common sense as it is regurgitating knowledge. Let's look at the research methods example questions below left:

a. All that is required is a statement of an appropriate *laboratory* experiment on misleading information, i.e. nothing about procedure, findings etc., just the researchers' names'.

b. This is *not* asking what an IV and DV are, but what they are *in this study*. Get into the habit of always operationalising your variables.

c. (i) As there are two marks available, a brief, muddled explanation (e.g. 'making sure the variables can be measured') would be worth 1 mark and a more elaborate explanation would be worth 2 (e.g. 'expressing variables in a way such that they can be tested in a precise manner').

   (ii) Hypotheses are a statement of the relationship between (in this case) an (operationalised) IV and an (operationalised) DV. They are also statements of how something *is* at the moment rather than what it *will* be.

d. Identifying any likely variable that might 'get in the way of' the relationship between IV and DV is where you need to do a bit of detective work. Perhaps the GCSE students would be aware of the study and acted accordingly? Having identified your extraneous variable, what would you do to minimise its impact?

e. Finally, there is a question about 'informed consent'. Students rarely seem to appreciate the importance of the word 'informed' in this context. What would *you* like to know about the study before agreeing to be a participant?

REVIEW

Craik and Lockhart (1972) proposed a theory of memory called the 'levels of processing model'. This model claimed that the more that information is elaborated, the more likely we will be able to access that information later on.

So... that means that just *reading* material doesn't make it particularly memorable. There are various ways of elaborating the material on this spread to make it more memorable. These include: writing out key points, explaining it to someone else, constructing a visual mind-map of information and so on. Try it and trust in psychology!

Tip: There is a wealth of useful revision videos on the Internet – take a look for some on mind-map construction.

Accuracy of eyewitness testimony: Anxiety

AO1 Description

- **Anxiety has a negative effect on memory** Automatic skills are not affected by anxiety, but performance on complicated cognitive tasks such as eyewitness memory tends to be reduced.

- Loftus *et al.* monitored eyewitnesses' eye movements and found that the presence of a weapon caused attention to be drawn towards the weapon itself and away from other things such as the person's face.

- **Anxiety has a positive effect on memory** Christianson and Hubinette (1993) found better than 75 per cent accurate recall in real witnesses to bank robberies. Witnesses who were most anxious (the victims) had the best recall.

- Deffenbacher (1983) reviewed studies of the effects of anxiety on eyewitness accuracy and concluded that when anxiety is only moderate then accuracy is enhanced. In conditions of extreme anxiety, accuracy is reduced.

Johnson and Scott (1976)

- **PROCEDURE** Participants heard an argument and saw a man carrying a pen covered in grease (low anxiety condition) or a knife covered in blood (high anxiety, 'weapon focus' condition). They were later asked to identify the man from a set of photographs.

- **FINDINGS** The mean accuracy was 49 per cent in the low anxiety pen condition, compared to 33 per cent in the knife condition, supporting the idea of a weapon focus effect.

AO3 Evaluation/Discussion

The weapon focus effect may not be caused by anxiety...

Pickel (1993) argues that the weapon focus effect could be a consequence of surprise rather than anxiety.	Participants watched a thief enter a hairdressing salon carrying scissors (high threat, low surprise), a handgun (high threat, high surprise), a wallet (low threat, low surprise) or a whole raw chicken (low threat, high surprise). Identification was less accurate in the high surprise conditions than in the high threat conditions.	*This supports the view that it is surprise that leads to the weapon focus effect.*

Real-life versus lab studies...

Lab studies may not create the real levels of anxiety experienced by a real witness during an actual crime.	Deffenbacher *et al.* reviewed 34 studies and concluded that, in general, laboratory studies demonstrate that anxiety tended to reduce accuracy, and that real-life studies tend to find an even greater loss in accuracy.	*These findings are at odds with Christianson and Hubinette's findings but suggest that lab studies are valid as they are supported by real-life studies.*

Research doesn't always support the weapon focus effect...

Studies of EWT in real-life crimes do not support the idea of a weapon focus effect.	Halford and Milne (2005) found that victims of violent crimes were more accurate in their recall of crime scene information compared to victims of non-violent crimes. The consequence of anxiety in these violent crimes appears to be an increase in the accuracy of eyewitness memory.	*This shows that there is no simple rule about the effect of anxiety on the accuracy of eyewitness testimony.*

Individual differences in the effects of anxiety on EWT...

It is possible that the effects of anxiety on EWT are moderated by emotional sensitivity.	Bothwell *et al.* (1987) found that participants labelled as 'stable' in terms of their emotional sensitivity showed rising levels of accuracy as stress levels increased, whereas those labelled as 'neurotic' showed decreasing levels of accuracy with increasing stress levels.	*This suggests that a key extraneous variable in studies of anxiety is participants' personality, particularly their emotional sensitivity.*

AO3 PLUS

APPLY: Exam skills

AO2: An example

SCENARIO Train passengers travelling home after a football match witnessed a fight among rival supporters in one of the carriages. One of the supporters drew a knife and threatened a fan from the other team. Passengers who witnessed the incident were asked by police to look at a series of photographs to identify the supporters involved in the confrontation.

From your knowledge of the effects of anxiety, what advice can you give the police about whether they can expect passengers to correctly identify the fans? **(4 marks)**

ANSWER *Findings from lab studies suggest accurate recall of the supporters' identities would be poorer due to the presence of the knife. The weapon focus effect predicts that the passengers' attention would be focused on the knife rather than features of the scene, such as the faces of those involved in the fight. However, interviews with real-life victims of violent bank robberies found that those who were directly threatened showed more accurate recall than bystanders, meaning some passengers may be able to correctly identify the fans, especially if they were directly threatened.*

AO2: One for you to try

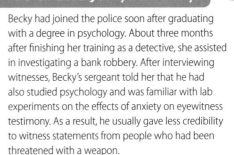

Becky had joined the police soon after graduating with a degree in psychology. About three months after finishing her training as a detective, she assisted in investigating a bank robbery. After interviewing witnesses, Becky's sergeant told her that he had also studied psychology and was familiar with lab experiments on the effects of anxiety on eyewitness testimony. As a result, he usually gave less credibility to witness statements from people who had been threatened with a weapon.

Using your understanding of the effects of anxiety on eyewitness testimony, explain what Becky might tell the detective sergeant to show him that his point of view might be incorrect. (6 marks)

AO2: Research methods

a. **Identify what type of graph is appropriate for each of these data sets.**

 (i) **Anxiety scores and recall scores for each participant, obtained from questionnaires.**

 (ii) **The number of participants who score 0–5, 6–10, 11–15, and 16–20 in a recall test.**

b. **Draw a suitable graph to represent the following data. Label your graph appropriately. (4 marks)**

Anxiety scores	16	12	11	17	8	10	4	15	14	7	11	18	4	12	16	6	14	8	11	15
Recall scores	10	16	14	6	11	14	8	12	18	9	14	4	6	17	7	11	12	5	13	10

c. **Draw a suitable graph to represent the following data. Label your graph appropriately. (4 marks)**

Recall score	0–5	6–10	11–15	16–20
n	2	7	8	3

How do I answer... application (AO2) questions?

Let's look again at the scenario of Becky in **AO2: One for you to try** above.

One way of answering questions such as this is to remember the 'Say one thing for 1 mark' and 'Say four things for 4 marks' strategy.

1 **Find a bit of appropriate psychology** For example, 'Pickel argues that the weapon focus effect could be a consequence of surprise rather than anxiety. She showed how participants who saw a thief carrying a chicken (high surprise) were less accurate in their recall than those who saw him carrying a gun (low surprise).'

2 **Use this to explain some aspect of the scenario** For example, 'This would challenge the detective sergeant's claim that anxiety has a detrimental effect on the accuracy of recall, because seeing a bank robber with a gun would not have been as surprising as seeing him with something more unexpected.'

3 **Find a second bit of psychology** For example, 'Studies of EWT do not always support the idea of a weapon focus effect. In fact, Halford and Milne found that victims of violent crimes were more, rather than less, accurate in their recall of crime scene information compared to victims of non-violent crimes.'

4 **Use this to explain the scenario** For example, 'The evidence of this research contradicts the detective sergeant's views. Becky could point out that, on the basis of psychological evidence, there is no simple rule about the effect of anxiety on the accuracy of eyewitness testimony.'

REVIEW

We have concentrated on one particular influence on eyewitness testimony – anxiety. In order to feel comfortable with this topic you should practise using the material in all the different ways that might be assessed in your exam.

1 Try constructing 3-mark, 4-mark and 6-mark descriptions of the relationship between anxiety and EWT.

2 How would you use the material on this spread to answer 8-mark, 10-mark and 16-mark extended writing questions?

3 If you are a little adventurous and would like to come up with a bit of evidence that challenges the 'high anxiety/less accurate recall' relationship, try entering 'An archival study of eyewitness memory of the Titanic's final plunge' in your search engine. Using the material in the abstract for this study, can you put together an AO3 point in the style we have constructed them on this spread?

Improving the accuracy of eyewitness testimony: The cognitive interview

 **RECAP**

AO1 Description

- **The cognitive interview** (CI) encourages witnesses to a crime to recreate the original context of the crime in order to increase the accessibility of stored information through the use of multiple retrieval strategies.

  > **1. Mental reinstatement of the original context** The witness is encouraged to mentally recreate the physical and psychological environment of the original incident. The aim is to provide contextual and emotional cues to retrieve memories.

  > **2. Report everything** The witness is encouraged to report every single detail of the event even though it may seem irrelevant. Memories are interconnected, so recollection of one item may then cue other memories.

  > **3. Change order** The interviewer tries alternative ways through the timeline of the incident, e.g. by reversing the order in which events occurred. The rationale is that this prevents pre-existing schema influencing recall.

  > **4. Change perspective** The witness is asked to recall the incident from multiple perspectives, e.g. by imagining how it would have appeared to other people present. This also disrupts the effect that schemas might have on recall.

- **The standard police interview** involves the interviewer doing most of the talking, asking specific questions that require specific answers. They may also ask leading questions that contaminate a witness's memory. These techniques disrupt the natural process of searching through memory, making memory retrieval inefficient.

Imagine yourself back in the bank. Tell me everything you remember. Start at the end and tell me what led up to that point. What would the cashier have seen?

AO3 Evaluation / Discussion

The cognitive interview is effective...

A strength of this approach is the amount of supporting research.

A meta-analysis by Köhnken *et al.* (1999) found an increase of 34 per cent in the amount of correct information generated in the CI. The effectiveness of the CI may be due to individual elements rather than the whole process, e.g. Milne and Bull (2002) found recall was significantly higher with just 'report everything' and 'mental reinstatement' components.

This suggests the cognitive interview is an effective technique for increasing the amount of information recalled.

Quantity rather than quality of recall...

A criticism of the cognitive interview is that effectiveness is often measured in terms of *quantity* of information recalled rather than *quality*.

Köhnken *et al.* not only found an increase in the amount of correct information generated, but also an increase in the amount of incorrect information (false positives) when using the enhanced CI.

This means that the results of this procedure need to be treated with caution, as it does not necessarily guarantee accuracy.

Problems with using the cognitive interview in practice...

A problem with the use of the cognitive interview is the amount of time and training needed to implement it.

Kebbel and Wagstaff (1996) report two issues with the CI: it requires more time than is often available, and it requires special training. Police often use strategies to limit an interview to save time and many forces have not provided the necessary training to conduct a CI.

A consequence is that the use of the cognitive interview in police interviews is not widespread.

Comparisons are difficult...

A problem in establishing the effectiveness of the cognitive interview is that only some aspects of it are used by some police forces.

Thames Valley Police use a version of the CI that does not include the 'changing perspectives' component. Greater Manchester Police have tended to use only the 'reinstatement of context' and 'report everything' components (Kebbell and Wagstaff).

This makes it difficult to establish the effectiveness of the technique as only parts of it are used in practice.

AO3 PLUS

APPLY: Exam skills

AO2: An example

SCENARIO

Saul was shopping in his local supermarket when he saw another customer hiding items in their jacket. The customer then tried to leave the store but security guards gave chase and eventually caught the customer just before they reached the store exit, at which point both guard and customer tumbled to the ground. When police arrived the customer accused the security guard of deliberately throwing him to the ground. The guard, however, argued they both tripped. Police officers decide to interview Saul to gain a better understanding of the incident.

What advice would you give police who wish to interview Saul using the cognitive interview technique? **(4 marks)**

ANSWER

Saul could consider events from another perspective. For example, what might shoppers nearer to the exit have seen? He could also change the order when recalling, such as starting from the moment the two fell to the ground and working backwards. These techniques aim to disrupt the effect that schemas have on Saul's recall of the event. Although the CI technique has been shown to increase the amount of correct information recalled, reporting of incorrect information also increases. Therefore Saul's recollections should be treated with caution by the police.

AO2: Research methods

This graph shows the relationship between anxiety and eyewitness accuracy of recall in one particular study.

a. **What can you conclude from this graph? (3 marks)**

The recall scores (out of 20) for individual participants in the three conditions were as follows:

Low anxiety condition: 12, 16, 13, 9, 14, 10, 15, 7, 11, 11, 8

Moderate anxiety condition: 14, 12, 18, 15, 14, 12, 17, 16, 14, 16, 18

High anxiety condition: 10, 8, 11, 6, 9, 10, 12, 7, 10, 12, 14

b. **Calculate the median and mode for each condition. (2 marks + 2 marks + 2 marks)**

c. **Use the median scores to construct a bar chart for the three conditions. Fully label your display. (4 marks)**

AO2: One for you to try

During one psychology lesson a man burst into the classroom and demanded to speak to the teacher. He told her that he was very angry about the way she had treated his son and continued shouting until the teacher managed to get him to leave. Afterwards the teacher asked the students to write down a description of everything they remembered.

Suggest how the teacher might use some of the techniques of the cognitive interview to question her students. (4 marks)

How do I answer... longer (12-mark or 16-mark) questions?

The difference between the three questions that follow lies in how you approach the AO3 evaluation/discussion.

Q1: Outline and evaluate the cognitive interview as a way of improving the accuracy of eyewitness testimony. (12 marks)

This requires an equal amount of AO3 to AO1, so there are two ways of doing this. Either you could use **two** complete AO3 points from those opposite (for a total of 150–180 words) *or* **one** complete and **two** other slightly less developed AO3 points.

Q2: Outline and evaluate the cognitive interview as a way of improving the accuracy of eyewitness testimony. (16 marks)

This question is more or less the same question but on an A Level paper, so this time it requires 10 marks' worth of AO3. The most effective way of matching this requirement would be to use all four AO3 points.

Q3: Discuss how the accuracy of eyewitness testimony can be improved. (16 marks)

The command word 'Discuss' requires AO3 that is a bit more 'discursive', e.g. looking at applications, implications, counterevidence, etc. We have tried to make our AO3 points 'discursive' to accommodate this. For example, the fourth AO3 point is 'discursive' because it goes beyond just saying that it *is* effective, and points out why it is difficult to establish this effectiveness.

In the previous chapter we advised you that, in these longer essay questions worth 12 or 16 marks, there will always be a requirement for 6 marks' worth of AO1, so we have provided you with the right amount of AO1 relevant to all three of these questions on the page opposite.

REVIEW

In this final **Review** section of this chapter, it is time for some more 'revision accounting'. This time we are reviewing the previous ten topics. When you feel you have mastered the AO1 and AO3 components of these and can cope with any of the different types of question that we have covered in the **How do I answer...?** sections, you will have earned a tick in the **Got it!** column. This list should include:

TOPIC	Got it!			Got it!	
	A01	A03		A01	A03
Short and long-term memory			Explanations for forgetting: retrieval failure		
The multi-store model of memory			Accuracy of EWT: misleading information		

Caregiver–infant interactions

RECAP

AO1 Description

- **Reciprocity** refers to where the actions of one partner elicit a response from the other partner, e.g. infants coordinate their actions with caregivers in a kind of conversation (Jaffe *et al.*, 1973).

- From birth, babies move in a rhythm when interacting with an adult, as if they were taking turns. Brazelton (1979) suggested that reciprocity is an important precursor to later communication.

- The regularity of an infant's signals allows the **caregiver** to anticipate their behaviour and respond appropriately.

- Sensitivity to infant behaviour is the foundation for later attachment between caregiver and infant.

- **Interactional synchrony** refers to how, when the infant and caregiver interact, they tend to mirror what the other is doing in terms of their facial and body movements.

- Meltzoff and Moore (1977) discovered that infants as young as two or three weeks imitated specific facial and hand gestures made by an adult model.

- In a later study, Meltzoff and Moore (1983) found evidence of interactional synchrony in babies as young as three days old, suggesting that this type of imitative response is more likely to be innate rather than learned.

AO3 Evaluation/Discussion

There are problems with testing infant behaviour…

There is reason to doubt the findings of research in this area because of difficulties in reliably testing infant behaviour.

Infants' mouths tend to be in constant motion, so it is difficult to distinguish between general activity and specific imitated behaviours. Meltzoff and Moore attempted to overcome this by using an observer with no knowledge of the behaviour being imitated, to make judgements of the infants' behaviour.

This highlights the difficulty in testing infant behaviour and one way in which this might be overcome.

There has been a failure to replicate…

Other studies have failed to replicate the findings of Meltzoff and Moore's findings.

Koepke *et al.* (1983) did not find the same evidence of interactional synchrony in very young infants. Meltzoff and Moore countered this by suggesting that Koepke *et al.*'s study was not as well controlled, which would account for the difference in findings.

Therefore, the findings from earlier studies have not been replicated in later studies, although differences in methodology might account for this.

The intentionality of infant behaviour is supported…

One way of testing the claim that infants' behaviour is intentional is to observe how they respond to inanimate objects.

Abravanel and DeYong (1991) observed infants interacting with two objects, one simulating tongue movements and the other a mouth opening/closing. Two groups of infants (aged 5 weeks and 12 weeks) made little response to the objects.

This suggests that infants do not imitate just anything they see, but that it is a specific social response to other humans.

There are individual differences in interactional synchrony…

A feature of interactional synchrony is that there is variation in infants in the degree they do this.

Isabella *et al.* (1989) found that more strongly attached infant–caregiver pairs showed greater interactional synchrony. Helmann (1989) showed that infants who demonstrate a lot of imitation have a better quality of relationship at three months.

This research shows that there are significant individual differences but does not indicate whether imitation is a cause or consequence of the relationship between infant and caregiver.

AO3 PLUS

APPLY: Exam skills

AO2: An example

SCENARIO Jacob was studying mothers interacting with their babies. He reported, 'Infant–Mother X: the mother sticks out her tongue. Her child imitates the action to an extent, partially protruding its tongue in response. The mother then quickly drops her lower jaw so her mouth opens wide. Again, the child copies. Infant–Mother Y: Infant Y shows distress through crying and holding its arms out towards the mother. The mother responds by picking the child up and holding him to her body. As she strokes her child's face the infant stops crying and smiles.'

Explain which infant–caregiver pair is displaying reciprocity and which pair is showing interactional synchrony. **(4 marks)**

ANSWER *Infant–Mother Y are showing reciprocity. This is because the actions of one elicit a response in the other. For example, the child cries and the mother responds by offering comfort, leading to a second response (smiling) from the infant. It is like a conversation. Infant–Mother X are showing interactional synchrony. This is because the infant is mirroring the mother's facial gestures. For example, the mother sticks out her tongue and the child copies the gesture.*

AO2: Research methods

Meltzoff and Moore (1977) conducted a controlled observation to investigate interactional synchrony in infants. The study was conducted using an adult model who displayed one of three facial expressions or hand movements where the fingers moved in a sequence. A dummy was placed in the infant's mouth during the initial display to prevent any response. Following the display the dummy was removed and the child's expression was filmed on a video.

a. **Briefly explain one strength of controlled observation as used in this study. (2 marks)**

b. **Briefly explain one limitation of controlled observation as used in this study. (2 marks)**

c. **Identify one ethical issue the researchers would need to consider in this research. Suggest how the researchers could deal with this ethical issue. (3 marks)**

AO2: One for you to try

Proud mother Nathalie was watching her partner, Darren, interacting with their baby daughter, Rebecca. Nathalie thought that it was really sweet how, whenever Darren smiled, Rebecca smiled back. Furthermore, whenever Darren moved his head, Rebecca also moved her head, perfectly in time with each other.

Using your knowledge of caregiver–infant interactions, explain what is happening in this situation. (3 marks)

How do I answer... selection (multiple choice) questions?

Which **one** of the following is **false** about interactional synchrony? (1 mark)

A It has been seen in three-day-old infants.

B It is probably a learned behaviour.

C It is probably an innate behaviour.

D It is not limited to the infant's mother.

Sometimes these questions require you to pick out the **one** statement that is correct, matches or defines a concept or idea. They may also (as here) ask you to pick out the **one** statement that is *false* or does *not* match or define a concept or idea.

Although these are generally worth only 1 mark, getting them correct is still important because that 1 mark can be the difference between one grade and another. So, some general advice on answering these:

* Read the question very carefully. Is it asking you to pick the statement that matches or the 'odd one out' that doesn't match?
* Make life easier by crossing out any that are obviously *not* going to be the correct answer, given the specific demands of the question.
* Applying this to the question above, we cross out **A** and **C** because that's what Meltzoff and Moore found (or concluded) in their study. That leaves a choice of **B** and **D** but **B** can't be true if **C** is true, so the 'untrue' one must be **B**.
* Questions asking which choice is 'false' are quite rare, however they are easy to miss if you don't read the question instructions carefully enough.

REVIEW

Knowing what is meant by reciprocity or interactional synchrony and being able to describe what psychologists know about these processes is vital for your understanding of this topic. There are a few things that you can do to help you with this.

1 Try explaining each of these processes to someone else (or even the dog, cat or teddy bear who won't be critical or snigger while you are doing it!).

2 Go back and read your notes again and then explain each in even more detail until you think Rover, Fang or Teddy would (had they *really* been listening) have a good understanding of both processes.

3 Try writing a few of your own selection (multiple choice) questions to consolidate this understanding.

 **RECAP**

AO1 Description

Stages of attachment

- Schaffer and Emerson (1964) carried out a study of infants in Glasgow. Infants were 5 to 23 weeks old at the start, and were studied until the age of one year. The researchers then described the stages of attachment:

- **Stage 1: Indiscriminate attachments** Infants initially produce similar responses to all objects, gradually developing a greater preference for social stimuli, such as a smiling face. Reciprocity and interactional synchrony help establish the infant's relationships with others.

- **Stage 2: The beginnings of attachment** At around four months, infants become more social, preferring human company to inanimate objects. As yet, they are still relatively easily comforted by anyone, and do not yet show **stranger anxiety**.

- **Stage 3: Discriminate attachments** By seven months, infants begin to display stranger anxiety and show **separation anxiety** when they are separated from one particular person, showing joy at reunion. This is their **primary attachment figure**.

- Schaffer and Emerson found that intensely attached infants had mothers who responded quickly and sensitively to their child's 'signals'. Infants who were poorly attached had mothers who failed to interact.

- **Stage 4: Multiple attachments** After the main attachment is formed, the infant also develops a wider circle of secondary attachments, depending on how many consistent relationships (other parent, grandparents, siblings etc.) he/she has.

The role of the father

- Schaffer and Emerson found that fathers were less likely to be primary attachment figures than mothers.

- Lamb (1977) reported there was little relationship between the amount of time fathers spend with their infants and infant–father attachment.

- There are biological reasons why fathers are less likely to be primary attachment figures: the female hormone oestrogen underlies caring behaviour.

- There are also cultural expectations and sex stereotypes that affect male behaviour. These include the belief that it is 'feminine' to be sensitive to others' needs.

- Research (e.g. Heermann *et al.*, 1994) has found that men are less sensitive to infant cues. Other research (Frodi *et al.*, 1978) has shown there is no difference in the *physiological* responses of males and females to an infant crying.

- There is evidence of males forming secure attachments with their children or sharing the role of primary attachment (Frank *et al.*, 1997), although biological and cultural factors may make this less likely.

AO3 Evaluation/Discussion

Data may not be reliable…

| The data collected by Schaffer and Emerson might be unreliable. | This is because the study was based on mothers' reports of their infants' behaviour. Because some mothers would have been less sensitive to their infants' protests, they would have been less likely to report them. | *This would create a systematic bias, which would challenge the validity of Schaffer and Emerson's conclusions.* |

Schaffer and Emerson's sample was biased…

| This included the nature of the population studied and the time in which the study took place. | The sample was drawn from a working-class population and the findings may not apply to other social groups. The sample was from the 1960s, yet parental care has changed a great deal since then, with many children being cared for outside the home. | *This suggests that if a similar study were carried out today, the results might be different.* |

The concept of monotropy is challenged…

| It may not be the case that the infant has one special and important attachment (monotropy), with other secondary attachments being less important. | Rutter (1995) argues against this, claiming that all attachment figures are equivalent. All attachments (e.g. with mother, father and siblings) are important because they serve different needs and are integrated to produce an infant's attachment type. | *This suggests that Bowlby may have been wrong in his claim that there is a hierarchy of attachments.* |

There are cultural variations in the attachment process…

| Because of differences between individualist and collectivist cultures, we would expect multiple attachments to be more common in collectivist rather than individualist cultures. | Sagi *et al.* (1994) found that infants raised in family-based arrangements (individualistic cultures) were twice as close to their mothers, in comparison to those raised in communal environments (collectivist cultures), where multiple attachments were the norm. | *This suggests that Schaffer and Emerson's stage model of attachment may apply specifically to individualist cultures.* |

AO3 PLUS

APPLY: Exam skills

AO2: An example

SCENARIO Danielle and Kristy were chatting about their children's development. 'I can't leave her with anyone at the moment,' Kristy explained. 'Every time my sister tries to hold her she screams and reaches out for me. When I hold her it's as if her whole face lights up.' Danielle mentioned she doesn't seem to have that difficulty with her son. 'He seems to enjoy being held by everyone. As long as he is having a cuddle or being fed, he's happy in anyone's arms.'

Explain which stages of attachment, as identified by Schaffer and Emerson, Kristy and Danielle's children seem to have reached. **(4 marks)**

ANSWER *Kristy's child is at stage 3: discriminate attachment. She is displaying separation anxiety by crying when separated from her primary attachment figure. Kristy seems to be her primary attachment figure as she shows joy when she is reunited with her. Danielle's child is probably younger than Kristy's child as he seems to be at stage 2: the beginnings of attachment. He has yet to form one specific attachment and so is happy to be comforted by anyone; he shows general sociability rather than stranger anxiety.*

AO2: Research methods

A psychologist compared two groups of adolescent participants who had either had secure or insecure attachments as infants. He used a questionnaire to identify their attachment type but also to rate the quality of their friendships. The higher the rating, the more positive the friendships were for the participant. The results of the study are shown below.

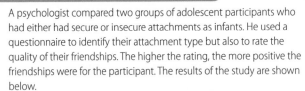

	Secure	Insecure
Median rating for quality of friendship	12.1	10.3

a. **Explain why this study is an example of a quasi-experiment. (2 marks)**
b. **Outline one limitation of using a questionnaire to collect the data in this study. (2 marks)**
c. **Sketch a bar chart to show the median ratings for quality of friendships in response to this question in Table 1. Fully label this chart. (4 marks)**

AO2: One for you to try

Gary lives in a community with very traditional views on parenting, and he couldn't remember his own father having much to do with his early childhood. When he found he was going to be a father himself he was thrilled, and looked forward to having the sort of relationship with his child that had been lacking between him and his own father. He was disappointed when, no matter how much time he spent with his young son Adam, Adam seemed to prefer the company of Gary's wife and her mother, and would always seek one of them when upset.

Explain why Adam's attachment with Gary might not be as strong as the one that he has formed with his mother and grandmother. (4 marks)

How do I answer... research methods (AO2) questions?

Questions requiring research methods knowledge can appear in any section of any paper in the AS or A Level exams. They could include any aspect of research methods, data analysis or ethical issues. Doing well in research methods questions is as much a case of thinking clearly and using common sense as it is regurgitating knowledge. Let's look at the **AO2: Research methods** example questions on the left:

a. There are 2 marks available for this question, so you should make it clear what is meant by a quasi-experiment. For the second mark you should add why *this* study fits that definition.
b. Although this is a fairly low mark tariff question, it still pays to read it carefully. There are a number of requirements, namely (i) it asks for **one**... (ii) **limitation**... of using (iii) **a questionnaire**... in (iv) **this study**. So, if you look at limitations of questionnaires on p.132, select one of these and apply it to this particular study, making sure it is expressed in the context of this study rather than just as a general limitation.
c. You need to know the difference between different types of graph, as drawing any other type of graph would not gain marks. Also, be aware of what 'labels' you need to add to gain the full 4 marks. These are: an appropriate title; accurately plotted data; accurate y-axis label; accurate x-axis label with appropriate key for the two bars.

REVIEW

Being able to describe something concisely, while maintaining accuracy, is not as easy as it sounds. On the opposite page, we have stripped down the descriptive detail you will find in the main Student Book to give you some guidance about how to do just that. Follow these steps to make it a bit more familiar.

1 Try answering the questions above using the advice given. How long did it take you and would you be able to reproduce this in exam conditions?
2 If the answer is 'no', then read over the material again and see how much you can reproduce just from memory.
3 Repeat Step 2 frequently over the coming weeks until the whole process becomes second nature.

Animal studies of attachment

AO1 Description

Lorenz (1935)

- **PROCEDURE** One group of gosling eggs were left with their natural mother while the other eggs were placed in an incubator.
  - > When the incubator eggs hatched, the first living moving thing they saw was Lorenz, and they started following him.
  - > Lorenz marked the two groups to distinguish them and placed them together, with him and their natural mother.
- **FINDINGS** The non-incubator goslings started following their natural mother and the incubator goslings ignored their natural mother and followed Lorenz.
  - > If goslings were not exposed to a moving object during a specific time period, the critical period, the animals did not imprint.
  - > Lorenz noted that the process is irreversible and long lasting, and that this early imprinting had an effect on later mate preferences, called sexual imprinting.

Harlow (1959)

- **PROCEDURE** Harlow created two wire mother 'surrogates'. One of these surrogates was wrapped in soft cloth to provide 'contact comfort'.
  - > Eight motherless infant rhesus monkeys were studied for 165 days. A milk bottle was placed on the cloth-covered 'mother' for one group and on the plain wire 'mother' for the other group.
  - > Measurements were made of the amount of time each infant spent with the two different 'mothers', and of their responses when frightened.
- **FINDINGS** All the motherless monkeys spent most time with the cloth-covered surrogate whether she had milk or not, and when frightened, all clung to the cloth-covered mother.
  - > Harlow found that the motherless monkeys developed to be socially and sexually abnormal in their interactions with other monkeys.
  - > If the motherless monkeys spent time with monkey 'peers' they could recover, but only if this happened before they were three months old.

AO3 Evaluation / Discussion

There is research support for imprinting…

Lorenz's concept of imprinting has been replicated in studies with other bird species.	Guiton (1966) found that chickens, exposed to yellow rubber gloves for feeding, became imprinted on the gloves. This shows that young animals are not born with a predisposition to imprint to a specific type of object, but develop their imprinting behaviour to any moving object within a critical window of development.	*Therefore, Guiton's findings provide clear support for Lorenz's conclusions about imprinting.*

There are criticisms of the concept of imprinting…

There is some dispute over the characteristics of imprinting.	The original concept of imprinting was that an image is stamped irreversibly on the nervous system. It is now believed that imprinting is more flexible, e.g. Guiton found he was able to reverse imprinting in chickens.	*This suggests that imprinting is no different from other types of learning and the effects are not irreversible, as Lorenz had originally proposed.*

There are confounding variables in Harlow's study…

The two wire surrogates varied in more ways than just being cloth-covered or not.	The heads used on the two surrogates were very different. One possibility is that the cloth-covered surrogate was more attractive to the infants simply because it had a more pleasing head.	*This suggests that Harlow's study lacked internal validity as differences between the two monkey surrogates were not sufficiently controlled.*

The results of Harlow's study with monkeys can be generalised to humans…

Despite differences between humans and animals, Harlow's findings about attachment have been mirrored in humans.	Harlow's findings that monkeys were *not* most attached to the wire 'mother' that provided food has also been demonstrated in the work of Schaffer and Emerson, which emphasised the importance of sensitive responding in the development of attachments.	*This shows that, although animal studies such as Harlow's provide useful pointers to explaining human behaviour, we should seek confirmation through research with humans.*

AO3 PLUS

APPLY: Exam skills

AO2: An example

SCENARIO The following passage appeared in an article on a parenting website:

'Attachment formation is not dependent on feeding. The person who feeds the infant is not necessarily the person who will become the child's main source of comfort. Instead, it seems to be the amount of comfort a caregiver offers that determines whether an attachment is formed.'

Consider the extent to which attachment research supports the claims made by the above passage. **(5 marks)**

ANSWER *Harlow's research into infant rhesus monkeys supports the claims made in the passage. He found that the infants spent the majority of time clinging to the cloth-covered mother, regardless of whether it provided food or not. They seemed to use the cloth mother as a safe base: running to it when startled and keeping in close proximity when playing with new toys. This suggests comfort rather than food was the basis of attachment formation as suggested by the website article. However, Harlow studied rhesus monkeys not human infants and therefore caution should be taken when generalising to humans. Although Schaffer and Emerson's research agreed with Harlow's as they found infants were not most attached to the person who fed them, rather it was the quality of the relationship that mattered (the comfort the caregiver offered).*

AO2: Research methods

Researchers used the Strange Situation test in order to investigate whether cats were more attached to their owners than to a random human. Cats were placed in a room and experienced being alone, being with their human owner and being with an unknown human. The cats were more exploratory and moved around more when their owner was in the room compared to when the stranger was present. When alone and with the stranger, the cats spent most of their time sitting by the door and vocalising.

a. **What was the aim of this study? (2 marks)**

b. **Write a non-directional hypothesis for this study. (2 marks)**

c. **What conclusions could the researchers draw from this study? (2 marks)**

AO2: One for you to try

As part of the 'hatch and release' scheme at San Diego Zoo, endangered California condor chicks (a type of vulture) are fed with the help of a condor-shaped hand puppet. Keepers explain that the purpose of the glove is to cover their hands so that the chick does not imprint on human beings or get too close to human beings when released back into the wild.

Using your knowledge of Lorenz's work on imprinting, explain the psychology behind the decision to use hand puppets to feed the condor chicks. (3 marks)

How do I answer... description only (AO1) questions?

There is a fairly simple formula in answering description only questions. For 2 marks, say two things (i.e. two points' worth), for 3 marks say three things and so on. Work through the sample questions below, using the AO1 material on the opposite page.

Q1: Outline the main findings of Harlow's attachment study. (2 marks)

Use the first **two** points for Harlow's **findings** (all three if three mark question).

Q2: Outline the findings of Lorenz's study of imprinting. (3 marks)

Use all **three** points for Lorenz's **findings**.

Q3: Outline Harlow's study of attachment. (4 marks)

Use the first **two** points for Harlow's **Procedure** and the first **two** points for **Findings**.

Q4: Outline one or more animal studies of attachment. (6 marks)

When given this sort of choice, it is wise to go for the **one** option (so description is more detailed). Include all **six** points for either Lorenz *or* Harlow's study.

This approach adds an appropriate level of detail to each answer and gives the examiner a useful way of discriminating between your answer and one that would be worth fewer than the maximum marks for that question.

REVIEW

One way of making sure you understand all the appropriate aspects of Lorenz's and Harlow's study is to do a bit of 'revision accounting'. When you feel you have mastered these different aspects, you have earned a tick in the **Got it!** column. This list should include:

TOPIC	Got it!		Got it!
The procedure of Lorenz's study (AO1)		The procedure of Harlow's study (AO1)	
The findings of Lorenz's study (AO1)		The findings of Harlow's study (AO1)	
Evaluation of Lorenz's study (AO3)		Evaluation of Harlow's study (AO3)	

Explanations of attachment: Learning theory

AO1 Description

Classical conditioning

- In attachment, food is an unconditioned stimulus (UCS) and pleasure is an unconditioned response (UCR).

- Certain things (such as the infant's mother) become associated with food because they are present at the time when the infant is fed. These are called neutral stimuli (NS).

- If the NS (mother) is consistently associated with the UCS (food) it takes on the properties of the UCS and produces the same response. The NS is now a conditioned stimulus (CS) and produces a conditioned response (CR).

- Just seeing this person gives the infant a feeling of pleasure (a CR). Learning theorists called this newly formed stimulus-response 'mother love'.

Operant conditioning

- When an animal is uncomfortable this creates a drive to reduce that discomfort. In the case of a hungry infant there is a drive to reduce the accompanying discomfort associated with hunger (Dollard and Miller, 1950).

- Consequently, when the infant is fed, this discomfort is reduced and the feeding produces feelings of pleasure, known as positive reinforcement.

- The food becomes a primary reinforcer and the person who supplies the food becomes a secondary reinforcer (through classical conditioning) and a source of pleasure in his/her own right.

- As a result, attachment occurs because the child seeks the person (usually the mother) who can supply the reward (food).

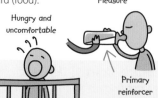

AO3 Evaluation/Discussion

Learning theory explanations are based on animal studies...

| A criticism of the learning theory of attachment is that it is based on animal studies (e.g. Skinner's research). | Although behaviourists believe that humans are no different to animals in the way they learn, critics argue that a human behaviour as complex as attachment cannot be explained in this way. It involves innate predispositions and mental activity that cannot be explained by conditioning. | *This suggests that the learning theory explanation is oversimplified and ignores factors such as contact comfort.* |

Attachment is not based on food alone...

| The main limitation of learning theory explanations is that they suggest food is the key element of attachment. | Evidence from Harlow's study with rhesus monkeys suggested that contact comfort rather than food was the most important factor in attachment. Schaffer and Emerson's research with human children found that 'sensitive responding' from the caregiver was more important than the provision of food. | *This suggests that learning theory presents only a limited explanation of attachment.* |

Learning theory has some explanatory power...

| A strength of learning theory is that it is able to explain some aspects of attachment. | Infants do learn through association and reinforcement, but food may not be the most important reinforcer. It is possible that parental attention and responsiveness are more important factors that assist in the formation of attachment, thus supporting the basic principles of learning theory. | *This shows that even though learning theory does not provide a complete explanation of attachment, it still has some value.* |

Bowlby's theory offers an alternative explanation...

| Learning theory was rejected as an explanation of attachment because a better theory appeared. | Bowlby's theory has many advantages in comparison to learning theory. E.g. it can explain *why* attachments form, whereas learning theory only explains *how* attachments form. Bowlby's also explains the benefits of attachment (e.g. protection from harm), which are not explained through learning theory. | *This shows that Bowlby's theory provides a more complete explanation of attachment than learning theory.* |

AO3 PLUS

APPLY: Exam skills

AO2: An example

SCENARIO Huw and his partner Meghan are new parents. When their daughter Victoria was born, Meghan gave up work to care for her full-time. Huw has to work long hours as he is the sole source of income for the family. Huw feels his daughter has a much stronger bond with Meghan than with him.

How would learning theory explain Victoria's attachment behaviour?
(4 marks)

ANSWER *Meghan is likely to be the person who feeds Victoria. Classical conditioning explains that food (UCS) gives Victoria feelings of pleasure (UCR). With repeated feeding, Meghan has become associated with this pleasure and so becomes the conditioned stimulus (CS) leading to 'mother love'. Huw works long hours so feeds his daughter less often, making it less likely Victoria will form an attachment with him. The operant conditioning explanation would be that food is a primary reinforcer as it reduces the uncomfortable feeling of hunger. Meghan has become a secondary reinforcer as Victoria has associated food with Meghan and the removal of hunger. Because Huw is not as involved in feeding he is less likely to become the secondary reinforcer and less likely to form an attachment.*

AO2: Research methods

A researcher wanted to carry out a study to see if there was any difference in the strength of attachment formed between mother and infant in a sample of working mothers compared with stay-at-home mothers. The 'working mothers' group left their children with a childminder during the day, but were there to feed their infants at the beginning and end of the day. The 'stay-at-home' mothers fed their infants, but also spent the days in the company of their infants. Researchers used a measure of attachment to assess attachment in infants when they reached the age of one year. This measure produces an overall score for each child ranging from +1.0 (very secure) to -1.0 (very insecure).

a. **Identify two ethical issues associated with this study. (2 marks)**

b. **Suggest how psychologists could deal with each of these issues. (4 marks)**

c. **Explain the purpose of the BPS Code of Ethics. (3 marks)**

The results of the study are as follows:

	Mean Attachment Q-set score	Standard deviation
'Working mother' infants	0.70	0.28
'Stay-at-home' infants	0.76	0.11

d. **Explain what is meant by the mean and standard deviation. (4 marks)**

e. **What do the data in the above table show about the strength of attachment in the two groups? (4 marks)**

AO2: One for you to try

When baby Nathan was born, his father Jon stopped working to stay at home and look after him, while Nathan's mother Sophie returned to work. Sophie continues to work full-time and does not have much to do with his care. Now that Nathan is ten months old, he has a particularly close relationship with his father.

Use your knowledge of learning theory to explain why Nathan became attached to his father. (3 marks)

How do I answer... 'Distinguish between' questions?

There are some fairly simple rules for answering this sort of question. If you are asked to 'Distinguish between…', 'Compare…' or 'Explain the difference between…', then these rules apply.

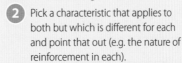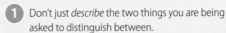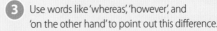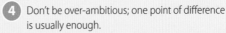

1 Don't just *describe* the two things you are being asked to distinguish between.

2 Pick a characteristic that applies to both but which is different for each and point that out (e.g. the nature of reinforcement in each).

3 Use words like 'whereas', 'however', and 'on the other hand' to point out this difference.

4 Don't be over-ambitious; one point of difference is usually enough.

So… how might we distinguish between operant and classical conditioning in the context of attachment using these rules?

In classical conditioning, an association is learned between a stimulus (such as food) and an involuntary response (feelings of pleasure). Operant conditioning, on the other hand, involves a learned association between a voluntary behaviour (feeding) and its consequence (reducing the hunger drive).

REVIEW

In order to feel comfortable with this topic you should practise using the material in all the different ways that might be assessed in your exam.

1 Try constructing 3-mark, 4-mark and 6-mark descriptions of the classical conditioning *and* operant conditioning explanations of attachment.

2 How would you use the material on this spread to answer 8-mark, 10-mark and 16-mark extended writing questions (or a 12-mark question if you are studying psychology at AS Level)?

Issues/Debates
Free will versus determinism. The learning theory of attachment is an example of environmental determinism because of its emphasis on conditioning and provision of food.

Explanations of attachment: Bowlby's theory

 **RECAP**

AO1 Description

- Attachment behaviour serves an important survival function: an infant who is not attached is less well protected. Parents must also be attached to their infants in order to ensure that the infants are cared for and survive.

- Infants who do not have the opportunity to form an attachment during the **critical period** (around three to six months) seem to have difficulty forming attachments later on.

- Attachment is determined by sensitivity, i.e. infants who are most strongly attached are the ones whose mothers are most responsive and most accessible.

- **Social releasers** are features of the infant, such as smiling and having a 'babyface', which elicit caregiving.

- Bowlby proposed that infants have one special emotional bond (**monotropy**), as well as many secondary attachments.

- An infant has one special relationship and forms a mental representation of this relationship (**internal working model**). This enables them to influence the caregiver's behaviour and acts as a template for future relationships.

- The **continuity hypothesis** proposes that individuals who are strongly attached in infancy continue to be socially and emotionally competent throughout childhood and adulthood compared to infants who are not strongly attached.

> **Issues/Debates**
> Free will versus determinism. Bowlby's theory of attachment is an example of biological determinism because of its emphasis on survival and critical periods.

AO3 Evaluation/Discussion

Attachment is adaptive...

A strength of Bowlby's theory is that it explains why human infants form attachments during the critical period rather than when they are first born.	Infants become attached during the critical period of three to six months, at the same time that they begin to crawl. It is therefore vital that infants form and maintain an attachment during this time, so that their caregivers can protect them.	*This supports Bowlby's claim that attachments are adaptive.*

A sensitive period rather than a critical period...

Bowlby's claim that attachments can only form within the three- to six-month 'critical' period has been challenged by Rutter *et al.*'s research.	Rutter *et al.* found that although infants were maximally responsive to attachment formation during the critical period, it was still possible for attachments to form outside this narrow window.	*As a result of this finding, the term 'sensitive period' is now preferred as an alternative to 'critical period'.*

There is research support for Bowlby's concept of monotropy...

The multiple attachment model, which claims that all attachment figures are equivalent, appears to contradict Bowlby's concept of monotropy.	However, in a review of research, Prior and Glaser (2006) concluded that a hierarchical model of attachment, which places emphasis on one central person 'higher' than others, is more likely than multiple attachments.	*This supports Bowlby's concept of monotropy and his claim that one special attachment plays a more significant role in emotional development.*

There is support for the continuity hypothesis...

Bowlby's claim that early attachment affects subsequent relationships is supported by research.	The Minnesota parent–child study (Sroufe *et al.*, 2005) followed participants from infancy to late adolescence and found continuity between early attachments and later emotional/social behaviour. Individuals who were securely attached in infancy were more socially competent, more popular and more empathetic later in childhood.	*This supports Bowlby's continuity hypothesis, as it shows a clear link between early and later attachments.*

AO3 PLUS

APPLY: Exam skills

AO2: An example

SCENARIO Aisha loves her baby sister and tells everyone about her big eyes and little squashy nose. Aisha enjoys feeding her and helps out with nappy changes. However, she sometimes finds it difficult to soothe her when she cries. Aisha's mother seems to instantly know what the baby needs and is able to calm her much more quickly than other family members.

How could Bowlby's attachment theory explain Aisha's experience?
(4 marks)

ANSWER Aisha's baby sister has social releasers such as big eyes and a little nose that encourage attachment formation. Aisha is motivated to remain in close proximity and interact with her. Although Aisha is involved in caregiving she may lack the level of sensitivity needed to become the primary attachment figure (she often finds it difficult to soothe her). Aisha's mother, however, can quickly identify the baby's needs and so is more likely to form that one special relationship (monotropy) during the critical period of three to six months. Aisha's sister is likely to form a secondary attachment to her, which will play a role in the infant's social development.

AO2: Research methods

A psychologist investigated the relationship between type of attachment in childhood and success in later adult relationships. He published a questionnaire in a local newspaper. The participants were people who read the newspaper, who filled in the questionnaire and sent it to the psychologist. Participants' answers to the questions were used to decide whether they had been securely or insecurely attached as children. The participants who were identified as securely attached children were more likely to have successful adult relationships than those identified as insecurely attached children.

a. **Construct an appropriate non-directional hypothesis for this study. (3 marks)**

b **Identify one ethical issue the researcher would need to consider in this research. Suggest how the researcher could deal with this ethical issue. (3 marks)**

c. **Identify one possible extraneous variable in this study and explain how this might affect the validity of the study. (3 marks)**

AO2: One for you to try

Hania is three years old and has strong bonds with both of her parents and her grandparents too.

Toby is four months old and likes attention but shows no preference for any person in particular.

Lola is five years old and shows little distress when her parents leave her and hardly responds when they return.

Victor is two years old and only has one strong bond and that is with his mother.

a. **Name the child who demonstrates a monotropic attachment. (1 mark)**

b. **Name the child who demonstrates an indiscriminate attachment. (1 mark)**

c. **Name the child who demonstrates an insecure-avoidant attachment. (1 mark)**

How do I answer... evaluation only (AO3) questions?

Like the description only questions on p.45, evaluation questions come in all sorts of shapes and sizes. Terms like 'Evaluate', 'Discuss', 'Explain', 'Criticism', 'Strength' and 'Limitation' all indicate that AO3 is required. Let's look at some examples.

Q1: Briefly explain **one** limitation of Bowlby's theory of attachment. (2 marks)

Using one of the AO3 points opposite as your material for this question, you would use the first two columns (the main critical claim and its expansion).

Q2: Explain **one** limitation of Bowlby's theory of attachment. (3 marks)

This simply requires a little more elaboration, so you would add in the material in the third column to access the third mark on offer.

Q3: Evaluate Bowlby's theory of attachment. (6 marks)

You would take the same approach as with **Q2:**, but this time using **two** of the AO3 points on the opposite page. Don't try to use more than two; it would make your answer too superficial.

REVIEW

On p.35 we introduced you to Craik and Lockhart's 'level of processing model' – the more that information is elaborated, the more likely we will be able to access that information later on. So... that means that just *reading* about Bowlby's theory doesn't make it particularly memorable.

There are various ways of elaborating the material on this spread to make it more memorable. These include: writing out key points, explaining it to someone else, constructing a visual 'mind-map' of information and so on. Try it and trust in psychology!

Tip: There is a wealth of useful revision videos on the Internet – take a look for some on mind-map construction.

Ainsworth's Strange Situation: Types of attachment

AO1 Description

Ainsworth (1971)

- Ainsworth *et al.* devised the **Strange Situation** to test the nature of attachment in order to see how infants behave under conditions of mild stress and novelty.
- **PROCEDURE** The procedure consists of eight episodes. The key feature of these episodes is that the caregiver and stranger alternately stay with the infant or leave.
  - > This enables observation of the infant's response to: separation from the caregiver (separation anxiety); reunion with the caregiver (reunion behaviour); response to a stranger (stranger anxiety).
  - > Observers record what the infant is doing every 15 seconds using five behavioural categories, with each item scored for intensity on a scale of 1 to 7.

- **FINDINGS** They found evidence of three different types of attachment.
  - > *Securely attached infants* (Type B) use their caregivers as a secure base to explore. They are not likely to cry if their caregiver leaves, and show some distress when left with a stranger. When feeling anxious they are easily soothed by their caregivers.
  - > *Insecure-avoidant infants* (Type A) are happy to explore with or without their caregiver. They show little response to separation and show little or no social interaction and intimacy with others.
  - > *Insecure-resistant infants* (Type C) seek and resist social interaction with others. They show high levels of separation anxiety and stranger anxiety. When reunited with their caregivers, they show conflicting behaviours and resist being picked up.

AO3 Evaluation/Discussion

There are more than three attachment types...

Subsequent research has suggested that Ainsworth overlooked a fourth type of attachment.	Main and Solomon (1990) proposed a fourth attachment type, the insecure-disorganised Type D. These infants do not conform to any of Ainsworth's original attachment types, as they show very strong attachment behaviour which is often followed by avoidant behaviour.	*This suggests Ainsworth's original conclusions were incomplete and do not account for all attachment behaviours.*

A strength of the Strange Situation is the reliability of the observations...

In observational studies such as Ainsworth's, reliability of observations is important.	Ainsworth *et al.* found almost perfect inter-observer reliability of .94, suggesting high agreement among the different observers when rating exploratory behaviour. High inter-observer reliability suggests that observations can be accepted as being reliable and Ainsworth's observations had almost perfect reliability.	*This suggests that the Strange Situation is a reliable method for examining attachment behaviour and determining attachment type.*

A real-world application of the Strange Situation...

A strength of the Strange Situation is that intervention strategies can be developed to help children with disordered patterns of attachment.	The Circle of Security Project (Cooper *et al.*, 2005) teaches caregivers to understand their infants' signals of distress. This project showed a decrease in the number of caregivers classified as disordered and an increase in the number of infants classified as securely attached.	*The success of strategies such as this emphasises the value of attachment research as it leads to an improvement in children's lives.*

Low internal validity of the conclusions...

The Strange Situation may simply measure the quality of one particular relationship rather than the child's attachment type.	Main and Weston (1981) found that children behaved differently in the Strange Situation, depending on which parent they are with. Therefore, the Strange Situation may be measuring an infant's relationship with a particular parent and not a personal characteristic – their attachment type.	*This suggests that the Strange Situation may lack internal validity as the observation may be measuring individual relationships.*

AO3 PLUS

 APPLY: Exam skills

AO2: An example

SCENARIO Tom and his mother participated in a Strange Situation study. Observers noted that Tom showed high willingness to explore and only a moderate level of distress when approached by a stranger. Amelia and her mother also took part. Unlike Tom, Amelia did not explore and showed intense distress when with a stranger. Compared to Amelia, Tom showed great enthusiasm when reunited with his mother. Amelia sought comfort but reacted angrily when held.

Based on the behaviours displayed, how would observers classify each child's attachment type? **(3 marks)**

ANSWER *Tom would be classified as securely attached as he uses his mother as a safe base from which to explore the room. He is comfortable with social interactions, showing enthusiastic reunion behaviour and only moderate distress when with a stranger. Amelia is showing behaviours associated with insecure-resistant attachment. She shows low willingness to explore and becomes very upset in the presence of a stranger. Her reunion with her mother suggests she is seeking, but at the same time rejecting, interaction.*

AO2: One for you to try

Ashley and Alex are 18 months old. They are observed individually using Ainsworth's Strange Situation. Ashley moves around the room and plays with toys in the corner. She pays little attention to her mother and does not even notice her mother leave the room. She then avoids her mother when she later returns. Alex, however, does not move around the room and cries intensely when her mother leaves. When her mother returns, she angrily resists being picked up and is difficult to comfort.

Use the information in the description above to suggest Ashley and Alex's attachment types. Explain how you reached your decision. (4 marks)

AO2: Research methods

Topál *et al.* (1998) used the Strange Situation technique to explore attachments between dogs and their owners. Two observers sampled eight behaviour categories every 10 seconds. The findings were that dogs, like people, were either securely or insecurely attached.

a. **What was the aim of this study? (2 marks)**

b. **Identify the sampling procedure used in this study and give one limitation of this. (3 marks)**

c. **Explain why two observers recorded behaviours. (1 mark)**

d. **Explain how the researchers might assess inter-observer reliability in this study. (2 marks)**

How do I answer... description and evaluation (AO1 + AO3) questions?

Q1: Briefly outline the nature of the Strange Situation and give one limitation of this research technique. (4 marks)

Q2: Outline and evaluate the Strange Situation as a way of studying attachment type. (6 marks)

Q3: Outline and discuss findings from research using the Strange Situation. (6 marks)

- **Step 1** in answering mixed AO1 + AO3 questions is recognising that this is what you are being asked to do! Having two different command words (e.g. Outline – an AO1 term – and evaluate – an AO3 term) is usually a good clue.
- **Step 2** is planning how much you should write for each. In mixed AO1 + AO3 questions up to 6 marks, the division is half and half (it is different with mark totals higher than this as we will see on p. 59).
- **Step 3** is deciding *what* to write. If you have followed the advice in the previous spreads, this should be easy to work out. For **Q1:**, this would mean using the first two points ('Ainsworth et al…' and 'The procedure consists of…') associated with the Strange Situation together with the first two columns of **one** of the AO3 points on the opposite page.
- For **Q2:**, the words 'as a way of' would alert you to the fact that the question is asking about the technique itself rather than its findings. Consequently, you would use the first three points associated with the **PROCEDURES** of the technique. For the AO3 content you might use one complete AO3 point from the Strange Situation opposite, or the first two columns from both of the AO3 points for this study.
- Although 'Discuss' is more commonly used as an AO1 + AO3 term in its own right, in **Q3:** it is being used just as an AO3 term. You have a number of ways to answer this, but whichever route you take, there should be about 75–90 words of AO1 and 75–90 words of AO3. This time you should use the **FINDINGS** associated with the Strange Situation plus AO3 material (as above).

REVIEW

Being able to summarise something concisely, while maintaining accuracy, is not as easy as it sounds. On the opposite page, we have stripped down the descriptive and evaluative detail from the Student Book to give you some guidance about how to do just that. Here's some tips to make the content a bit more familiar.

1. Try answering the three questions in **How do I answer... ?** above using the advice given. How long did it take you and would you be able to reproduce this in exam conditions (allowing approximately one minute of writing time per mark)?

2. If the answer is 'no', then read over the material again and see how much you can reproduce just from memory.

3. Repeat Step 2 frequently over the coming weeks until the whole process becomes second nature.

Cultural variations in attachment

AO1 Description

van IJzendoorn and Kroonenberg (1988)

- **PROCEDURE** van IJzendoorn and Kroonenberg conducted a meta-analysis of the findings from 32 studies of attachment behaviour. This involved over 2000 Strange Situation classifications in eight different countries.

- **FINDINGS** Differences were small, with secure attachment the most common classification in every country. Insecure-avoidant attachment was the next most common except in Israel and Japan, where insecure-resistant attachment was the next most common. Variation *within* cultures was 1.5 times greater than variation *between* cultures.

    > The conclusion was that the global pattern across cultures appears to be similar to that found in the US, i.e. secure attachment is the 'norm'.

    > The presence of these cultural similarities supports the idea that secure attachment is 'best' for healthy social and emotional development.

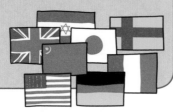

Cultural similarities and differences

- **Cultural similarities** Tronick *et al.* (1992) studied an African tribe, the Efe, who live in extended family groups. Despite differences in childrearing practices the infants, at six months, still showed one primary attachment.

- **Cultural differences** Grossmann and Grossmann (1991) found higher levels of insecure attachment amongst German infants than in other cultures.

    > German culture involves keeping some interpersonal distance between parents and children. This means infants do not engage in proximity-seeking behaviours in the Strange Situation and so appear to be insecurely attached.

    > Takahashi (1990) found similar rates of secure attachment in Japanese infants to those found by Ainsworth *et al.* However, the Japanese infants showed no evidence of insecure-avoidant attachment and high rates of insecure-resistant attachment.

    > In Japan, infants rarely experience separation from their mothers, which would explain why they were more distressed in the Strange Situation than their American counterparts.

AO3 Evaluation/Discussion

Similarities may be due to global culture…

Bowlby claims that the reason for such similarities of attachments across cultures is because attachment is an innate mechanism.	van IJzendoorn and Kroonenberg later concluded that some of the similarities across cultures could be explained by the effects of mass media. This spreads ideas about parenting so that children in different cultures are exposed to similar parenting styles.	*This suggests that cultural similarities in attachment are not due to innate influences but to our increasingly global culture.*

Research focuses on 'countries' rather than 'cultures'…

An issue with van IJzendoorn and Kroonenberg's research is that they were studying differences in countries rather than cultures.	For example, a Japanese study found a similar distribution of attachment types to Western studies in Tokyo, but an increase in insecure-resistant individuals in a rural sample (van IJzendoorn and Sagi, 2001).	*These results demonstrate that 'country' and 'culture' are not the same thing, and provide support to the claim that there is more variation within than between cultures.*

The 'tools' of cross-cultural research may not be appropriate…

An issue for cross-cultural research is that the 'tools' used for assessment may not be valid in that culture.	The Strange Situation has assumptions that are specific to its country of origin (USA). It assumes 'willingness to explore' is a sign of secure attachment. However, in Japan, dependence rather than independence is a sign of this (van IJzendoorn and Sagi).	*This means that research using the Strange Situation may lack validity in cultures other than the US.*

Attachment theory itself is culturally biased…

Rothbaum *et al.* argue that it is not just the methods used in research that are culturally biased, but also the underlying theory.	Bowlby believed that securely attached infants become socially and emotionally competent children and adults. In the West, this is defined in terms of independence and self-oriented behaviour, but in Japan, 'competence' is represented by a preference for group- rather than self-oriented behaviour and the inhibition of emotional expression.	*Therefore, the high levels of insecure-resistant attachment in Japanese children may simply represent a different form of 'competence'.*

AO3 PLUS

APPLY: Exam skills

AO2: An example

SCENARIO A researcher carried out cross-cultural research to compare attachment types across two countries: Germany and Japan. Mother-infant pairs were observed in the Strange Situation enabling classifications of secure, insecure-avoidant and insecure-resistant to be made.

a. *Based on van IJzendoorn and Kroonenberg's research, what do you think the researchers would find in this study?* **(2 marks)**

b. *Why should the researcher treat their findings with caution?* **(4 marks)**

ANSWER a. The researcher may find that for both countries secure attachment is the most common classification. Germany is likely to show more insecure-avoidant than insecure-resistant attachments, while Japanese infants are more likely to be classified as insecure-resistant than insecure-avoidant.

b. However, these findings should be treated with caution as the Strange Situation is based on Western ideas of childcare and attachment behaviours. It is unlikely that the Japanese infants would have been left alone before experiencing the Strange Situation and so show extreme distress compared to German children whose parents have encouraged independence. This could result in Japanese children being incorrectly classified as insecure-resistant. Furthermore, the researcher should not mistake culture for country. van IJzendoorn and Kroonenberg found more variation within cultures than between them so one study of Germany or Japan cannot be said to represent a whole culture due to the influence of subculture on childrearing practices.

AO2: Research methods

van IJzendoorn and Kroonenberg's study described on the opposite page is an example of a 'meta-analysis'.

a. **Explain what is meant by a 'meta-analysis'. (2 marks)**

b. **Why was a meta-analysis the most suitable approach for van IJzendoorn and Kroonenberg's study? (2 marks)**

c. **Briefly explain one strength and one limitation of meta-analysis as a research approach in psychology. (4 marks)**

REVIEW

On this spread we have looked at cultural variations in attachment and focused on how to answer AO2 application questions. To enhance your practical expertise in questions on this topic further, there are a few other useful things you can do, including planning what you would write for:

• 'Outline' questions on cultural variations in attachment worth 4 marks and 6 marks
• 'Outline' questions on van IJzendoorn and Kroonenberg's study worth 3 marks, 4 marks and 6 marks.

Using the format of bullet pointed material (for AO1) and AO3 points, write a plan for an 8-mark, 12-mark and (if you are taking the A Level) a 16-mark essay question for: 'Discuss cultural variations in attachment.'

AO2: One for you to try

Intervention programmes aimed at helping children who are insecurely attached tend to be based on Western beliefs about the nature of attachment. These programmes emphasise the development of independence and self-efficacy in these children. However, such programmes are viewed more positively in the United States than in Japan. Japanese parents do not value either the programmes or their intended outcomes, and Japanese experts are less likely to recommend them.

Using your knowledge of cultural variations in attachment, explain why the type of intervention programme described above is less valued in Japan than in the US. (4 marks)

How do I answer... essay questions with an AO2 component?

Q1: Yumi is 18 months old and has just moved from Japan to the UK. On her first day at nursery she cries when her mother leaves and will not allow the helpers to comfort her.

Briefly discuss cultural variations in attachment. Make reference to Yumi's behaviour in your answer. (8 marks)

Q2: Jack is 18 months old and has just moved from the UK to Japan. At nursery, he copes well when his mother leaves and is content and happy with the helpers.

Discuss cultural variations in attachment. Make reference to Jack's behaviour in your answer. (12/16 marks)

Essay questions with an AO2 (application) component, are essentially the same as a straightforward essay (see p.55) *but* two of the marks available are diverted for your ability to explain the scenario outlined in the question in the context of the material you are discussing.

For example, for **Q1:**, there would be 3 marks for AO1, 3 marks for AO3 *and* 2 marks for AO2. For example, for this question you might write the following for the AO2 component:

van IJzendoorn and Kroonenberg's research found that, although secure attachment was the most common classification in every country studied, insecure-resistant attachment was the next most common in Japan. Yumi is Japanese, and the behaviour she is exhibiting at nursery is characteristic of this form of attachment, i.e. she is displaying separation anxiety and stranger anxiety.

For **Q2:**, if a 12-marker, it would be 6 marks for AO1, 4 marks for AO3 *and* 2 marks for AO2.

Finally, if you meet this question as a 16-marker (at A Level), then you should write 6 marks' worth of AO1, 6 marks' worth of AO3 *and* 4 marks' worth of AO2.

Bowlby's theory of maternal deprivation

AO1 Description

- Deprivation refers to the loss of emotional care that is normally provided by a primary caregiver.
- Bowlby proposed that prolonged emotional **deprivation** would have long-term consequences in terms of emotional development.
- **The value of maternal care** Children need a 'warm, intimate and continuous relationship' with a mother figure to ensure continuing normal mental health.
- **Critical period** A child who has frequent and/or prolonged separations may become emotionally disturbed but only if this happens before the age of about two-and-a-half years, and if there is no substitute mother-person available.

- Bowlby suggested the **long-term consequence** of deprivation was emotional maladjustment or even mental health problems such as depression.

44 juvenile thieves (Bowlby, 1944)

- **PROCEDURE** Bowlby analysed case histories of 88 emotionally maladjusted children attending a Child Guidance Clinic – half had been caught stealing (the 44 'thieves') and the other half were a control group.
  - > Bowlby suggested 14 of the 'thieves' were affectionless psychopaths – they lacked normal signs of affection, shame or sense of responsibility.
- **FINDINGS** Bowlby found that, of the 14 individuals diagnosed as affectionless thieves, 12 had experienced frequent early separations from their mothers.
  - > Almost none of the control participants experienced early separations whereas 39 per cent of the thieves had experienced early separations. This suggests that early separations are linked to affectionless psychopathy.

AO3 Evaluation/Discussion

Emotional separation could be more important than physical separation…

Infants can still experience deprivation even if they are not physically separated from their caregiver.	A mother who is severely depressed may find it difficult to provide appropriate levels of emotional care. Radke-Yarrow *et al.* (1985) found that 55 per cent of children with severely depressed mothers were insecurely attached, in comparison to 29 per cent of children with non-depressed mothers.	*This suggests that psychological separation can also lead to deprivation, in the same way as physical separation.*

There is research support for the long-term effects of deprivation…

Research suggests that early maternal deprivation increases the likelihood that individuals will experience later negative outcomes.	Bifulco *et al.* (1992) found that 25 per cent of women who had experienced separation from their mothers later developed depression or an anxiety disorder, compared to 15 per cent of those with no experience of separation. The severity of these problems was much greater in women whose loss was before the age of six.	*This shows that early deprivation can make people more vulnerable to later mental health problems.*

There are real-world applications of Bowlby's theory…

Bowlby's work has had a positive impact on the way children are looked after in hospitals.	Prior to Bowlby's research, children were separated from their parents when they went into hospital. However, Bowlby's and the Robertsons' (1952) research (filming the distress of young children in hospital) led to major changes. Parents are encouraged to visit their children and there is greater flexibility in terms of visiting hours.	*This demonstrates the positive application of Bowlby's work to improve the lives of children.*

There is a difference between deprivation and privation…

Rutter (1981) claimed that Bowlby did not make it clear whether the child's attachment bond had formed but been broken (deprivation), or had never been formed in the first place (privation).	Rutter believed that the *lack* of an attachment bond would have far more serious consequences for the child than the *loss* of an attachment bond.	*This is important because there is a key distinction between deprivation and privation, and a lack of clarity may affect the validity of research findings.*

AO3 PLUS

APPLY: Exam skills

AO2: An example

SCENARIO Jamie lost his mother to a terminal illness when he was three years old. Before her death she had spent a long time in hospital. Jamie rarely visited her as his father felt it would be too upsetting for him to see his mother.

Using Bowlby's theory of maternal deprivation explain how Jamie might be affected by this separation from his mother. **(4 marks)**

ANSWER *Bowlby believed that a child who experiences deprivation during the critical period is at risk of later emotional disturbance. As Jamie experienced separation from his mother before the age of five, he could develop difficulties in childhood and adulthood. Bowlby claimed, 'mother-love in infancy is as important for mental health as are vitamins and proteins for physical health', implying Jamie would experience poorer mental health than children who have not experienced deprivation. Jamie experienced prolonged separation from his mother prior to her death and so may develop affectionless psychopathy as identified by Bowlby in his study of 44 thieves. This means Jamie might lack normal signs of affection, shame or a sense of responsibility.*

AO2: Research methods

Bowlby studied 88 children who were patients at the Child Guidance Clinic in London. Bowlby conducted interviews with the parents to find out if the children had experienced early childhood separation.

Identify one issue with the use of interviews that the researcher would need to consider in this research and explain how the researcher may overcome this issue. (3 marks)

Hint: 1) You should state an issue in this research study. 2) You should explain why this is an issue. 3) Finally, you should state how the researcher can overcome this issue.

AO2: One for you to try

Sally's one-year-old son Max has to go into hospital for a minor operation and stay there for a week. She is worried what effect this may have on him, especially as she has to go to work during the day so cannot be with him.

Suggest what Sally might do to ensure Max's emotional well-being while he is in hospital. Use psychological research to support your answer. (4 marks)

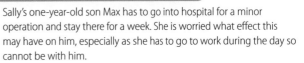 **How do I answer... longer (12-mark or 16-mark) essay questions?**

Q1: Outline and evaluate Bowlby's theory of maternal deprivation. (12 marks)

Q2: Discuss Bowlby's theory of maternal deprivation. (16 marks)

1. The first thing you need to do is work out how much AO1 and how much AO3 you should write. For a 12-mark question, this is a straightforward half and half, so half your content should be half AO1 (outlining) and half AO3 (evaluating). For the 16-mark questions (found at A Level), AO1 is worth 6 marks and AO3 10 marks, so you would write a little less than double the amount of AO3 compared to AO1.

2. The second thing is to decide *what* to write. It will always be 6 marks' worth of AO1, so we have provided you with the right amount of AO1 on the page opposite. Practise writing this AO1 material (legibly) to see if you can do it in 7 ½ minutes. Then you have the choice of what to write for either 6 marks' worth of AO3 (in a 12-mark question) or 10 marks' worth of AO3 (in a 16-mark question). We have aimed to make each AO3 point around 60–75 words, so that would be three points for a 12-mark question and four for a 16-mark question.

3. The command word 'Discuss' still has the same AO1 requirement, but requires AO3 that is a bit more 'discursive', e.g. looking at applications, implications, counterevidence. We have tried to make our AO3 points 'discursive' to accommodate this.

 REVIEW

On the opposite page, we have stripped down the detail you will find in the main Student Book to give you some guidance about how to answer questions on Bowlby's maternal deprivation theory. To prepare yourself for possible questions on this topic, make sure you can use this material effectively. Practise the following examples.

1. Write a 6-mark description of the model (this could include details of the juvenile thieves study).

2. Write a 4-mark description of the juvenile thieves study (for questions that ask specifically for this).

3. Write three elaborated AO3 points (if you are doing psychology at AS) or four points (if you are following the A Level course).

RECAP

AO1 Description

Rutter and Sonuga-Barke (2010)

- Rutter and Sonuga-Barke studied 165 Romanian orphans who spent their early lives in Romanian institutions. Of these, 111 were adopted before the age of two and 54 by the age of four.
- **PROCEDURE** Adoptees were tested at regular intervals to assess physical, cognitive and social development, and compared to a control group of 52 British children adopted in the UK before the age of six months.
- **FINDINGS** Romanian orphans lagged behind the British adoptees on all measures of development. By the age of four, some of the children had caught up with their British counterparts, particularly those adopted before the age of six months.
  - > Follow-ups confirmed that significant deficits (disinhibited attachments and problems with peer relationships) remained in individuals who experienced institutional care beyond the age of six months.

Other studies of Romanian orphans

- Le Mare and Audet (2006) carried out a longitudinal study of 36 Romanian orphans adopted to families in Canada. They were physically smaller than a matched control group at age four-and-a-half years, but this difference disappeared at ten-and-a-half.
- Zeanah *et al.* (2005) compared 136 Romanian children aged 12–31 months, who had spent 90 per cent of their lives in an institution, to a control group of children who had never been in an institution. The institutionalised children showed signs of disinhibited attachment.

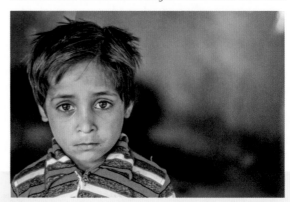

AO3 Evaluation/Discussion

There are individual differences in the effects of institutionalisation...

Not all children who experience institutionalisation fail to recover.	Although some research suggests that individuals who do not form an attachment within the sensitive period are unable to recover, this is not true of all children who experience institutionalisation. Rutter suggested that some children in institutions might receive special attention and so have some type of attachment experience.	*This suggests that institutionalisation does not affect all children in the same way.*

There are real-life applications of research into institutionalisation...

Insights from research into institutionalisation has been used to improve the lives of children.	The process of adoption has changed so that mothers who give a baby up for adoption do so within the first week of birth. This enables children to form a secure attachment with their adoptive families during the sensitive period.	*The result is that adoptive mothers and their children are just as securely attached as in non-adoptive families (Singer et al. 1985).*

The value of longitudinal studies in institutionalisation research...

A strength of longitudinal studies such as the one carried out by Rutter and Sonuga-Barke is that they follow the lives of children over many years.	Longitudinal studies such as this allow researchers to assess the long-term effects of institutionalisation and whether these effects may disappear after sufficient time with suitable high-quality care.	*These studies have demonstrated that it would be wrong to conclude that institutionalisation inevitably causes negative effects.*

Emotional deprivation is only one factor...

A limitation of research using Romanian orphans is that there were inevitably confounding variables.	Orphans were faced with more than just emotional deprivation. The appalling physical conditions affected their health and lack of cognitive stimulation would have affected their development. Many orphans went on to experience poor subsequent care, such as living in poverty.	*This suggests that researchers should be cautious when interpreting the effects of these studies, as there are many factors that could have affected the orphans' development.*

AO3 PLUS

 # APPLY: Exam skills

AO2: An example

SCENARIO Nadia and Aaron are in the process of adopting a four-month-old infant. The birth mother was unable to look after the child and so the child has been cared for by a state orphanage in Serbia. Due to a lack of funding, the orphanage has few staff and poor conditions, with limited resources to provide a good standard of physical care and cognitive stimulation.

What insights can institutional research offer Nadia and Aaron regarding their upcoming adoption? **(4 marks)**

ANSWER *Due to the lack of resources in the orphanage the child may be underdeveloped both physically and cognitively. Research suggests lack of emotional care and mental stimulation can lead to developmental delays. Nadia and Aaron should also be aware that the child may demonstrate disinhibited attachment, showing overfamiliarity with strangers and attention seeking as they age. However, the child is currently four months old and so still within the sensitive period for attachment formation. Therefore, the effects of institutionalisation may not be as extreme if the adoption is completed quickly. Furthermore, research suggests that, if Nadia and Aaron can provide high-quality emotional care, the effects of institutionalisation can be overcome.*

AO2: Research methods

The scenario in **AO2: One for you to try** above, about Alin, is an example of a case study. A case study is a detailed study of a single individual, institution or event. Many research methods may be used, such as observations, interviews, psychological tests or experiments. Case studies are often longitudinal, following an individual over an extended period of time.

Identify one strength and one limitation with the use of a case study in this example. (4 marks)

AO2: One for you to try

Using your knowledge of Romanian orphan studies and the effects on institutionalisation, answer the following:

Research has shown that institutionalisation can have numerous negative effects on children. In the 1990s, many children were found living in awful conditions in Romanian orphanages. Alin lived in one of these orphanages from birth, but was adopted at 18 months old. Alin's development was studied for a number of years and he developed into a healthy young child.

Explain why Alin later developed into a healthy young child. You should refer to psychological research in your answer. (4 marks)

How do I answer... application (AO2) questions?

Let's look again at the question about Alin in **AO2: One for you to try** above.

One way of answering questions such as this is to remember the 'Say one thing for 1 mark' and 'Say four things for 4 marks' strategy.

1. **Find a bit of appropriate psychology** (e.g. 'Rutter and Sonuga-Barke found that significant deficits (e.g. disinhibited attachments) remained in individuals who experienced institutional care beyond the age of six months.').

2. **Use this to explain some aspect of the scenario** (e.g. 'As Alin wasn't adopted until 18 months, it might be expected that he would experience similar problems as a consequence of his early institutionalisation.').

3. **Find a second bit of psychology** (e.g. 'Le Mare and Audet carried out a longitudinal study of Romanian orphans adopted to families in Canada. Although they were physically smaller than a matched control group at age 4 ½, this difference disappeared at 10 ½.').

4. **Use this to explain the scenario** (e.g. 'The results of this study might explain why Alin showed no lasting developmental deficits, despite the fact he was not adopted until age 18 months.').

REVIEW

In the first topic of this chapter (p. 41), we suggested that you could explain the content of that spread to someone else (or dog, cat or teddy bear) as a way of elaborating the material, thus making it more memorable.

Now is the time to try that technique again but in a slightly different way. Take a large sheet of paper (A3 works well here) and construct a mind-map so that all your material on Romanian orphan studies is linked together in a wonderfully visual way. This serves several purposes.

1. It *elaborates* the material, making it more memorable.

2. The act of constructing the mind-map counts as *revision*, again making it more likely you can recall it in an exam.

3. You have a *visual* image of the material, which, for many people, is a much easier way of remembering complex material.

The influence of early attachment

AO1 Description

- **The internal working model** An infant learns what relationships are and how partners in a relationship behave towards each other from experience. This is used to predict the behaviour of other people in the future.

    > The internal working model also affects childhood friendships (the Minnesota child–parent study found continuity between early secure attachment and later emotional and social competence), parenting and mental health.

Hazan and Shaver (1987)

- **PROCEDURE** Hazan and Shaver placed a 'Love Quiz' in a newspaper. This asked questions about current attachment experiences and about attachment history to identify current and childhood attachment types.

    > The quiz also asked questions about attitudes towards love: an assessment of the internal working model. They analysed 620 responses, 205 from men and 415 from women, from a cross-section of the population.

- **FINDINGS** They found that the prevalence of attachment styles was similar to that found in infancy: 56 per cent were classified as secure, 25 per cent as avoidant and 19 per cent as resistant.

    > Securely attached adults described their love experiences as happy, friendly and trusting, and their relationships were more enduring than adults who were insecurely attached.

    > They also tended to have a positive internal working model of relationships.

AO3 Evaluation/Discussion

Research is only correlational…

Research linking early attachment to later relationships is correlational so cannot show a causal effect.	Attachment style *and* later love styles might be caused by a third variable, such as innate temperament. An infant's temperament affects the way a parent responds, and so it is a determining factor in attachment style. Temperament may also explain issues with relationships later in life.	*This means that researchers cannot claim that the internal working model determines later relationships without considering other intervening variables.*

Studies rely on retrospective classification…

A criticism of studies is that they rely on retrospective classification for attachment style.	Studies such as Hazan and Shaver's rely on adults answering questions about their early lives in order to assess their early attachment style. Such recollections may be flawed because memories are not always accurate.	*However, longitudinal studies do tend to support Hazan and Shaver's finding that early attachment style predicts relationships in adult life.*

Attachment research is deterministic…

A criticism of theory and research related to attachment is that it is overly deterministic.	Hazan and Shaver's research suggests that early experiences have a fixed effect on later adult relationships. An infant who is insecurely attached is doomed to experience negative relationships. However, Simpson *et al.* (2007) found that many individuals experience happy adult relationships despite having been insecurely attached as infants.	*This suggests that an individual's past does not unalterably determine the future course of their relationships.*

There are alternative explanations for adult attachment type…

Feeney (1999) suggests that adult attachment types may be properties of the relationship rather than the individual.	Feeney argued that, rather than early relationships causing later attachment type, an alternative explanation is that individuals seek out others who confirm their expectations of relationships. Being in a secure adult relationship causes adult attachment type rather than the other way round.	*This means that there may be a better explanation for the findings of early attachment research.*

A03 PLUS

⚙ APPLY: Exam skills

A02: An example

SCENARIO As an infant, Marco seemed to avoid social interaction and intimacy with others. He showed little tendency to cling to his caregiver and was happy to explore with or without the caregiver's presence. This behaviour resulted in Marco being classified as insecurely attached.

How might Marco's behaviour as an adult be influenced by his internal working model? **(4 marks)**

ANSWER *Marco's internal working model may mean he has lower expectations than those of securely attached people that others are friendly and trusting. Therefore, he may have fewer friendships than people who showed secure attachments in infancy. Marco may also have shorter romantic relationships than securely attached people. Hazan and Shaver found relationships lasted, on average, 6 years for insecure-attached individuals compared to 10 years for those classified as securely attached. Should he become a father, he may experience parenting difficulties as his internal working model may not provide a reference point from which to form relationships with his own children.*

A02: One for you to try

Researchers wanted to assess the relevance of Bowlby's 'internal working model' by exploring whether early attachment styles predicted individuals' experiences with close relationships in adulthood. They constructed a questionnaire to assess whether a sample of adult respondents were securely or insecurely attached as infants, and other questions about the success (or otherwise) of their romantic relationships in adulthood.

Using your knowledge about the internal working model, explain what would be the most likely findings of this study? (3 marks)

A02: Research methods

In the study above, the researchers used a questionnaire to gather information about early attachment and also about participants' later experiences with relationships.

a. **Why might it be preferable to use an interview rather than a questionnaire in this study? (2 marks)**

b. **Why might it be preferable to use a questionnaire rather than an interview in this study? (2 marks)**

c. **Suggest one ethical issue that might arise if an interview was used in this study, and one that might arise if a questionnaire was used. (2 marks)**

d. **Explain how researchers might deal with each of these potential ethical issues. (4 marks)**

e. **Identify two possible extraneous variables that might prevent researchers measuring a clear relationship between early attachment experiences and later experiences with relationships. (2 marks)**

🐾 How do I answer... shorter (8-mark) essay questions?

Outline and evaluate research into the influence of early attachment. (8 marks)

Not all essays follow the 12-mark or 16-mark format. Some have a slightly lower tariff. Of these lower tariff essay questions, the 8-marker is the most common. It does help to know what you are dealing with, however, as they are not always straightforward.

For example, the first question, if it were on an AS paper, would be worth 4 marks for AO1 (four points) and 4 marks for AO3 (first two columns of two AO3 points). In fact, it is simply two thirds of a 12-mark question, so two thirds of the marks for each skill. However, it is *half* of a 16-mark question at A Level, so that would lead to a different mark division of 3 marks for AO1 and 5 marks for AO3. So, your division of content would depend on whether you are taking an AS or an A Level paper.

James and Robert work together and are good friends. James is happily married but Robert seems incapable of sustaining a steady romantic relationship. One evening, while having a drink together, Robert starts talking about his childhood, saying that he had been a lonely child and that his parents (both successful politicians) appeared almost resentful at times that he had come into their lives.

Discuss one way in which early attachment can influence later behaviour. Make reference to Robert's problems with relationships in your answer. (8 marks)

This question includes a scenario that is referred back to in the question. This is an indication that there is an additional AO2 requirement in the question. AO2 marks tend to be 'stolen' from the AO3 allocation, so this question would be 3 marks of AO1 (first three points), 3 marks of AO3 (one complete AO3 point) *and* 2 marks worth of AO2. Robert appears to have suffered from what Rutter referred to as 'privation' given that his parents had little interest in him. In keeping with Bowlby's continuity hypothesis, this would explain why he continues to have troubles in adulthood, as his internal working model makes him distrustful of relationships.

🔁 REVIEW

In this final **Review** section of this chapter, it is time for some more 'revision accounting'. This time we are reviewing the previous ten topics. When you feel you have mastered the AO1 and AO3 components of these and can cope with any of the different types of question that we have covered in the **How do I answer... ?** sections, you will have earned a tick in the **Got it!** column. This list should include:

TOPIC	Got it!			Got it!	
	A01	A03		A01	A03
Caregiver–infant interactions			Ainsworth's Strange Situation: Types of attachment		
The development of attachment			Cultural variations in attachment		
Animal studies of attachment			Bowlby's theory of maternal deprivation		
Explanations of attachment: Learning theory			Romanian orphan studies: Effects of institutionalisation		
Explanations of attachment: Bowlby's theory			The influence of early attachment		

Definitions of abnormality

RECAP

AO1 Description

Statistical infrequency

- **Statistical infrequency** defines abnormal behaviours as those that are extremely rare in the population.
    > For example, a House of Commons briefing paper in 2018 reported that 1 in 6 people in the UK had experienced a common mental disorder such as depression or anxiety in the previous week.
    > Statistically, therefore, 'normal' behaviours are defined as those that are found in the majority of people.
    > If 1 in 6 people had experienced a mental disorder in the week before the survey, the majority (5 in 6) had been mentally healthy in that period.

Deviation from social norms

- **Deviation from social norms** states that anyone who deviates from socially created norms (or unstated rules) is considered abnormal.
    > Some social norms, such as not laughing at a funeral, are implicit, so may indicate an underlying abnormality if broken. Other social norms, such as causing a disorder in public, are policed by laws which are explicit norms of behaviour.
    > An example of an implicit social norm is politeness. Impolite people are behaving in a socially deviant way because others find it difficult to interact with them.
    > Some abnormal behaviour, such as paedophilia, deviates from an implicit social rule *and* is also against the law.

AO3 Evaluation / Discussion

Statistical infrequency

Some statistically infrequent behaviours are desirable…

Not all 'abnormal' behaviours would be considered undesirable.	For example, very few people have an IQ over 150, but for those who do, this 'abnormality' would be considered desirable. Equally, some undesirable behaviours, such as depression, are relatively common.	*Therefore, using statistical infrequency to define abnormality means that we are unable to distinguish between desirable and undesirable behaviours.*

The cut-off point for statistical infrequency is subjective…

If abnormality is defined in terms of statistical infrequency, we need to decide where to separate normality from abnormality.	For example, one of the symptoms of depression is 'difficulty sleeping'. Some people might think abnormal sleep is less than 6 hours a night on average, others might think the cut-off should be 5 hours.	*This means it is difficult to define abnormality in terms of statistical infrequency, which is a limitation of this definition.*

Deviation from social norms

Social norms vary over time and are open to abuse…

In the past homosexuality was considered a mental disorder in DSM (Diagnostic and Statistical Manual of Mental Disorders), whereas today it is acceptable in most countries.	Similarly, 50 years ago in Russia, anyone who disagreed with the state ran the risk of being regarded as insane and placed in a mental institution.	*Therefore, if we define abnormality in terms of deviation from social norms, there is a real danger of creating definitions based on prevailing social morals and attitudes.*

Deviance is related to context and degree…

Another limitation is that judgements on deviance are often related to the context of a behaviour.	For example, wearing next to nothing on a beach is regarded as normal, whereas the same outfit in the classroom or at a formal gathering would be regarded as abnormal and possibly an indication of a mental disorder.	*This means that social deviance on its own cannot offer a complete definition of abnormality, because it is inevitably related to both context and degree.*

Cultural relativism…

A limitation of both definitions is that cultures differ in terms of statistical infrequency and social norms of behaviour.	Classification systems like DSM are mainly based on white middle-class Western cultures, yet are applied to other subcultures. However, DSM-V (2013) acknowledges cultural differences in symptoms for panic attacks: uncontrollable crying or difficulty breathing may be primary symptoms in different cultures.	*This shows that, although it is difficult to establish universal rules for labelling behaviours as abnormal, it is possible to include cultural relativism in diagnostic systems.*

AO3 PLUS

APPLY: Exam skills

AO2: An example

SCENARIO Pete spends up to 60 hours every week video-gaming. His parents complain that this is so extreme that he must be addicted to it.

Using the statistical infrequency definition of abnormality, explain whether Pete's behaviour could be considered abnormal. **(4 marks)**

ANSWER *First, Pete's behaviour would need to be compared to statistical norms of video-gaming time among his peers to determine whether 60 hours per week was rare. If it were not he would not be considered abnormal. Nevertheless, 60 hours might mean that he (and his peers) did not function adequately in other ways so statistical infrequency is an insufficient explanation on its own.*

AO2: Research methods

Interpreting data

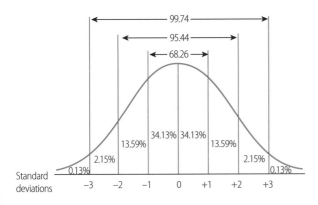

Standard deviations

This normal distribution curve shows IQ scores in a population.

a. **If intellectual disability is defined as having an IQ more than 2 standard deviations below the mean, what percentage of the population have an intellectual disability? (1 mark)**

b. **In the UK population of 66 million, how many people would you expect to fall into this category? (1 mark)**

AO2: One for you to try

Cheryl is 35 years old. At a relative's funeral she laughed and made phone calls throughout the service. When she talks to people she stands very close to them, making them feel uncomfortable.

Identify one definition of abnormality that could describe Cheryl's behaviour. Explain your choice. (3 marks)

 ## How do I answer... description only (AO1) questions?

There is a simple formula for answering AO1 questions, which only ask you to 'Describe', 'Outline' or 'Explain' something. For 2 marks, say two things; for 3 marks, say three things, and so on.

Work through the sample questions below, using the AO1 material on the opposite page.

Q1: Briefly explain how statistical infrequency can be used to define abnormality. (2 marks)

Use the first **two** 'Statistical infrequency' points.

Q2: Describe the use of statistical infrequency to define abnormality. (3 marks)

Use these first **two** points and add in a third point to elaborate further.

Q3: Briefly outline the deviation from social norms definition of abnormality. (2 marks)

Use the first **two** 'Deviation from social norms' points.

Q4: Explain how deviation from social norms can be used to define abnormality. (4 marks)

Use all **four** 'Deviation from social norms' points.

 # REVIEW

You will need to be able to answer questions with different mark allocations concisely but keeping enough detail to explain the concept clearly. Practise answering the questions above, but in timed conditions. You should spend about 1 ¼ minutes per mark, so for a 2-mark question you have 2 ½ minutes and for a 4-mark question you have 5 minutes. Make sure you allow time to plan your answers, to make sure you write them in a logical way.

1️⃣ Practise recalling the bullet points.

2️⃣ Practise writing the full answer, setting a timer to make sure you use the time available.

3️⃣ Check your answer is clear and logical, and has relevant key terms in each point.

Definitions of Abnormality (continued)

 **RECAP**

A01 Description

- Failure to function adequately means a person is not coping with their day-to-day life.
  - > In addition, their behaviour causes distress to the individual and/or others.
  - > For example, people with phobias may find their anxiety very distressing. On the other hand, people with schizophrenia generally lack awareness that anything is wrong, but their behaviour (hallucinations, believing that they are being persecuted) may well be distressing to others.
  - > The WHODAS (World Health Organisation Disability Assessment Schedule) can be used to measure functioning in areas such as self-care, getting along with people, life activities and participation in society.

- Deviation from ideal mental health proposes that certain criteria are needed for positive mental health. The absence of any of these would indicate abnormality.
  - > Jahoda (1958) identified six criteria for ideal mental health:
    1. positive self-attitudes
    2. self-actualisation
    3. integration (being able to cope with stressful situations)
    4. autonomy
    5. having an accurate perception of reality
    6. mastery of the environment (such as relationships, work and problem-solving).
  - > These six characteristics enable someone to feel happy and behave competently.
  - > If one or more of these criteria is absent, the person may be experiencing a mental disorder.

A03 Evaluation/Discussion

Failure to function adequately

The 'failure to function adequately' definition recognises the individual's subjective experience...

A benefit of this definition is that we view the disorder from the point of view of the person experiencing it.	In addition, we can use the WHODAS criteria to measure the ability of the individual to function adequately (e.g. dress themselves, prepare meals) and so measure abnormality objectively.	*This definition therefore has both sensitivity (considering subjective experience) and practicality (using objective measures).*

The behaviour may be functional...

A limitation is that some apparently dysfunctional behaviour can be beneficial for the individual.	For example, some mental disorders, such as eating disorders or depression, may lead to extra attention for the individual. Such attention is rewarding and thus quite functional rather than dysfunctional.	*This failure to distinguish between functional and dysfunctional behaviours means that this definition is incomplete.*

Ideal mental health

Unrealistic criteria...

One of the major criticisms of this definition is that, according to ideal mental health criteria, most of us are abnormal.	Jahoda presented them as *ideal* criteria, but how many need to be lacking before a person would be judged as abnormal? Furthermore, the criteria are quite difficult to measure, e.g. assessing an individual's capacity for personal growth or environmental mastery.	*This means that this approach may be an interesting concept but not really useable when it comes to identifying abnormality.*

It is a positive approach...

This definition offers an alternative perspective on mental disorder that focuses on the positives rather than the negatives.	Even though Jahoda's ideas were never really taken up by mental health professionals, the ideas have had some influence and are in accord with the 'positive psychology' movement.	*A strength of this approach, therefore, lies in its positive outlook and its influence on humanistic approaches.*

Cultural relativism...

A limitation of both definitions is that there are different cultural ideas of how life should be lived.	For example, 'adequate functioning' depends on cultural norms and people from non-dominant subcultures may have different lifestyles. Jahoda's criteria of self-actualisation may not apply to collectivist cultures.	*This could explain why people from non-middle class or minority ethnic groups are more often diagnosed with mental disorders.*

A03 PLUS

⚙ APPLY: Exam skills

AO2: An example

SCENARIO Mike's flatmate never cleans his room. It is so bad that visitors to the flat remark on the bad smell it causes. Mike's flatmate holds down a good job and is clean and well presented when he goes to work.

Using the 'failure to function adequately' definition of abnormality, explain whether Mike's flatmate could be considered abnormal. **(4 marks)**

ANSWER One aspect of the definition is that there is distress to the individuals or others around them. In this case, there appears to be no distress for Mike's flatmate but possible distress for Mike and others that visit.

Another aspect is about people coping with their day to day life. Mike's flatmate clearly can as he is going to work and is clean and well presented. Therefore he is unlikely to be considered abnormal.

AO2: Two for you to try

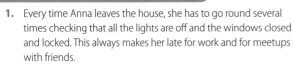

1. Every time Anna leaves the house, she has to go round several times checking that all the lights are off and the windows closed and locked. This always makes her late for work and for meetups with friends.

   Identify one definition of abnormality that could describe Anna's behaviour. Explain your choice. (3 marks)

2. Sandra and Vitaly were having a discussion about what 'abnormal' means. Sandra said 'People go to get help for their mental health when they feel distressed about their feelings or behaviour, because they aren't normal.' Vitality said, 'That's true, but I don't think that definition is perfect.'

   a. Identify the definition of abnormality Sandra was using. **(1 mark)**

   b. Give one example of a behaviour that causes people psychological distress or suffering. **(1 mark)**

   c. Vitaly doesn't think Sandra's definition is perfect. Explain one limitation of the definition of abnormality Sandra was using. **(2 marks)**

AO2: Research methods

A survey asked 8000 Australian adults aged 16–85 to complete the WHODAS questionnaire.

Some had existing diagnoses of mental or physical disorders. They were then grouped by type of disorder, and the results are shown below:

	Mental disorder	Physical disorder	No disorder
Mean	6.3	4.3	1.4
Standard deviation	7.1	6.1	3.6

a. **What can you conclude from this data? (4 marks)**

b. **Why was a stratified sample used in this survey? (2 marks)**

🐾 How do I answer... selection (multiple choice) questions?

Q1: Which **two** of the following are included in Jahoda's six characteristics of ideal mental health? Tick **two** boxes only.

A Fitting into a group. ☐

B Resistance to stress. ☐

C Physical health. ☐

D Owning your own house. ☐

E Self-actualisation. ☐

Q2: The following statements are all linked to different definitions of abnormality. Select the **two** statements that describe the 'failure to function adequately' definition of abnormality. Tick **two** boxes only.

A Behaviour that is different from the way most people in society act. ☐

B Not achieving self-actualisation. ☐

C Not following the standards set by society. ☐

D Behaviour that interferes with everyday life. ☐

E Not being able to resist stress. ☐

Some multiple choice questions require you to pick **one** statement which is true or which matches an idea or definition. Sometimes they are asking you to do the opposite: to pick the statement that is *false* or *does not* fit a definition or concept.

These two examples require you to select **two** statements, so make sure you follow the instructions carefully.

- Read the question carefully and make sure you have understood whether you are looking for a **true** or **false** statement, or **more than one** statement.
- Cross out any which are obviously wrong, to increase your chances of picking the right answer.
- Think about the remaining statements carefully, and if necessary just go with your hunch.
- Have a go at these two questions now!

🔄 REVIEW

Now you have learned four definitions of abnormality, make sure you are clear about the key features of each, so that you can distinguish between them. Some of the evaluation points are very similar. For example, cultural bias can be used as a criticism of all four definitions, but in different ways.

For each of the four definitions of abnormality (listed below) write down how cultural differences might compromise the effectiveness of each in defining abnormality:

- Statistical infrequency
- Deviation from social norms
- Failure to function adequately
- Deviation from ideal mental health

RECAP

AOI Description

Phobias

- A **phobia** is an anxiety disorder, and is an irrational fear of a specific object or situation. About 2.6 per cent of the UK population have a clinical phobia.

- The main **emotional** characteristic of a phobia is excessive and unreasonable fear of a specific object or situation (e.g. spiders, flying, heights). This is accompanied by anxiety and panic, which the individual recognises is disproportionate to the actual danger posed.

- Fear produces the **behavioural** characteristic of avoiding the phobic stimulus. This interferes with the person's usual social and occupational functioning over an extended period of time. Some people may also 'freeze' or faint in the presence of the phobic stimulus.

- A defining **cognitive** characteristic of phobia is irrational thinking about the phobic stimulus and resistance to rational argument about the actual danger it poses.

Depression

- **Depression** is a mood disorder.

- The main **emotional** characteristic of major depressive disorder is sadness and/or a loss of interest and pleasure in activities a person is normally interested in and takes pleasure from. Other negative emotional characteristics include feelings of despair, low self-esteem, lack of control, and inward- or outward-directed anger.

- **Behavioural** characteristics of depression include difficulties in concentrating, decreased or increased activity patterns, excessive sleep or insomnia, and increased or decreased appetite.

- The main **cognitive** characteristics of depression are irrational negative thoughts about the self, the world in general and the future.

OCD

- **Obsessive Compulsive Disorder (OCD)** is also an anxiety disorder. The two components of OCD are recurrent, persistent and intrusive thoughts or impulses (obsessions) and repetitive behaviours (compulsions).

- The thoughts or impulses are the main **cognitive** characteristic of OCD, and are recognised by sufferers as being excessive or unreasonable.

- Because OCD sufferers believe they have no control over these thoughts or impulses, they experience anxiety, and this is the main **emotional** characteristic of OCD. Sufferers also experience embarrassment and shame about their obsessions and compulsions.

- A person who is obsessed by a fear of being contaminated by germs may develop compulsive handwashing behaviour as a way of reducing anxiety. The repetitive behaviour is the main **behavioural** characteristic of OCD. It may be performed overtly (e.g. handwashing) or covertly (e.g. counting). Sometimes, though, compulsive behaviour is not a response to obsessional thoughts, and people may compulsively avoid certain stimuli.

APPLY: Exam skills

AO2: An example

SCENARIO A 55-year-old man, Tony, has suffered from appetite loss and has lost four stones in weight over the past six months. His loss of appetite has been accompanied by a burning pain in his chest, back and abdomen, which he is convinced indicates a fatal abdominal cancer. He is withdrawn and isolated, unable to work, uninterested in friends and family, and unresponsive to their attempts to make him feel better. He awakes at 4 am and is unable to fall back asleep. He claims to feel worse in the morning and to improve slightly as the day wears on. He is markedly agitated and speaks of feelings of extreme unworthiness. He says that he would be better off dead and that he welcomes his impending demise from cancer. (Adapted from Spitzer et al., 1981.)

Explain why Tony has been diagnosed with depression, identifying cognitive, emotional and behavioural characteristics. **(4 marks)**

ANSWER Tony's feeling of extreme unworthiness, and saying that he would be better off dead, are evidence of despair. He is uninterested in friends and family, showing he has lost interest and pleasure in normal things. These are emotional characteristics of depression. He has behaviour characteristics of change in sleep patterns, waking up at 4 am, and has lost his appetite. His cognitive characteristics are believing that his pain indicates fatal cancer (an irrational negative thought) and that he would be better off dead (negative thoughts about himself and the future). So Tony is showing clear signs of depression, a mood disorder.

AO2: Research methods

A psychologist compared the rates of phobias, depression, and OCD in three countries. The number of cases per hundred members of the population for the three countries is shown in the table below.

	Phobias	**Depression**	**OCD**
Country A	2.7	2.8	2.6
Country B	2.6	2.1	1.5
Country C	0.7	1.4	1.9

a. **Which country has the lowest number of cases of phobias? (1 mark)**

b. **Which country has the highest number of cases of depression? (1 mark)**

c. **In which country is the rate of depression twice as high as in Country C? (1 mark)**

d. **Calculate the mean rate of each disorder across the three countries. Which disorder has the highest mean rate overall? (2 marks)**

AO2: One for you to try

The billionaire Howard Hughes became a recluse and was never seen in public. He insisted that all of his employees wore white gloves when they handled documents that he would later have to touch. His employees were not allowed to look at him, let alone touch him.

All of his doors and windows were taped because of the distress he felt about being contaminated by germs. One employee said that she regularly heard him dictating the same phrases over and over again. Hughes said that he wanted to live longer than his parents, and that because everybody carries germs the only way he could do this was by avoiding germs.

Using your knowledge of OCD, identify a cognitive, behavioural and emotional characteristic shown by Howard Hughes in the passage above. (3 marks)

How do I answer... 'Distinguish between' questions?

Explain the difference between an obsession and a compulsion. (2 marks)

There are special requirements for answering questions which ask you to 'Distinguish between' two concepts, or to 'Compare' or 'Explain the difference between' them. Follow these three steps when answering these types of questions:

1. Don't just describe one thing and then the other.

2. Pick a characteristic which applies to both, but which is different for each, and point it out.

   (For example, both are characteristics of OCD, but obsessions are cognitive and compulsions are behavioural.)

3. Explain the difference, using words like 'whereas' or 'however' to distinguish between them clearly.

   For 2 marks, one difference is enough. For 4 marks, you would need to explain two.

An obsession is a cognitive characteristic of OCD, involving persistent or intrusive thoughts, whereas a compulsion is a behaviour characteristic of OCD, with the person carrying out repetitive behaviours as a way to reduce anxiety.

REVIEW

This spread looks at three types of mental disorder, and the emotional, behavioural and cognitive characteristics of each. This means you need to know a total of nine characteristics.

Practise recalling them in different ways, for example:

1. What are the cognitive characteristics of each of the three disorders? And what about the emotional and the behavioural characteristics?

2. Make a big table like a noughts and crosses board to fill in all nine elements from memory.

3. Then practise elaborating them – for example, in OCD the obsessions and compulsions are recognised by the sufferer as being excessive or irrational.

The behavioural approach to explaining phobias

RECAP

AO1 Description

The two-process model

- Mowrer (1947) proposed the two-process model to explain phobias.

- **Classical conditioning** explains how a phobia is acquired. An initially neutral stimulus (NS) is paired with an unconditioned stimulus (UCS), which produces the unconditioned response (UCR) of fear. The neutral stimulus then becomes a conditioned stimulus (CS) and produces fear as a conditioned response (CR) whenever the CS is presented.

- Watson and Rayner (1920) paired an initially neutral stimulus (a white rat) with an unconditioned stimulus (a loud noise). This produced the unconditioned response of fear in a baby known as Little Albert. After making this pairing four times, Little Albert produced a conditioned fear response when they presented him with the rat in the absence of the UCS.

- This demonstrated that a fear response to an initially neutral stimulus could be classically conditioned.

- **Operant conditioning** explains how phobias are maintained. If fear is lowered by avoiding the phobic stimulus, then avoidance behaviour becomes a negative reinforcer.

- For example, if someone was afraid of spiders because they had been previously frightened by one, the reduction in fear they experienced by avoiding spiders would lead them to continue avoiding them.

AO3 Evaluation/Discussion

The importance of classical conditioning…

The two-process model is supported by research asking people about their phobias.	Sue *et al.* (1994) found that some people *can* recall a specific event that led to their phobia developing. For example, agoraphobics are most likely to explain their phobia in terms of a specific event.	*This shows that classical conditioning can be involved in developing phobias.*

Issues/Debates
Think about nature (inherited factors) versus nurture (conditioning) in relation to biological preparedness and the diathesis–stress model of phobias.

Biological preparedness…

A limitation of the two-process model is that a phobia does not always develop after a traumatic incident. For example, Di Nardo *et al.* found that not everyone who is bitten by a dog develops a phobia of dogs.	The diathesis–stress model proposes that we inherit a genetic vulnerability for developing mental disorders, but a disorder is then triggered by a life event. In addition, fear is easier to condition to some things (e.g. spiders) than others (e.g. toasters).	*Seligman argues that we are genetically prepared to learn associations between fear and stimuli (such as snakes) that were life-threatening in our evolutionary past.*

Support for social learning…

An experiment by Bandura and Rosenthal (1966) supported the social learning explanation of the development of phobias.	In their experiment, a model acted as if he was in pain every time a buzzer sounded. Later on, those participants who had observed this showed an emotional reaction to the buzzer, demonstrating an acquired 'fear' response.	*This shows that imitating the behaviour modelled by others can lead to the acquisition of phobias.*

The two-process model ignores cognitive factors…

A limitation of the two-process model is that there are cognitive aspects to phobias that cannot be explained in a traditionally behaviourist framework.	For example, a person who thinks they might die if trapped in a lift might become extremely anxious and this may trigger a phobia about lifts. This shows that irrational thinking is also involved in the development of phobias.	*This would explain why cognitive therapies can be more successful in treating phobias than behavioural treatments.*

AO3 PLUS

APPLY: Exam skills

AO2: An example

SCENARIO A wasp becomes trapped in Becky's hair and stings her painfully several times before she is able to free it. Thereafter she is panicky and has to escape whenever she hears a buzzing insect, and she avoids going outdoors in case she encounters one.

Apply the two-process model of phobias to explain Becky's buzzing insect phobia. **(4 marks)**

ANSWER *Classical conditioning explains the initiation of Becky's fear of insects. She learned to associate the sound of buzzing (NS) with pain (UCS) and the fear it caused (UCR). As a result of this association, buzzing alone (now the CS) is able to elicit fear (CR). Operant conditioning maintained her fear of insects. Avoiding buzzing insects (and the potential fear associated with insects) keeps her calm and so is negatively reinforcing.*

AO2: Research methods

The chart below shows the prevalence (number of cases per thousand in a population) of dental fear relative to three other fears.

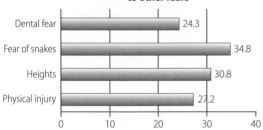

Prevalence of dental fear relative to other fears

Dental fear	24.3
Fear of snakes	34.8
Heights	30.8
Physical injury	27.2

a. **Which is the modal type of fear shown in the chart above? (1 mark)**

b. **How many extra cases (per thousand) of dental fear would need to occur for it to become the second most common fear in the chart? (1 mark)**

c. **How many fewer cases of fear of snakes (per thousand) are needed for it to become the least common fear in the chart? (1 mark)**

d. **What level of measurement is used in the chart? (1 mark)**

AO2: One for you to try

When Stuart was a young boy, his parents bought a Dalmatian puppy for Christmas. One day, the puppy was playing and bit Stuart on the leg. Ever since then, Stuart has been afraid of his parents' dog. Stuart's friend Dave has a Great Dane, but Stuart won't go round to Dave's house because the thought of doing so fills him with fear.

a. **Explain Stuart's behaviour in terms of Mowrer's two-process model. (4 marks)**

b. **Explain why Stuart is afraid of Dave's Great Dane even though the dog that bit him was a Dalmatian. (2 marks)**

How do I answer... evaluation only (AO3) questions?

You can recognise AO3 questions by their use of terms like 'Evaluate', 'Criticism', 'Strength', 'Limitation'. For example:

Q1: Give one criticism of the two-process model. (3 marks)

For **Q1:** choose one of the AO3 points and use all three columns to elaborate it fully.

Q2: Evaluate the two-process model as an explanation of phobias. (4 marks)

Q2: needs two elaborated points, so choose two AO3 points which you can explain clearly, making sure you state whether they are a strength or a limitation of the model, and why.

Q3: Explain a strength of the two-process model. (2 marks)

Q3: is just looking for one strength plus some brief elaboration. You could use the first AO3 point on the opposite page. Using this point, you would use the lead-in phrase and the first two columns (the main critical claim and its expansion). Alternatively, you could summarise the content in all three columns into about 50 words (i.e. including the 'link-back' conclusion).

 REVIEW

Make sure you are really clear about the processes of classical conditioning. You need to write out the terms fully first time, with the abbreviation in brackets, e.g. 'unconditioned stimulus (UCS)', then you can just use the abbreviation if you mention it again.

1. Check that you know the full names for: UCS, UCR, NS, CS, CR.

2. Can you explain the two-process model very briefly, for a 4-mark answer?

3. How would you use the material on this spread to answer a 16-mark extended writing question?

The behavioural approach to treating phobias

RECAP

AO1 Description

Systematic desensitisation

- **Systematic desensitisation (SD)** uses counterconditioning to replace fear with relaxation.
- Patients learn a relaxation technique, such as slow breathing or progressive muscle relaxation.
- The patient and therapist work out a hierarchy of phobic situations, from least to most feared.
- The patient imagines the least feared scene whilst simultaneously relaxing. When no anxiety is experienced, fear has been desensitised. The therapist and patient work through the hierarchy in a systematic way until the patient experiences no anxiety when imagining the most feared scene.
- In *in vivo* SD, the phobic is gradually exposed to the phobic stimulus rather than imagining it or using pictures (*in vitro*).
- SD is based on 'reciprocal inhibition' – being relaxed inhibits anxiety.

Flooding

- **Flooding** involves a single exposure to the most feared situation.
- The patient is exposed to the actual phobic stimulus or to a virtual reality version of it in one long session, until their anxiety has disappeared.
- Although intense fear is initially experienced, the fear response is eventually extinguished as adrenaline levels naturally decrease.
- A new stimulus-response link can be learned, and the feared stimulus is now associated with a non-anxious response.

Darn... she's obviously had SD

AO3 Evaluation / Discussion

Effectiveness of SD…

Research has found that SD is successful for a range of phobias. For example, McGrath *et al.* (1990) reported that about 75 per cent of patients with phobias respond to SD.	*In vivo* techniques are more successful than *in vitro* (Choy *et al.*, 2007). Often a number of different exposure techniques are involved – *in vivo*, *in vitro* and also modelling, where the patient watches someone else who is coping well with the feared stimulus (Comer, 2002).	*This demonstrates the effectiveness of SD, but also the value of using a range of different exposure techniques.*

Effectiveness of flooding…

Flooding can be an effective treatment for those who stick with it.	For example, Craske *et al.* (2008) concluded that flooding and SD were equally effective in treating phobias. However, it can be highly traumatic, and patients may quit during treatment.	*This shows that flooding can be useful for particular individuals as long as they are aware beforehand of the distress they are likely to experience, so that they complete the treatment.*

Strengths of behavioural therapies…

Behavioural therapies for phobias are generally faster, cheaper and require less effort on the patient's part than other psychotherapies.	For example, CBT requires a willingness for patients to think deeply about their mental problems, which is not the case for behavioural therapies. Self-administered SD can be as effective as therapist-guided SD, making it cheaper and more accessible.	*This means that behavioural therapies can be useful for children and people with learning difficulties.*

Relaxation may not be necessary…

It may be that the success of both SD and flooding is more to do with exposure to the feared situation than relaxation.	For example, Klein *et al.* (1983) compared SD with supportive psychotherapy for patients with either social or specific phobias. They found no difference in effectiveness, suggesting that the 'active ingredient' in SD or flooding may simply be the generation of hopeful expectancies that the phobia can be overcome.	*This suggests that cognitive factors are more important than the behavioural approach generally acknowledges.*

AO3 PLUS

APPLY: Exam skills

AO2: An example

SCENARIO A student with social phobia is terrified of giving presentations in class.

Using the principles of SD, explain how a therapist could help this student to overcome their fear. **(3 marks)**

ANSWER The therapist would apply counterconditioning to substitute fear with relaxation. The student would identify a hierarchy of feared situations relating to giving presentations. They would also be taught to master relaxation techniques. Each step of the hierarchy would then be faced while maintaining relaxation until the most feared step was manageable.

AO2: Research methods

Drawing conclusions

A researcher conducted a study to test the effectiveness of systematic desensitisation in the treatment of aviophobia (fear of flying). She recorded the percentage of participants who reported that they were still using aeroplanes three years after their treatment and the percentage who were not. She also recorded the percentage of participants who had refused to undergo either systematic desensitisation or flooding when it was offered, and who had to be referred for an alternative form of therapy.

	Systematic desensitisation	Flooding
Percentage still using aeroplanes	41	76
Percentage no longer using aeroplanes	59	24
Percentage who refused therapy when offered	15	37

a. **What do these results suggest about the relative effectiveness of the two forms of therapy? (1 mark)**

b. **What do the results imply about the usefulness of the desensitisation hierarchy? (2 marks)**

c. **Explain why the percentage of people refusing the therapies might be higher for one therapy than for the other. (2 marks)**

AO2: One for you to try

Celine's husband has planned a weekend away sightseeing in Paris. He is very keen to visit the Eiffel Tower and stand at the top admiring the views. Her husband doesn't know it, but Celine has a phobia of heights. This phobia is so bad that she has difficulty in going to her office on the third floor, and she cannot even sit on the top deck of a bus any more. Celine's husband has booked a romantic meal in the restaurant at the top of the Eiffel Tower, and she doesn't want to let him down. A friend suggests she tries flooding to overcome her phobia.

Explain how a therapist might use flooding to help Celine to overcome her phobia. (6 marks)

How do I answer... extended writing (8-mark) questions?

Q1: Outline and evaluate the use of systematic desensitisation in treating phobias. (8 marks)

Q2: Discuss the use of systematic desensitisation in treating phobias. (8 marks)

When you are asked for 8 marks' worth, stop and think what the question is requiring you to do. If you are taking an AS paper, the marks will be divided evenly between AO1 (4 marks) and AO3 (4 marks). In an A Level paper, however, an 8-mark question is half of a 16-mark essay, so you need to produce 3 marks' worth of AO1 and 5 marks' worth of AO3.

Your AO1 needs to be a very concise summary of all the steps of SD. Keep an eye on the balance of your answer: writing too much detail for AO1 is a common trap students fall into.

Q1 and Q2 are very similar, but the command word 'Discuss' is an instruction, which is looking for you to give both sides of the argument in your AO3 section. In this case, you can use any of the AO3 points on the opposite page, but develop the points using the elaboration in the three columns so that you have a more detailed analysis, and include a strength and a limitation of SD.

REVIEW

The first four bullet points in the explanation of SD are all essential when you are describing the process of SD and how it works.

1. Which key terms would you need to include if you were explaining how SD works?

2. Which points would you need if you were explaining how SD is carried out by a therapist?

3. Can you explain the difference between *in vivo* and *in vitro* techniques?

4. Some simple phobias can be self-treated: try applying this process to something you feel anxious about. Applying the process to a real-life situation should help you to remember them.

 **RECAP**

AO1 Description

Ellis' ABC model (1962)

- Ellis' (1962) **ABC model** proposed that when an activating event (A) leads to an irrational belief (B), the consequences of this (C) may be depression.

- For example, being fired at work (A) might lead to the irrational belief (B) that the company had it in for you, which could lead to the consequence (C) of depression.

- Musturbatory thinking is the source of irrational beliefs such as 'I must be approved of by important people', 'I must do well or I am worthless', and 'The world must give me happiness'. People who hold these beliefs may become depressed.

Beck's negative triad (1967)

- Beck's (1967) **negative triad** model described how childhood experiences, such as continual parental criticism or rejection by others, lead to negative cognitive **schemas** developing. These are activated in situations similar to those present when these schemas were learned.

- These systematic negative schemas, and cognitive biases such as generalisation, lead to depression.

- Negative schemas maintain the negative triad of beliefs. These concern the self (e.g. 'I'm unattractive and boring'), the world (e.g. 'No one wants my company'), and the future (e.g. 'I'll always be on my own').

AO3 Evaluation/Discussion

Support for the role of irrational thinking…

The view that depression is linked to irrational thinking is supported by research by Hammen and Krantz (1976).

They found that depressed participants made more errors in logic when asked to interpret written material than did non-depressed participants. In addition, Bates *et al.* (1999) found that depressed participants who were given negative automatic-thought statements became more and more depressed.

This research supports the view that negative thinking leads to depression. However, negative thinking may also be a consequence of depression.

Blames the client rather than situational factors…

The cognitive approach suggests that it is the client who is responsible for their disorder. This gives the client the power to change the way things are.

However, this stance may lead the client or therapist to overlook situational factors, life events or family problems which may have contributed to the mental disorder.

The strength of the cognitive approach therefore lies in its focus on the client's mind and recovery, but other aspects of the client's life may also need to be considered.

Practical applications in therapy…

The effectiveness of Cognitive Behaviour Therapy (CBT) supports the usefulness of the cognitive approach.

CBT is consistently found to be the best treatment for depression, especially when used in conjunction with drug treatments (e.g. Cuijpers *et al.*, 2013).

If depression is alleviated by challenging irrational thinking, then this suggests such thoughts had a role in the depression in the first place.

Alternative explanations…

AO3 PLUS

Depression can also be explained biologically, in terms of genetic factors and neurotransmitters.

Studies have found low levels of the neurotransmitter serotonin in depressed people. A gene related to low levels of serotonin is ten times more common in depressed people. Research shows that drug therapies, which raise serotonin levels, are successful in the treatment of depression.

This means that neurotransmitters also play a role in causing depression, and so a diathesis-stress model could be a better approach to take.

Issues/Debates
Link to nature-nurture. Diathesis-stress is a model of interaction between nature and nurture

APPLY: Exam skills

AO2: An example

SCENARIO Anita is the youngest child in a family of high achievers and has never matched their accomplishments. She often feels very low in spirits. During her first driving lesson, she experiences road rage from other drivers and immediately decides to give up.

Apply Beck's (1967) concepts of negative schema and negative triad to explain the cognitive processes that led to Anita's decision. **(4 marks)**

ANSWER *Anita's history of feeling like a failure has led her to develop a pessimistic framework (negative schema) for interpreting events in her life. When she encounters a new failure, such as what happened in her driving lesson, this schema is activated. Consequently she thinks in a self-defeating way by activating the negative triad of thoughts that are a characteristic of depression: 'I am a bad driver. Everyone thinks so. I will never be able to drive.'*

AO2: Research methods

Does therapy make a difference? A psychologist tests whether mood scores improve after a course of CBT (high scores indicate better mood). To compare 'before' and 'after' scores, she conducts a sign test:

Participant	Mood score before therapy	Mood score after therapy	Difference ('after' minus 'before')	Sign
1	6	7	1	+
2	3	4	1	+
3	4	6	2	+
4	5	6	1	+
5	6	5	-1	-
6	5	7	2	+
7	5	5	0	
8	5	8	3	+
9	4	7	3	+
10	5	4	-1	-
11	4	6	2	+
12	3	7	4	+

Level of significance for a one-tailed test	0.05	0.01
Level of significance for a two-tailed test	0.10	0.02
N		
10	1	1
11	2	1

Table of critical values

a. **Work out the value of *S* from the table above. (1 mark)**
b. **Use the table of critical values of *S* to decide whether there is a significant effect at the 5 per cent level of significance (the hypothesis is directional). (2 marks)**
c. **What can be concluded about the effect of CBT on mood scores? (2 marks)**

AO2: One for you to try

Boris had a spare ticket for a music concert. Rather than let it go to waste, he thought he'd phone Becky and ask her if she wanted to go with him. 'I'd love to, but I'm afraid I can't,' said Becky, 'I've got loads of psychology homework to do tonight.' Boris put the phone down and thought: 'These tickets are like gold dust. Becky must really hate me to turn a free ticket down.' Boris was so upset he decided not to go to the concert himself.

Using your knowledge of Ellis' ABC model, explain why Boris didn't go to the concert. (3 marks)

How do I answer... application questions?

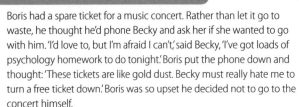

STEM	Millie left school after her GCSEs and hasn't been able to find a job. She is convinced she is unemployable, and often sits crying in her room as her friends have all moved on and she thinks no one cares about her, and she feels she has no future. Sometime she wishes she could disappear altogether.
QUESTION	Discuss the cognitive approach to explaining depression, referring to Millie's situation. (8 marks)

In an 8-mark discussion question with a stem, you still need to outline and evaluate the explanation of depression, but you also need to refer to Millie (AO2). This means that you need a little less AO3. For A Level the split is 3:2:3 (3 marks AO1, 2 marks AO2, 3 marks AO3), so you need one fully expanded AO3 point or two shorter ones.

The best way to bring in AO2 is to link each AO1 point you make, clearly explaining how it applies to Millie.

For example:

Millie is showing all three elements of Beck's negative triad. She has negative views about the world (no one cares about her), the future (she feels she has no future) and the self (she is convinced she is unemployable).'

This is more efficient than explaining all the theory then going through it again to explain Millie's depression.

REVIEW

Choose one of the example application questions on this page. Try writing an AO1/AO2 explanation in different ways:

1 Explain the theory (AO1) then explain how it links to the stem (AO2).

2 Explain the theory and link as you go.

3 Start with the stem, and introduce theory to explain it.

Count the words you have used in each version. Which version is most efficient? Remember, the more concise you can make your answer while retaining enough detail, the better, as it will give you more time to answer other questions.

The cognitive approach to treating depression

AO1 Description

Cognitive behaviour therapy (CBT)

- Ellis' rational emotive behaviour therapy (REBT), a type of **cognitive-behavioural therapy** (CBT), aims to turn **irrational thoughts** into rational thoughts, and resolve emotional and behaviour problems.

- Ellis' model was expanded to ABCDEF. D: disputing irrational thoughts and beliefs. E: effects of disputing and effective attitude to life. F: the new feelings that are produced.

- REBT focuses on challenging or disputing irrational, self-defeating thoughts and replacing them with effective, rational beliefs. Logical disputing (Does thinking this way make sense?), empirical disputing (What is the evidence for this belief?) and pragmatic disputing (How is this belief likely to help me?) can be used.

- Clients complete homework assignments between therapy sessions, such as asking someone out on a date when they had feared rejection. Homework enables irrational beliefs to be tested against reality (empirical disputing).

- Behavioural activation encourages clients to engage in pleasurable activities that they used to enjoy.

- Therapists provide clients with unconditional positive regard, to convince clients of their value as humans. Another feature is for the client to become more active, since being active leads to rewards that are an antidote to depression.

AO3 Evaluation/Discussion

Research support for REBT...

Ellis (1957) claimed a 90 per cent success rate for REBT in the treatment of depression. In addition, a review by Cuijpers *et al.* (2013) of 75 studies found that CBT was superior to no treatment.

However, Ellis recognised that the therapy was not always effective, as some clients did not put their revised beliefs into action (Ellis, 2001). Therapist competence also explains some of the variation in CBT outcomes (Kuyken and Tsivrikos, 2009).

This suggests that REBT is effective, but its effectiveness depends on both client and therapist.

Support for behavioural activation...

Babyak *et al.* (2000) randomly assigned people with depression to a course of aerobic exercise, antidepressant drug treatment, or both.

All three groups exhibited significant improvement after four months. The exercise group had significantly lower relapse rates than the medication group.

This shows that a change in physical activity can indeed be beneficial in treating depression.

Alternative treatments are available...

The most popular treatment for depression is the use of antidepressants such as SSRIs. Drug therapies also require less effort by the client than CBT.

Drug treatment could enable a depressed client to cope better with the demands of CBT. The review by Cuijpers *et al.* (above) found that CBT was especially effective if it was used in conjunction with drug therapy.

This suggests that using both CBT and drugs might be the best option.

All methods of treatment for mental disorder may be equally effective...

Luborsky *et al.* (2002) reviewed over 100 studies comparing different therapies and found only small differences between them in terms of their effectiveness.

Sloane *et al.* (1975) showed that psychological therapies share many common factors such as being able to talk to a sympathetic person and express one's thoughts.

The lack of difference between psychotherapies might be a result of the commonalities they share. It is known as the 'Dodo Bird effect'.

Everyone has won and all must have prizes

 # APPLY: Exam skills

AO2: An example

SCENARIO A psychologist had a client in poor physical condition who believed that they will never be any better.

How might a cognitive therapist encourage a depressed client to dispute this conclusion on logical, empirical and pragmatic grounds, and with what aim in mind? **(4 marks)**

ANSWER *Logically it does not follow from the person's current ill health that they cannot change their situation and become healthy in the future. Empirically, there is abundant evidence that many people in a similar position have made big improvements and a lack of evidence to support the person's belief that their health cannot improve. Pragmatically, maintaining the irrational belief is self-destructive and so the person is not motivated to try and improve their situation. The therapist's aim would be to replace the person's irrational belief with a rational one that leads to more positive thoughts and actions.*

AO2: Research methods

A researcher was recruited by a regional hospital trust, which wanted to know the most effective form of treatment for the two most common forms of disorder dealt with by their mental health team – depression and anxiety.

She gathered data from therapists working across the region, representing three forms of therapy, CBT (REBT), psychoanalytic therapy and counselling. After six months of receiving therapy, clients were asked to rate (as a percentage) how much they felt they had improved as a result of receiving therapy. The results are shown in the bar chart below. The researcher also interviewed each client in order to gather qualitative data on the effects of their therapy.

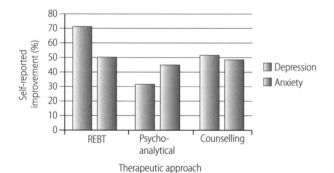

a. **Briefly explain one advantage of gaining qualitative data in this study. (2 marks)**

b. **Outline two factors that, unless they were controlled for, would make it difficult to compare the effectiveness of the different types of therapy in this study. (4 marks)**

c. **State two findings and for each one draw a conclusion. (4 marks)**

AO2: One for you to try

Although Sophie was a very good student, she told her friends that she felt she needed to prove her competence all the time. If things didn't go the way she wanted them to, it felt like an absolute disaster to her. Sophie's best friend told her not to be so silly, but Sophie reacted to this, telling her friend that she felt like she needed everybody to approve of her all the time.

Using your knowledge of CBT, identify three irrational thoughts in the above passage and suggest a way in which each of those thoughts could be disputed. (6 marks)

How do I answer... description and evaluation (AO1 + AO3) questions?

Describe and evaluate how challenging irrational thoughts can be used to treat depression. (6 marks)

First you need to be aware of how much AO1 and AO3 you need to include. In questions up to 6 marks, the division is half and half. (This is different in higher mark questions.)

Next you need to plan what to write. For this question, AO1 bullet points 2, 3 and 4 on the opposite page are relevant, and this would be plenty for 3 marks of AO1. For AO3, the first evaluation point gives an interesting discussion about effectiveness, and this would be plenty for 3 marks of AO3.

REVIEW

You will have to be selective in learning names of researchers. Key studies with researchers named in the specification, such as Ellis, are vital. However, you will also want to use evidence from other research, and the name can be a useful tag to make it clear that you know what you are talking about.

Select which researchers' names you want to try to learn, for example Cuijpers carried out an important review of CBT so is worth learning. Make a table of names and summaries of findings of their research. Keep testing yourself both ways round: cover the names, look at the research summary and try to remember the name. And vice versa.

If you struggle with names, it's much more important to know the key terms of theory and summaries of evidence, along with other evaluation points such as comparisons with alternative treatments.

The biological approach to explaining OCD

AOI Description

Genetic explanations

- The COMT **gene**, which regulates dopamine production, may contribute to OCD. A less active form of this gene is more common in OCD patients, and produces higher dopamine levels.

- The SERT gene may also contribute to OCD by reducing serotonin levels. A mutation of this gene has been found in two unrelated families where six of the seven members had OCD (Ozaki *et al.*, 2003).

- Diathesis-stress: each gene only creates a vulnerability (a diathesis) for OCD. Other factors, such as childhood experience, provide the trigger (stress) for the condition to develop.

Neural explanations

- High **dopamine** levels and low serotonin levels are associated with OCD.

- High doses of drugs that enhance dopamine induce stereotypical movements in rats, whilst antidepressant drugs, which increase serotonin activity, reduce the symptoms of OCD.

- The orbitofrontal cortex (OFC) of the frontal lobes and the caudate nucleus, part of the basal ganglia, are thought to be abnormal in people with OCD. Damage to the caudate nucleus fails to suppress minor 'worry' signals from the OFC, creating a worry circuit.

- Serotonin plays a key role in the operation of these structures, and low serotonin levels may cause them to malfunction. Dopamine is the basal ganglia's main **neurotransmitter**, so high dopamine levels lead to overactivity of this region.

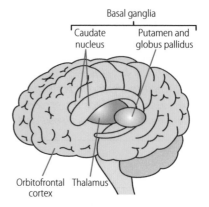

The worry circuit

AO3 Evaluation / Discussion

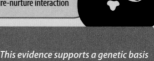

Evidence for the genetic basis of OCD comes from family and twin studies...

Nestadt *et al.* (2000) found that people with a first-degree relative with OCD had a five-times greater lifetime risk of OCD themselves, compared to risk levels in the general population.

A meta-analysis found that identical (monozygotic, MZ) twins were more than twice as likely to develop OCD if their twin had the disorder than non-identical (dizygotic, DZ) twins (Billett *et al.*, 1998).

This evidence supports a genetic basis for OCD, but the concordance rates are never 100 per cent so environmental factors must also play a role.

Research support for genes and the role of the OFC...

Menzies *et al.* (2007) used MRI to produce images of brain activity in OCD patients and their immediate family members without OCD.

OCD patients and their close relatives had reduced grey matter in key regions of the brain, including the OFC.

This supports the view that inherited anatomical differences may lead to OCD in certain individuals. In the future, brain scans may be used to detect OCD risk.

Other disorders with genetic links to OCD...

Research suggests that OCD may be an expression of genes linked to other disorders such as Tourette's and autism and so would be a characteristic of a number of different disorders.

Pauls and Leckman (1986) studied patients with Tourette's syndrome and concluded that OCD is one form of expression of the same gene that determines Tourette's. Obsessional and compulsive behaviour is also found in children with autism, and people with anorexia nervosa.

This supports the view that there are not specific genes unique to OCD, but they merely act as a predisposing factor towards obsessive-type behaviour.

Alternative psychological explanations...

The two-process model can be applied to OCD: a neutral stimulus (such as dirt) is associated with anxiety. Compulsive behaviours (such as handwashing) maintain the association by negative reinforcement.

Exposure and response prevention (ERP) is a similar treatment to systematic desensitisation. Patients experience their feared stimulus and are prevented from performing their compulsive behaviour.

Albucher et al. (1998) report that most adults with OCD improved considerably using ERP, suggesting that OCD has psychological as well as biological causes.

 APPLY: Exam skills

AO2: An example

SCENARIO Della shows symptoms of OCD, while her identical twin, Delia, is symptom-free.

Using your knowledge of the genetic explanation, explain why this might be the case. **(4 marks)**

ANSWER *Della and Delia are genetically identical so they may have inherited the COMT or SERT gene. These genes affect dopamine and serotonin production respectively and are implicated in OCD. The difference between the twins might be explained by the diathesis–stress model. This model would suggest that both Della and Delia may have the same inherited vulnerability (a diathesis) for OCD, but only Della experienced a stressor which had triggered the expression of this gene. Delia, on the other hand did not experience the same stressor, and so escaped expression of this gene. Consequently, unlike Della, Delia suffered no ill effects.*

AO2: Research methods

In a study designed to investigate the effectiveness of different kinds of drug therapy, thirty participants with OCD were randomly divided into three groups. The first group were given a course of SSRI drugs. The second group were given tricyclic drugs, and the third group received a placebo. None of the participants were told which group they had been assigned to. A measure was taken of the severity of the participants' symptoms before the study began, and a second measure was taken after three months had elapsed. The lower the score, the more the symptoms were reduced. The results of the study are shown in the table below.

	Mean severity of symptoms before drug therapy began (max. = 100)	**Mean severity of symptoms after 3 months of drug therapy (max. = 100)**
SSRI drugs	70	58
Tricyclic drugs	70	37
Placebo	70	56

State two findings from the study and for each finding draw one conclusion. (4 marks)

AO2: One for you to try

Leon, Andy and Allegra were discussing the biological causes of OCD. 'Of course it's genetic,' said Leon. 'Look at the evidence from family studies. You're five times more likely to develop OCD if you have a first-degree relative who has the disorder. That proves it's genetic.' 'He's right,' said Andy, 'twin studies prove it as well. The concordance rate for twins who share the same genes is really high.' As confident as Leon and Andy seemed, Allegra wasn't convinced by their arguments.

Explain why Allegra might not be convinced by Leon and Andy's arguments. (6 marks)

How do I answer... longer (12-mark or 16-mark) questions?

Q1: Outline and evaluate the biological approach to explaining OCD. (12 marks)

In the AS exam you will be asked 12-mark questions. These require 6 marks' worth of AO1 and 6 marks' worth of AO3.

Q2: Discuss biological explanations of OCD. (16 marks)

In the A Level exam, a 16-mark question requires 6 marks' worth of AO1 and 10 marks' worth of AO3. This means that, at A Level, you should aim to write almost twice as much AO3 as AO1.

We have given you enough AO1 points on the opposite page for 6 marks of AO1. Practise writing this in 7 ½ minutes.

For your AO3, you need to write three effective points for 6 marks, or four effective points for 10 marks.

Watch out for the command word 'Discuss', which is looking for a more balanced and wide-ranging discussion, not just a list of strengths or limitations of an explanation or treatment. This could include applications, implications, counterevidence, and any relevant issues and debates. In this topic, the issues of biological reductionism, biological determinism, and the nature side of the nature–nurture debate are all relevant. Pick one and explain **how** it is relevant.

REVIEW

Make sure you are comfortable with biological explanations. Revising the biological approach would be helpful here, making sure you can explain the role of genes in behaviour, the action of neurotransmitters, how SSRIs work, and the structure of the brain. You could practise drawing a diagram of synaptic transmission and explaining it to yourself verbally. You could also sketch a brain with the main regions labelled.

The biological approach to treating OCD

 **RECAP**

AO1 Description

Drug therapy

- SSRI antidepressants (e.g. Prozac) are the most commonly used drugs to reduce the anxiety associated with OCD. They block the reuptake of **serotonin** in the presynaptic membrane, increasing serotonin concentration at receptor sites on the postsynaptic membrane.

- Since low serotonin levels are implicated in the brain's 'worry circuit', increasing serotonin may have the effect of normalising this circuit.

- Tricyclic antidepressants (e.g. Anafranil) block the transporter mechanism that reabsorbs both serotonin and **noradrenaline** into the presynaptic cells that released them. The effect of this is to increase both serotonin and noradrenaline levels.

- Tricyclics have more side effects than SSRIs, and so are used as a second-line treatment when SSRIs have not been effective.

- Benzodiazepine (BZ) anti-anxiety drugs (e.g. Valium) are also used to treat OCD. They enhance the activity of **gamma-aminobutyric acid (GABA)**, which has a general quietening effect on many brain neurons.

- BZs react with GABA receptors on the receiving neuron. This makes it harder for the neuron to be stimulated by other neurotransmitters. The neuron's activity is slowed down, and induces feelings of relaxation.

AO3 Evaluation/Discussion

There is considerable evidence for the effectiveness of drug treatments…

Soomro et al. (2008) reviewed 17 studies of the use of SSRIs with OCD patients and found them to be more effective than placebos in reducing the symptoms of OCD up to three months after treatment.

However, most studies only last three to four months (Koran et al., 2007), and many patients relapse within a few weeks if medication is stopped (Maina et al., 2001).

Therefore, while drug treatments have been shown to be effective in the short term, they may not provide a lasting cure.

Drug therapies are preferred to other treatments…

An advantage of drug therapies is that they involve little input from the user in terms of effort and time, and require little monitoring by doctors.

In contrast, therapies such as CBT require the patient to attend regular meetings and put considerable thought into tackling their problems, as well as requiring therapists' time.

These benefits mean that drug therapies are more economical for the health service than psychological therapies.

All drugs have side effects, some more severe than others…

Nausea, headache and insomnia are common side effects of SSRIs (Soomro et al., 2008). Tricyclics can have worse side effects, such as hallucinations and irregular heartbeat.

BZs can cause increased aggressiveness and long-term memory impairment. They are also addictive, so BZs should be limited to a maximum of four weeks of treatment (Ashton, 1997).

These side effects can be enough to make a patient stop taking the drug, and therefore limit the usefulness of drugs as treatments for OCD.

The effectiveness of drugs may be exaggerated by publication bias…

AO3 PLUS

Turner et al. (2008) claim there is a publication bias toward studies that show a positive outcome of antidepressant drugs in the treatment of OCD.

A consequence of this publication bias is that research may exaggerate the beneficial effects of these drugs. Drug companies also have a strong interest in the success of their products and much of the research is funded by these companies.

Selective publication can lead doctors to make inappropriate treatment decisions that may not be in the best interest of their patients.

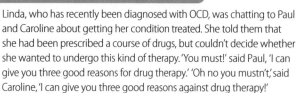 APPLY: Exam skills

AO2: An example

SCENARIO

Imagine that you are a health professional who has been asked to help a patient with OCD decide on the best treatment.

What key points would you make to help the patient decide between drug treatments and CBT? **(4 marks)**

ANSWER *Drug treatments are a relatively quick and cost-effective way of treating the symptoms associated with OCD. However, they have side effects of differing severity, for example nausea and headaches or even memory impairment. They may also be a 'quick fix' lasting only a few months. CBT requires much greater investment of time and effort but may be more effective than drug treatments in the long term. A compromise position might be to try drug therapy in the short term to enable the patient to take a more considered view of their situation and decide what to do in the longer term.*

AO2: Research methods

In a study designed to investigate the effectiveness of different kinds of drug therapy, 30 participants with OCD were randomly divided into three groups. The first group were given a course of SSRI drugs. The second group were given tricyclic drugs, and the third group received a placebo. None of the participants were told which group they had been assigned to. A measure was taken of the severity of the participants' symptoms before the study began, and a second measure was taken after three months had elapsed. The lower the score, the more the symptoms were reduced.

Outline three ethical issues that the researcher should have considered in this research, and suggest how they could be dealt with. (6 marks)

AO2: One for you to try

Linda, who has recently been diagnosed with OCD, was chatting to Paul and Caroline about getting her condition treated. She told them that she had been prescribed a course of drugs, but couldn't decide whether she wanted to undergo this kind of therapy. 'You must!' said Paul, 'I can give you three good reasons for drug therapy.' 'Oh no you mustn't,' said Caroline, 'I can give you three good reasons against drug therapy!'

a. **Outline three reasons Paul might have given Linda for using drug therapy. (3 marks)**

b. **Outline three reasons Caroline might have given Linda for not using drug therapy. (3 marks)**

How do I answer... research methods questions?

Questions requiring research methods knowledge can appear in any section of any paper in the AS or A level exams. They could include any aspect of research methods, data analysis or ethical issues. Here are a few tips:

- Take time to think – remember the relevant research methods key terms.
- When you are interpreting data, make comparisons between different values such as 'higher', 'lower' or 'similar', don't simply quote the numbers.
- Most research methods questions require you to link your knowledge to the stem information. They use phrases like 'in this study', and you must link explicitly or give relevant examples from the study.

For example, in the **AO2: Research methods** question on the left, you must refer to ethical issues that are relevant to a study testing drug effectiveness. You must then suggest how the researcher could deal with the ethical issues, again in a way that would work in this particular study. The issues of privacy or confidentiality would be less relevant than talking about informed consent or deception.

REVIEW

Practise thinking through research methods issues when you are learning studies from this chapter. You should be able to identify some issues to do with internal or external validity in any study, and think how you would make a specific, relevant point (e.g. the researcher may have known which drug the participants were taking, leading to a researcher effect if an unconscious behaviour affected the responses of participants) rather than a basic, generic point (field experiment, so good ecological validity). You should also know strengths or limitations of the type of research method, the sampling, and the research design. Ethical issues are always important: what they are, and how to deal with them.

RECAP

AO1 Description

Wilhelm Wundt (1832–1920)

- Wilhelm Wundt was the first person to call himself a psychologist. He believed that the human mind could be studied scientifically, using a technique called **introspection**.

- Introspection means 'looking into' and is the process by which a person gains knowledge about their mental and emotional states.

- Wundt believed that, with appropriate training, mental processes such as memory and perception could be observed systematically. Participants were presented with a stimulus (e.g. a visual image) and asked to describe their inner thought processes.

- Wundt then compared these responses to generate theories of perception. This is a structuralist approach.

The emergence of psychology as a science

- **Empiricism** is the belief that knowledge comes from observation and experience alone. When Wundt applied empirical methods to the study of human beings, psychology began to emerge as a science.

- This new approach – psychology – was based on two major assumptions. First, that all behaviour is 'caused'. Second, that it is possible to 'predict' behaviour in different conditions.

- The process used to explore these assumptions became known as the **scientific method**. The scientific method uses investigative methods that are objective, systematic and replicable.

From now on, Psychology will be experimental science

AO3 Evaluation/Discussion

Wundt's methods were unreliable...

A criticism of Wundt's research was that participants could only report conscious experiences. Behaviourists considered that processes such as memory or perception were unobservable constructions.	Wundt's approach failed because of the poor reliability of his methods. Introspective 'experimental' results were not reliably reproducible by researchers in other laboratories.	*In contrast, behaviourists such as Pavlov and Thorndike were already achieving reliably reproducible results and discovering explanatory principles that could be generalised to human beings.*

A scientific approach tests assumptions about behaviour and makes generalisations...

Because of the scientific method's reliance on empirical observation, psychological theories can be refined or abandoned in response to new evidence.	However, much human behaviour is unobservable, so cannot be directly measured. Also, human behaviour may not follow universal laws, so generalisation may be inappropriate.	*This means that much of psychological knowledge is inferential: there is a gap between the actual data obtained in research investigations and the theories put forward to explain this data.*

Introspection is still useful in scientific psychology...

Csikszentmihalyi and Hunter (2003) used bleepers to prompt teenagers to write down their thoughts and feelings at random points in the day.	The teens were more often unhappy than happy, but when their energies were focused on a challenging task, they tended to be happier.	*Introspection therefore offers researchers a way of measuring participants' conscious thoughts and feelings.*

Introspection is not particularly accurate...

Nisbett and Wilson (1977) claim that we lack knowledge of the causes and processes underlying our behaviour and attitudes.	This problem is evident in the study of implicit attitudes, i.e. unconscious attitudes or stereotypes. For example, unconscious racism influences the way someone behaves and thinks.	*Because such attitudes are unconscious, self-reports through introspection would not reveal them. This challenges the value of introspection in exploring attitudes and beliefs.*

AO3 PLUS

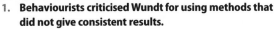

APPLY: Exam skills

AO2: An example

SCENARIO In a study of perception, several participants are asked to describe their inner sensations and experiences while viewing a visual illusion, and what they say is recorded.

How would a structuralist, such as Wundt, use the records to construct an understanding of this experience? What difficulty might the researcher experience in this process? **(4 marks)**

ANSWER *The researcher would combine accounts and look for patterns among them, which would give clues about the nature of this type of perception. Understanding of this is likely to be poor because participants are using introspection: everyone's reports are likely to be different and not everyone is equally aware of their inner thought processes.*

AO2: Research methods

A student wants to study sexism, and plans to use an introspective method, asking participants to count how many times they have a judgemental thought about another person based on their sex. Her teacher suggests the data may not be very reliable, and there could be ethical issues with this research.

a. Why might the data have poor reliability? **(3 marks)**

b. What ethical issues could there be in this research? **(3 marks)**

AO2: Two for you to try

1. **Behaviourists criticised Wundt for using methods that did not give consistent results.**

   a. Why were Wundt's results inconsistent? **(2 marks)**

   b. How did the behaviourists overcome these issues and carry out research that was more reliable? **(2 marks)**

2. **Which of the following are features of Wundt's method of introspection? Tick two boxes. (2 marks)**

   a. Introspection is based on the belief that the mind can be studied scientifically. ☐

   b. Introspection is a self-report method. ☐

   c. Wundt believed that anyone can collect data about their own perceptions using introspection. ☐

   d. Introspection produces reliable data about mental processes. ☐

How do I answer... description only (AO1) questions?

There is a simple formula for answering AO1 questions that only ask you to 'Describe', 'Outline' or 'Explain' something. For 2 marks, say two things; for 3 marks, say three things, and so on. Try working through the sample questions below, using the AO1 material on the opposite page.

Q1: Outline Wundt's contribution to the development of psychology. (4 marks)

Use AO1 bullet points 1, 2, 3 and 5.

Q2: Explain what is meant by *introspection*. (2 marks)

A simple definition needs a little elaboration for 2 marks. Use AO1 bullet points 2 and 3.

Q3: Outline how Wundt used introspection to investigate mental processes. (3 marks)

Use AO1 bullet points 1, 2 and 3.

Q4: Explain how empirical research in psychology makes use of the scientific method. (3 marks)

Use the last three AO1 bullet points, about **empiricism**.

REVIEW

Learning key terms is vital for getting high marks in answers. You need to use specialist terminology effectively to get Level 4 (top marks) in extended writing answers, or to get full marks in short answers. Learn these key terms by keeping an up-to-date glossary, and testing yourself on the definitions frequently. If you use two columns, you can cover the definition and recall the word, or read the word and see if you can state the definition accurately:

Term	Definition
Empiricism	Introspection
A belief that knowledge comes from observation and experience alone.	The process by which a person gains knowledge about their mental and emotional states by observing conscious thoughts and feelings.

The behaviourist approach

A01 Description

Classical conditioning

- Pavlov discovered **classical conditioning** in his research with dogs. Pavlov repeatedly presented a bell, a neutral stimulus (NS), with food, an unconditioned stimulus (UCS), which led to an unconditioned response (UCR) of salivation.

- After many pairings the NS produces the same response as the UCS. The NS becomes a conditioned stimulus (CS) producing a conditioned response (CR).

- If the CS is presented without the UCS a few times, extinction occurs and the CR is no longer produced. Spontaneous recovery can then occur if the CS and UCS are paired again.

- Conditioned animals will also respond to other stimuli that are similar to the CS; this is stimulus generalisation.

Operant conditioning

- Skinner's theory of **operant conditioning** suggests that whether or not an animal repeats a particular behaviour depends on its consequences.

- Positive **reinforcement** occurs when a behaviour produces a consequence that is rewarding.

- Negative reinforcement occurs when a behaviour removes an unpleasant consequence. Reinforcement increases the likelihood of the behaviour being repeated.

- **Punishment** occurs when a behaviour is followed by an unpleasant consequence, and decreases the likelihood of the behaviour being repeated.

A03 Evaluation/Discussion

Classical conditioning has been applied to the treatment of phobias…

Systematic desensitisation is a therapy based on classical conditioning. It works by eliminating the learned anxious response (the CR) that is associated with a feared object or situation.	The learned response (anxiety) is replaced with another (relaxation) so the patient is no longer anxious in the presence of the feared object or situation.	*This therapy is effective for a range of phobias such as fear of spiders (arachnophobia) and fear of flying (aerophobia).*

Operant conditioning is based on experimental research…

A particular strength of Skinner's research was his reliance on the experimental method, using controlled conditions to discover causal relationships between variables.	He used 'Skinner boxes' to manipulate the consequences of behaviour (the independent variable), so he could accurately measure the effects on a rat's behaviour (the dependent variable).	*This allowed him to establish a cause-and-effect relationship between the consequences of a behaviour (i.e. positive or negative) and the future frequency of its occurrence.*

Over-reliance on non-human animals in research…

Skinner's research has received some criticism because his experiments involved the study of rats and pigeons, rather than humans.	Critics claim that human beings have free will rather than having their behaviour determined by positive and negative reinforcement.	*However, Skinner argued that free will is merely an illusion, and what we believe are behaviours chosen by free will are actually the product of environmental conditioning.*

Issues/Debates
Free will and determinism

A limited perspective on behaviour…

Behaviourists have been accused of ignoring other levels of explanation such as cognitive factors or emotional states.	Treating human beings as a product of their conditioning alone means that we ignore the evidence for the role of these other factors in shaping behaviour.	*However, Skinner argued that even complex behaviours, such as our interactions with the opposite sex or pathological behaviour, could be better understood by studying the reinforcement history of the individual.*

Issues/Debates
Holism and reductionism

AO3 PLUS

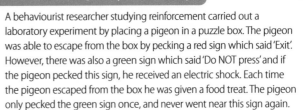

APPLY: Exam skills

AO2: An example

SCENARIO Shortly after eating breakfast with coffee, while listening to music, a traveller is seasick during a ferry crossing. Following this the smell and taste of coffee induce nausea.

Apply what you know about classical conditioning to explain this outcome. **(4 marks)**

ANSWER *Sickness is a natural unconditioned response to the unconditioned stimulus of disorienting motion. The previously neutral stimulus of coffee has become a conditioned stimulus for nausea due to its accidental pairing with the sea motion, and seasickness is the conditioned response. We are biologically prepared to associate smells and tastes with potentially toxic, nausea-inducing substances.*

AO2: Research methods

The behaviourist researcher (in **AO2: One for you to try**) noticed that at first the pigeon escaped rather slowly; however, with each attempt made, the time taken to escape decreased. The data from his experiment is shown in the table below.

Attempt	Time taken for the pigeon to escape from the puzzle box (seconds)
1	54
2	45
3	36
4	22
5	15
6	11
7	6

a. **The experimenter chose to calculate the mean time taken. Explain why the mean is an appropriate measure of central tendency for the above data. (2 marks)**

b. **Calculate the mean time taken for the pigeon to escape from the puzzle box. (1 mark)**

c. **Calculate the range of scores, in seconds. (1 mark)**

AO2: One for you to try

A behaviourist researcher studying reinforcement carried out a laboratory experiment by placing a pigeon in a puzzle box. The pigeon was able to escape from the box by pecking a red sign which said 'Exit'. However, there was also a green sign which said 'Do NOT press' and if the pigeon pecked this sign, he received an electric shock. Each time the pigeon escaped from the box he was given a food treat. The pigeon only pecked the green sign once, and never went near this sign again.

Use your knowledge of operant conditioning to explain the pigeon's behaviour. (4 marks)

How do I answer... 'Distinguish between' questions?

There are special requirements for answering questions which ask you to 'Distinguish between' two concepts, or to 'Compare' or 'Explain the difference between' them:

1. Don't just describe one thing and then the other.

2. Pick a characteristic which applies to both, but which is different for each, and point it out.

3. Explain the difference, using words like 'whereas' or 'however' to point out the difference clearly.

For 2 marks, one difference is enough. For 4 marks, you would need to explain two.

Q1: Distinguish between classical and operant conditioning. (2 marks)

Both are forms of learning within the behaviourist approach, but classical conditioning is learning by association and operant conditioning is learning from the consequences of behaviour.

Q2: Explain the difference between reinforcement and punishment. (2 marks)

Reinforcement is a consequence of a behaviour which makes that behaviour more likely to be repeated, whereas punishment makes it less likely to be repeated.

REVIEW

You need a secure knowledge of the process of classical conditioning. Practise writing out the steps in diagram form, as this will help you to remember it, although you would need to write it out in words in an exam. Make sure you know the full terms, not just the abbreviations, and you can explain which is the bell, the food, and the response of salivation in Pavlov's experiment.

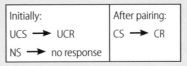

Initially:	After pairing:
UCS → UCR	CS → CR
NS → no response	

Social learning theory

AO1 Description

- **Social learning theory** (SLT) is learning through observation of others and imitating behaviours that are rewarded.

- **Modelling** is a form of learning in which a person (the model) performs a behaviour and another individual observes them.

- **Mediational processes** enable the observer to store mental representations of this behaviour and its probable consequences.

- **Imitation** is the process of copying an observed behaviour and is more likely to occur when **identification** takes place. Children are more likely to identify with and learn from models who are similar to them.

- Children who observe a model receiving rewards are also much more likely to imitate their behaviour. This is known as **vicarious reinforcement**.

Bandura *et al.* (1961)

- **PROCEDURE** Bandura *et al.* conducted an experiment to examine SLT in children. Children observed an aggressive or non-aggressive adult model interacting with a Bobo doll, and were then tested for imitative learning.

- **FINDINGS** The children who observed the aggressive model reproduced much of the model's aggressive behaviour (both verbal and physical). Children who had observed the non-aggressive model showed almost no aggression.

  > In a follow-up study, children who saw the model being rewarded for their aggressive acts (vicarious reinforcement) were more likely to demonstrate aggression in their own play.

AO3 Evaluation / Discussion

Social learning theory has useful applications, including understanding criminal behaviour...

The probability of someone engaging in criminal behaviour increases when they identify with models who commit crimes and develop the expectation of positive consequences for this behaviour (Akers, 1998).	Ulrich (2003) found that the strongest predictor of violent behaviour in adolescence was association with delinquent peers, where violence was both modelled and rewarded.	*However, Siegel and McCormick (2006) suggest that young people with deviant attitudes (e.g. low self-control) seek out peers with similar attitudes and behaviours, as they are more fun to be with than their less reckless counterparts.*

Research support for identification...

Fox and Bailenson (2009) used computer-generated 'virtual' humans, who looked similar or dissimilar to participants, engaging in exercise or merely loitering.	Participants who viewed their virtual model exercising engaged in more exercise in the 24 hours following the experiment than participants who viewed their virtual model merely loitering, or a dissimilar model exercising.	*They concluded that greater identification with a model leads to more learning because it is easier to visualise yourself in the place of the model.*

Social learning theory disregards other potential influences on behaviour...

For example, in explaining the development of gender role behaviour, social learning theorists would emphasise the importance of gender-specific modelling.	In real life, however, a child is exposed to many different influences, which interact in complex ways. These include genetic predispositions, conditioning, personality factors, and media portrayals of gender.	*This presents a serious problem for social learning researchers. It is very difficult to show that one particular thing (social learning) is the main causal influence.*

The importance of identification in social learning...

Health campaigns have made the most of the identification process by matching characters that model the desired behaviour with the target audience in terms of physical characteristics, attitudes and behaviours.	Greater identification with the model is expected to influence social learning. For example, Andsager *et al.* (2006) found that perceived similarity to a model in an anti-alcohol advertisement was positively related to the message's effectiveness.	*Based on this finding, the researchers suggest that some of a message's potency may be lost if the individual finds it difficult to identify with a given model.*

AO3 PLUS

APPLY: Exam skills

AO2: An example

SCENARIO Jack and Jess are 10-year-old siblings. Jack tends to be badly behaved after watching violent television programmes and has been fighting at school. Jack's mum is puzzled because Jess watches the same programmes but doesn't appear to be as affected by them.

Using social learning theory, explain Jack's behaviour and suggest why Jess does not behave in the same way after watching television programmes where males are shown acting violently. **(4 marks)**

ANSWER *It is likely that Jack identifies more strongly than Jess does with the violent role models on TV, most probably because most of these models are male, like Jack. As a result, he is more likely to internalise their behaviour and imitate it, especially if he expects the consequences to be rewarding (e.g. praise from peers). Jess, as a girl, is less likely to identify with the male violent models on TV. She does not imitate them because she does not anticipate any rewards associated with such violent behaviour.*

AO2: Research methods

A study looked at the behaviour of twins to see how similar they were. Each twin was rated for aggressiveness on a scale of 1 to 10. The results are displayed in the table below.

Twin pair	A	B	C	D	E	F	G	H	I
Twin 1	8	6	4	5	2	8	9	6	7
Twin 2	6	5	8	6	5	4	8	5	7

a. **How many people were tested in this study? (1 mark)**

b. **Draw an appropriate scattergram to display this data. Give a title for your graph. (4 marks)**

c. **What does your graph show about the twins in terms of their aggression? (2 marks)**

d. **Two students are discussing the findings. Fred says, 'This clearly shows that aggressiveness is inherited in genes.' Katrina disagrees, and thinks there could be another explanation. What other explanation could there be for these findings? (3 marks)**

AO2: One for you to try

Mrs Watkins is a secondary school teacher. She notices that some of the students in her class constantly call out answers without raising their hands, which ruins the learning for other students.

How might Mrs Watkins use vicarious reinforcement to change the behaviour of these students? Explain your answer with reference to both positive reinforcement and punishment. (4 marks)

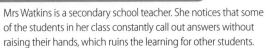

How do I answer... research methods (AO2) questions?

Questions requiring research methods knowledge can appear in any section of any paper in the AS or A Level exams. They could include any aspect of research methods, data analysis or ethical issues. Here are a few tips:

*   Take time to think. What research method is being used? What design? What sampling?
*   Research methods questions require you to link your knowledge to the stem information. They use phrases like 'in this study', and you must link clearly or give relevant examples from the study.
*   Drawing graphs – don't forget to use an appropriate scale on the axes (use up at least half of the height and width of the graph paper provided in the exam paper); label the axes (the names of the two variables); plot points or bars carefully. A scattergram just has points; don't join them or try to draw a line of best fit or any other line.

For example, in the **AO2: Research methods** question on the left, take your time to think – there are nine sets of twins. The scattergram should have 'Twin 1' on the y-axis and 'Twin 2' on the x-axis. For part **c** you need to describe the correlation between the aggressiveness scores of pairs of twins: weak/strong? Positive/negative? Part **d** then asks you to apply your knowledge. 'The twin pairs have had the same environment. They were exposed to the same models and reinforcement for their behaviour if they were brought up in the same family, so another explanation would be social learning. Maybe they have both imitated the aggressiveness level of their parents, and been reinforced for that behaviour within their family.'

REVIEW

Students often write far too much when they know a study very well, such as Bandura's Bobo doll study. You need to be very selective and concise, while giving enough detail and specialist terminology to get the marks.

Practise selecting points to use in different specific questions, such as Bandura's findings, procedure, and theory of social learning. However, long descriptions and evaluation of Bandura's study will not get much credit if the question is about social learning theory itself.

You also need to be able to evaluate the methodology and findings of the study. For example, he carried out a lab experiment with highly controlled variables, but the task was very artificial and children may have been affected by demand characteristics. What kinds of validity could you comment on?

The cognitive approach

AO1 Description

The study of internal mental processes

- Cognitive processes include memory, attention, perception, emotion and awareness. These processes cannot be studied directly, but must be understood by **inference** and logical reasoning from measuring observable behaviour.

- The **cognitive** approach studies the mind as an information processor, with inputs, processing, storage, retrieval and outputs.

- For example, in a **computer model** of memory, we input information via our senses, working memory is like the computer's RAM (random access memory), and long-term memory is similar to information stored on a hard drive.

- Cognitive psychologists often develop theoretical models, for example the working memory model, to visually represent a mental process.

- A **schema** is a cognitive framework that helps organise and interpret information. Schemas allow us to take shortcuts when interpreting large amounts of information, but can lead to stereotypes as we make assumptions about people based on incomplete information.

The emergence of cognitive neuroscience

- **Cognitive neuroscience** studies the living brain, using brain imaging technology such as positron emission tomography (PET) and functional magnetic resonance imaging (fMRI), showing which parts of the brain are active during different tasks.

AO3 Evaluation / Discussion

The cognitive approach has many useful applications...

In social psychology, research in social cognition has helped psychologists better understand how we interpret the actions of others.	The cognitive approach to psychopathology has been used to explain how much of the dysfunctional behaviour shown by people can be traced back to faulty thinking processes.	*These insights have led to the successful treatment, using cognitive-based interventions, of people suffering from disorders such as depression and OCD.*

The cognitive approach uses scientific methods...

The use of the experimental method provides researchers with a rigorous method for collecting and evaluating evidence in order to reach accurate conclusions about how the mind works.	Carefully designed controlled laboratory experiments produce large quantities of empirical data which form the basis of theories about cognitive processes.	*This means that conclusions about how the mind works are based on objective evidence, not just self-report or conscious introspection.*

The computer model is a limited analogy...

Terms such as 'coding', 'storage' and 'retrieval' are borrowed directly from the field of computing. However, there are important differences between the way computers and humans process information.	Computers do not make mistakes, nor do they ignore or forget information. Human behaviour, on the other hand, is affected by emotion and motivation as well as systematic cognitive biases.	*This limits the usefulness of explaining human thought and behaviour using computer models.*

Studies may lack ecological validity...

AO3 PLUS

Many studies of cognitive psychology tend to use tasks that have little in common with participants' natural everyday experiences.	For example, memory experiments use test materials such as random word lists or digits. These are quite different from how we use memory in everyday life (e.g. remembering appointments or conversations).	*Therefore, much of the research in cognitive psychology can be criticised as lacking ecological validity; it fails to reflect behaviours that occur in real-life settings.*

APPLY: Exam skills

AO2: An example

SCENARIO After observing real counsellors at work, cognitive scientists develop a computerised counsellor which they claim can ask questions in a way that is indistinguishable from real counsellors. In pilot tests, participants rate the capability of the computerised counsellor as very low.

Apply what you know about cognitive models of human behaviour to explain the clients' dissatisfaction. **(4 marks)**

ANSWER *Cognitive models of complex human behaviour tend to concentrate on information flow through predictable systems. However, real human interaction is much more complex than this. For example, computer models fail to incorporate unpredictable, emotional and motivational influences on behaviour. These include mood, anxiety and so on, things that influence human behaviour. A computerised counsellor would not respond to subtle cues related to these states and so would not closely resemble real-life, everyday interactions. Clients' dissatisfaction could therefore be due to the fact that the computerised counsellor did not seem human-like enough.*

AO2: Research methods

A cognitive psychologist conducted a laboratory experiment to see how memory works.

Condition 1: Eight participants were presented words with pictures.

Condition 2: Eight different participants were presented the same words, without pictures.

The participants were then tested on their recall of the words ten minutes later. The following results were obtained:

Participant	Number of words recalled: Condition 1	Participant	Number of words recalled: Condition 2
1	15	9	7
2	14	10	10
3	11	11	4
4	15	12	9
5	8	13	4
6	6	14	6
7	4	15	4
8	15	16	4
Mean		Mean	
Standard deviation	4.47	Standard deviation	2.29

a. **Calculate the mean scores for both conditions. Show your calculations. (4 marks)**

b. **Outline one conclusion that could be drawn from the standard deviation scores in the table above. (2 marks)**

c. **Which experimental design was used in this study? (1 mark)**

d. **(A level only) The psychologist wants to test the signficance of the difference in the numbers of words recalled between the two conditions. Name a suitable statistical test, and give reasons for your answers. (3 marks)**

AO2: One for you to try

Maisie was in a restaurant when a fight broke out at the next table. She hadn't noticed the people at that table until the fight broke out.

Explain how Maisie's schemas relating to eating a meal in a restaurant may affect her memory of this incident. (3 marks)

How do I answer... evaluation (AO3) questions?

Evaluation questions use terms like 'evaluate', 'strength', 'criticism', 'limitation'. For example:

Q1: Outline two strengths of the cognitive approach in psychology. (6 marks)

For this question the first two AO3 points should be fully elaborated.

Q2: Explain two limitations of the cognitive approach in psychology. (6 marks)

This time use the third and fourth AO3 points.

Q3: Briefly evaluate the use of computer models in psychology. (4 marks)

For this question you could first explain how computer models are useful. For example, 'they help to describe complex mental processes by using the analogy of information processing, with input, output and memory storage'. Then explain the limitations of this using the third AO3 point.

REVIEW

This would be a good opportunity to remind yourself about the cognitive explanation and treatments for depression. The multi-store model and working memory model are also cognitive models, so evaluation points you have learned relating to these topics may also apply to the cognitive approach generally. Have a look at those sections in this book (pages 70–73 and 24–27), and think about how the theory and evaluation match up with this spread. It's more efficient to learn some points that can be used in various ways in different topics, and it helps you to cross-reference your knowledge. Making interconnected mental maps will give you more pathways for retrieving vital information in the pressure of the exam.

The biological approach

RECAP

AOI Description

- The biological approach views human beings as biological organisms and provides biological explanations of all aspects of psychological functioning.

- **Genes** carry instructions for a particular characteristic (such as intelligence). The **genotype** is the genetic code in the DNA and the **phenotype** is the physical appearance that results from this inherited information.

- How these characteristics develop depends on an interaction between genes and the environment.

- Biological structures also play an important role in behaviour. The nervous system carries messages around the body in the form of electrical signals in neurons.

- **Neurotransmitters** are molecules that transmit messages from one neuron to the next. They diffuse across the synapse and bind to receptors, where they may cause excitation or inhibition of an impulse.

- Behaviour can also be influenced by hormones, chemicals produced by endocrine glands such as the pituitary gland. Hormones are secreted directly into the bloodstream where they travel to their target cells, causing a physiological reaction.

- Darwin's theory of **evolution** describes how behaviours that make individuals more likely to survive and reproduce are passed on through genes. As a result these genes and their associated behaviours become more common in future generations. This is the process of **natural selection**.

> Well, we've finally got the tablet, but now we'll have to wait until we've evolved enough to invent Facebook

> **Issues/Debates**
> Nature-nurture debate

AO3 Evaluation/Discussion

The biological approach uses the scientific method and experiments to investigate behaviour...

Experimental studies take place in highly controlled environments so that other researchers are able to replicate research studies, adding to the validity of the original findings if they can be reproduced.

The use of sophisticated imaging and recording techniques has increased the precision and objectivity of experimental research in this area.

As a result, these techniques have contributed to the scientific validity of the biological approach.

The biological approach has useful applications in the real world...

A strength of the biological approach is that it provides clear predictions, e.g. about the effects of neurotransmitters or biological rhythms on behaviour.

For example, research into the role of neurochemical imbalance in depression has led to the development of effective drug treatments.

This further demonstrates the value of adopting a biological approach, as treatments can benefit people's health and well-being.

The biological approach is reductionist...

The biological approach is criticised for its belief that complex behaviour can be broken down into the action of genes, neurochemicals and hormones.

For example, many explanations of mental disorders are reductionist because genes or neurochemical imbalances are believed to be the main cause of these disorders.

We cannot fully understand a behaviour without also taking account of the other factors that influence it. These include cognitive, emotional and cultural factors.

> **Issues/Debates**
> Reductionism and holism

The dangers of genetic explanations of criminal behaviour...

AO3 PLUS

Critics claim this may lead to genetic screening of the population and discrimination against those with a genetic predisposition for criminality.

This also creates the danger that genes might then be used to explain criminality, despite the fact that the connection between genes and complex behaviours is far from straightforward.

However, there may be positive consequences too; if individuals have a genetic predisposition for criminality, they could be helped to develop coping skills to protect them from its influence.

> **Issues/Debates**
> Free will and determinism

APPLY: Exam skills

AO2: An example

SCENARIO Laura's friends describe her as a fitness fanatic. She spends most of her spare time preparing for, and running in, increasingly demanding marathons, which she finds personally very rewarding.

How might this behaviour be explained on genetic and neurochemical levels? **(4 marks)**

ANSWER *Laura is described as a fitness fanatic as she spends most of her time training and running. She may have genes which predispose her to athleticism, so that her body shape and metabolism are suited to this activity. She also finds it very rewarding, which indicates that she is experiencing neurochemical benefits, such as the effects of serotonin and dopamine resulting from exercise, which make her feel good. This acts like operant conditioning, reinforcing the behaviour and making it more likely that she will keep running more and more.*

AO2: Research methods

In a study of criminality, researchers checked the school records of 50 pairs of twins, and recorded the number of detentions each twin had received for poor behaviour.

Twenty-two twin pairs had received the same number of detentions. Twenty-eight twin pairs had received different numbers of detentions.

Use your knowledge of genotypes and phenotypes to explain these findings. (4 marks)

AO2: One for you to try

Samuel and Daniel are identical twins who were separated at birth. When they meet each other at the age of 18 they are surprised by their slight differences in looks and their huge differences in personality. Samuel is much more outgoing than Daniel, who has always been rather shy.

Use your knowledge of genotype and phenotype to explain the differences in their personality. (4 marks)

How do I answer... selection (multiple choice) questions?

Which of the following terms is *not* true of a phenotype?

A It is affected by the environment.

B It is affected by genes.

C It refers to behaviour that is not inherited.

D It demonstrates the nature-nurture interaction.

To answer multiple choice questions, follow these steps:

- Read the question carefully – are you being asked to identify **one** or **two** statements? Are you looking for statements that are correct or that are **not** correct? In this question you need to find one statement which is **not** true of a phenotype.
- Cross out any which are obviously wrong. Phenotype is affected by genes and environment, so cross out **A** and **B**.
- Think carefully about what remains. **C** is tricky as it gives you a double negative to consider, but the statement is the opposite of **B** so could be correct.
- If you can rule out **D** as well, you are left with **C**. Think carefully and check – yes, this is correct as it is **not** true that phenotype refers to behaviour that is not inherited. In other words, phenotype refers to behaviour that is (partially) inherited.

REVIEW

Several of the big debates in Psychology are relevant here: nature-nurture, biological reductionism and biological determinism. If you are taking A Level Psychology, you will know about these from the **Issues and debates** topic. If you are taking AS, you will not know so much about them. Reductionism just means breaking things down into their simplest parts in order to investigate them. This is useful as it allows us to investigate the causes and mechanisms of complex behaviours, but it can give a

limited understanding if we don't also take into account other levels of explanation. So you can see that 'reductionism' is a strength as well as a limitation. In other words, it is a discussion point with two sides to it, rather than just a straight criticism of this approach. The same is true for determinism and nature-nurture. To access high-level AO3 marks you will need to be able to use subtle discussion points like this.

The psychodynamic approach

RECAP

AOI Description

Freud's theory of psychoanalysis

- **Psychodynamic** theories emphasise change and development in the individual, unconscious motives and desires, and the importance of early childhood experiences in shaping personality.

- Freud's theory of **psychoanalysis** suggests that the **unconscious** mind reveals itself through 'Freudian slips', creativity and neurotic symptoms.

- Freud described the **structure of personality**, with three parts in conflict: The id (impulsive physical appetites, including the libido); the ego (mediates between the id and the superego); and the superego (consisting of conscience, which internalises societal rules, and ego-ideal, determined by parental expectations).

- **Defence mechanisms** prevent traumatic memories from becoming conscious and causing anxiety. For example, repression is unconscious blocking of unacceptable thoughts and impulses. Denial is refusal to accept reality. Displacement involves redirecting hostile feelings onto an innocent person or object.

- The **psychosexual stages** emphasise that libido (sexual energy) is the main drive, but is expressed differently at each stage of development: oral, anal, phallic, latent and genital.

- For example, during the phallic stage (age 3–6), sexual energy is focused on the genitals. Boys experience the Oedipus complex, a desire to possess their mother and get rid of their father, causing castration anxiety.

AO3 Evaluation / Discussion

A pioneering approach to understanding human behaviour...

It suggested new methodological procedures for gathering evidence (case studies) and the development of the approach was based on observations of behaviour rather than introspection.	From these observations, Freud and his followers were the first to demonstrate the potential of psychological treatments for disorders such as depression and anxiety.	*This approach has led to successful treatments; for example, de Maat et al.'s (2009) large-scale review of psychotherapy studies concluded that psychoanalysis produced significant improvements in symptoms.*

However, psychoanalysis is a gender-biased approach...

Freud seemed content to remain ignorant of female sexuality and how it may differ from male sexuality.	This led psychoanalysts such as Karen Horney, who broke away from Freudian theory, to criticise his work, particularly his views on women and their development.	*Dismissing women and their sexuality in such a way is problematic, not only because Freud treated many female patients, but also because his theories are still so influential today.*

Issues/Debates
Gender bias

Psychoanalysis is a culture-biased approach...

Sue and Sue (2008) argue that psychoanalysis has little relevance for people from non-Western cultures.	They claim that many cultural groups do not value discussion and insight in the same way that Western cultures do. In China, for example, a person who is depressed or anxious avoids thoughts that cause distress rather than being willing to discuss them openly.	*This contrasts with the Western belief that open discussion and insight are always helpful in therapy.*

Issues/Debates
Culture bias

Psychoanalysis: a comprehensive theory...

As well as its therapeutic applications, psychoanalysis can be used to explain many other aspects of human behaviour outside of the realm of psychology.	Psychoanalysis has been used as a form of literary criticism. For example, in Shakespeare's play *Hamlet*, many aspects of Hamlet's psyche are seen as a projection of Shakespeare's own mind.	*As a result, we are able to interpret these works using psychoanalytic concepts, delving into the mind of the author or the fictional character.*

APPLY: Exam skills

AO2: An example

SCENARIO Gerry is trying to quit smoking because he knows it is bad for him. For several weeks he succeeds but then he meets an old smoking companion who presses him to smoke. Gerry successfully resists and feels pleased.

Apply Freud's concepts of id, ego and superego to explain Gerry's resistance to the temptation to smoke. **(4 marks)**

ANSWER *Gerry enjoys smoking and this satisfies the immediate, pleasure-seeking id. However, because his ego is in touch with reality he knows it is bad for his health. This leads to a tension between the id and ego, the urge to engage in a pleasurable activity against the reality of the harm it may be causing. The superego stands in judgement of his actions. Resistance to the temptation to smoke satisfies his ego-ideal which makes Gerry feel good about himself, whereas giving in to the temptation would activate his conscience, making him feel guilty.*

AO2: Research methods

A researcher looked at the effectiveness of treatment in two groups of patients suffering from symptoms of depression.

One group received psychoanalytic therapy and the other group received cognitive behavioural therapy, both over a two-year period. These two groups were compared to a control group of patients who received no treatment over the same two-year period.

The graph below shows the percentage of patients who reported a 'significant improvement' in the depressive symptoms at three months, six months and one year.

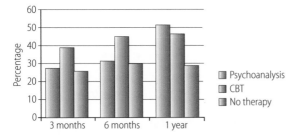

State two findings and for each one draw a conclusion. (4 marks)

AO2: One for you to try

Sadie is a 40-year-old woman who has experienced high levels of anxiety since her teenage years. She doesn't remember much about her childhood but she knows it was traumatic and she tries not to think about it. However, her symptoms are now making it impossible to carry out normal everyday tasks like going shopping or meeting friends. She decides to try psychoanalysis after reading about it on the Internet.

What explanations might a psychoanalyst suggest for her symptoms, and how might the analysis help her? (4 marks)

How do I answer... longer (16-mark) questions?

In A Level, a 16-mark question needs 6 marks of AO1 and 10 marks of AO3, so you should aim to write almost twice as much AO3 as AO1. We have given you enough AO1 points for 6 marks of AO1. Practise writing this in 7 ½ minutes. For your AO3, you need to write four effective points for 10 marks.

Q1: Outline and evaluate the psychodynamic approach in psychology. (16 marks)

This is a straightforward 'Outline and evaluate' question, but you will have to be selective, as there is more than enough theory. Remember the maximum number of marks you can get for AO1 is 6, so don't try to cover all the aspects of theory in detail. Our summary bullet points are sufficient.

Q2: Discuss the role of the unconscious in the psychodynamic approach to psychology. (16 marks)

Q2: seems to be asking something very specific about the unconscious, but in fact the entire psychodynamic approach is based on the role of the unconscious, so you can also describe psychosexual stages and defence mechanisms, which operate in the unconscious. Just make sure you explicitly explain the unconscious nature of these aspects of the theory.

Watch out for the command word 'Discuss', which is looking for a more balanced and wide-ranging discussion, not just a list of strengths or limitations of the approach. This could include applications, implications, counterevidence, and any relevant issues and debates. In this topic, the issues of psychic determinism, scientific method, gender and cultural bias are all relevant. Pick one and explain **how** it is relevant.

 REVIEW

How much to write: You could practise writing 2-mark, 4-mark and 6-mark descriptions of psychodynamic theory, or a 2-mark or 4-mark answer focusing on only one aspect such as psychosexual stages or the structure of the personality. For 2 marks, use two bullet points, etc. For 6 marks you should be writing about 150 words. If you try to cover all aspects of the theory thoroughly, you will run out of time for AO3 in an extended answer, so be selective and concise. We have helped you by summarising the key content in the bullet points, but you still need to include enough detail and specialist terminology if you want to get marks in the top band.

Humanistic psychology

A LEVEL ONLY ZONE

RECAP

AO1 Description

- The basic assumption of **humanistic** psychology is that we have **free will**: the ability to make significant personal choices within biological/societal constraints.

Maslow's theory

- Maslow described a **hierarchy of needs** in which people must fulfil each level before moving to the next: physiological, safety, love/belonging, esteem, and **self-actualisation** at the top.

- People who attain self-actualisation are creative and accepting, and have peak experiences of extreme inspiration and ecstasy.

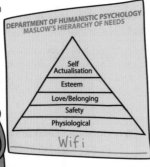

DEPARTMENT OF HUMANISTIC PSYCHOLOGY
MASLOW'S HIERARCHY OF NEEDS

Self Actualisation
Esteem
Love/Belonging
Safety
Physiological

Wifi

Rogers' theory

- Humanistic psychology focuses on the **self**. Rogers claimed that our two basic needs, unconditional positive regard from other people and feelings of self-worth, develop from childhood interactions with parents. **Conditions of worth** are a perception that acceptance from others depends on meeting their expectations.

- The more similar our self-concept and our ideal self, the greater our psychological health and state of **congruence**. Most people experience some incongruence, and use defence mechanisms to feel less threatened.

- Rogers believed that people can creatively solve their own problems and become more authentic (true to self). Humanistic therapists provide empathy and unconditional positive regard, facilitating the client in finding self-actualisation.

AO3 Evaluation/Discussion

Research with adolescents supports Rogers' theory of conditions of worth...

Individuals who experience conditional positive regard are likely to display more 'false self behaviour' – doing things to meet others' expectations even when they clash with their own values.	For example, teenagers who feel they have to fulfil certain conditions in order to gain their parents' approval frequently end up disliking themselves.	*Consistent with Rogers' predictions, adolescents who created a 'false self', pretending to be the kind of person his or her parents would love, were more likely to develop depression.*

However, humanistic research methods do not establish causality...

Evaluating the humanistic approach scientifically is difficult because most of the evidence used to support this approach fails to establish a causal relationship between variables.	Rogers in particular was an advocate of non-experimental research methods, arguing that the requirements of experimental methods make it impossible to verify the results of counselling.	*Although some studies have shown personal growth as a result of receiving humanistic counselling, these do not show that the therapy necessarily caused the changes.*

Humanistic psychology gives an overly idealised and unrealistic view of human nature...

Critics argue that people are not as inherently 'growth oriented' as humanistic theorists suggest, and the approach does not adequately recognise people's capacity for self-destructive behaviour.	The view that personality development is directed only by an innate potential for growth is seen as an oversimplification, as is the assumption that all problems arise from blocked self-actualisation.	*This suggests that encouraging people to focus on their own self-development rather than on situational forces may not be realistic in modern society.*

Cultural differences in the hierarchy of needs...

In a later development to his theory, Maslow did acknowledge that, for some people, needs may appear in a different order. This is borne out by cross-cultural evidence.	For example, a study in China found that 'belonging' took priority over physiological needs, and 'self-actualisation' related to contributions to the community rather than individual development.	*Many studies confirm that Europeans and Americans focus more on personal identity in defining their self-concept, whereas Chinese, Japanese and Koreans define self-concept more in terms of social relationships.*

Issues/Debates
Cultural bias

90

⚙ APPLY: Exam skills

AO2: An example

SCENARIO Beth knows her parents are proud of the career she has chosen but she is unhappy in it. If she ever suggests she wants to leave her job, her parents seem very disapproving. One day she has a serious accident. As soon as she recovers, she leaves her job to pursue her dream of travelling the world.

Apply Rogers' concepts of conditions of worth and congruence to explain Beth's decision. **(4 marks)**

ANSWER *Beth has conditions of worth from her parents, as they disapprove when she talks about leaving her job. Beth attempted to fulfil her parents' conditions of worth by pursuing the career that they valued rather than doing what she really wanted to do. However, this ideal self was a poor fit to her self-concept and the incongruence between the two left her feeling unfulfilled. The accident made her reassess her life choices, allowing her to achieve greater congruence between her self-concept and her ideal self. This greater congruence allowed her to become a fully functioning, authentic person.*

AO2: Research methods

Langer and Rodin (1976) studied nursing home residents ranging in age from 65 to 90 years. The residents were asked to complete a self-report questionnaire about their sense of personal agency and happiness levels. They were then given a talk from the director of the nursing home, emphasising personal agency and choice. A control group listened to a talk emphasising the staff's responsibility in caring for them. Three weeks later another self-report questionnaire was administered to the residents.

The 'agency' group reported feeling happier, more alert, more sociable and more in control whereas the 'control group' had declined in all of these areas.

a. **Why were the questionnaires administered by nursing staff who did not know the aims or the two conditions of this field experiment? (2 marks)**

b. **What conclusion would you draw from these results? (2 marks)**

AO2: One for you to try

Jasmine has been feeling very low since her relationship breakdown, and has gone to see a counsellor. The counsellor uses concepts from humanistic psychology in their practice.

Explain how the counsellor might try to help Jasmine. (6 marks)

🐾 How do I answer... application questions with a stem (AO1, AO2 and AO3)?

Beth knows her parents are proud of the career she has chosen but she is unhappy in it. One day she has a serious accident. As soon as she recovers, she leaves her job to pursue her dream of travelling the world.

Outline and evaluate the humanistic approach. Refer to Beth's behaviour in your answer. (16 marks)

Here is a longer version of the question in **AO2: An example**, which requires you to set your analysis of Beth's behaviour in the context of an 'Outline and evaluate' essay about the humanistic approach. You will need 6 marks' worth of AO1, 4 marks of AO2 and 6 marks of AO3 discussion. The best way to tackle the AO1/AO2 is to introduce aspects of theory which you can link to Beth, and explain the links as you go.

For example:

Maslow described the hierarchy of needs, in which each level must be fulfilled before the person can move to higher levels. At the top is self-actualisation. Beth achieved lower levels, such as meeting her physiological, safety, love/belonging and esteem needs in her career, but re-evaluated her need for self-actualisation after her accident and decided to pursue her dream of travelling the world.

This effectively describes Maslow's theory while linking it efficiently to the stem. You could then do the same with aspects of Rogers' theory of the self and congruence.

You would need three effective evaluation points in this application essay, and these do not need to necessarily link to Beth. Remember that you can slot in issues/debates where possible: free will is a key concept, and cultural bias in theory is also relevant.

🔄 REVIEW

Be ready to explain each of the key terms within this section. Some of them seem quite similar, so make sure you can explain the difference between conditions of worth and unconditional positive regard, or between congruence and authenticity, for example.

Also test yourself on Maslow's hierarchy of needs: practise saying them in order from the bottom of the pyramid, visualising or drawing the structure, or using your hands to build an imaginary pyramid. This will help you to memorise the correct order as you are using multiple coding in your memory.

Comparison of approaches

A01 Description

- The different approaches can be usefully compared (and contrasted) in terms of their stance on three fundamental issues concerning human behaviour.

Free will or determinism?

- **Determinism** refers to the belief that behaviour is caused by forces other than the individual's will to do something. Examples of determinism in the different approaches are: reinforcement (environmental determinism – the behaviourist approach), neurochemical or genetic factors (biological determinism) or unconscious factors (psychic determinism – the psychodynamic approach).

- **Free will** is the alternative end of the spectrum, as seen in the humanistic approach, where the individual is seen as being capable of self-determination.

Issues/Debates
Free will and determinism

Nature or nurture?

- The **scientific method** refers to the use of investigative methods that are objective, systematic and replicable, and the formulation, testing and modification of hypotheses based on these methods.

- The **nature-nurture** debate considers to what extent human behaviour is the product of a person's genes (nature) or experiences (nurture). For example, the behaviourist approach takes a *nurture* stance, whereas the biological approach looks at the influence of innate factors, i.e. *nature*.

Issues/Debates
Nature-nurture

The scientific method

- The six approaches take different positions in relation to their commitment to the **scientific method**. Behaviourist, social learning, cognitive and biological approaches use objective scientific methods such as experiments. The psychodynamic approach is based more on case studies and subjective interpretation. Humanistic psychology rejects a scientific approach to research, as human consciousness and experience are too complex.

The approaches compared

- Basic assumptions of the approaches can also be used as comparison points.

APPROACH	Basic assumptions
Behaviourist	• External forces in the environment shape our behaviour (i.e. it is determined).
	• Explanations of behaviour emphasise the role of nurture more than nature.
	• Behaviourism aligns itself strongly with the scientific method.
Social learning	• Behaviourism is learned as a result of the observations of others (i.e. it is determined).
	• Explanations of behaviour emphasise the role of nurture more than nature.
	• Social learning aligns itself with the scientific method but research can lack validity.
Cognitive	• Thought processes determine behaviour (i.e. some degree of control over behaviour).
	• Explanations of behaviour emphasise the role of nature *and* nurture.
	• Cognitive psychology aligns itself with the scientific method despite some inference.
Biological	• Physiological and/or inherited factors determine behaviour.
	• Explanations of behaviour emphasise the role of nature more than nurture.
	• Biological psychology aligns itself strongly with the scientific method.
Psychodynamic	• Unconscious factors beyond our conscious control determine behaviour.
	• Explanations of behaviour emphasise the role of nature *and* nurture.
	• Psychodynamic psychology does not really align itself with the scientific method.
Humanistic	• Behaviourism is under our conscious control (i.e. we have free will).
	• Explanations of behaviour emphasise the role of nature *and* nurture.
	• Humanistic psychology mostly rejects the use of the scientific method.

APPLY: Exam skills

A02: An example

SCENARIO Jason's teacher thinks he is turning out to be an aggressive boy like his big brother Jake.

Suggest explanations from two contrasting approaches for this similarity between the brothers' behaviour. **(4 marks)**

ANSWER The biological approach might suggest that Jason and Jake both have a shared genetic basis for their aggression. This would determine their behaviour, by causing changes in neurotransmitter levels associated with aggressive behaviour.

Jason and Jake may have learned their behaviour as a result of a shared environment, having been exposed to the same aggressive role models, either in the home or on TV. This would mean they had experienced similar social learning. If their role models were seen to benefit from their aggressive behaviour, this would lead Jason and Jake to anticipate similar rewards for their aggressive behaviour.

A02: Research methods

a. **Identify one area of psychological research from the cognitive approach in psychology and consider how this research may have beneficial effects for the economy. (4 marks)**

b. **Identify one area of psychological research from the biological approach in psychology and consider how this research may have beneficial effects for the economy. (4 marks)**

A02: One for you to try

Alex is determined to carry out a scientific experiment as part of his Extended Project Qualification research. His teacher explains that it is better to start with a research question and then decide on an appropriate research method. However, Alex is not deterred.

a. **Using your knowledge of the different approaches to psychology, what explanations might psychologists give for Alex's determination to carry out an experiment as part of his project? (3 marks)**

b. **Suggest an area of psychology that might be appropriate for Alex to study using an experimental method and explain why this would be suitable. (3 marks)**

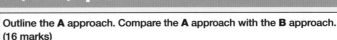

How do I answer... comparison (A03) questions?

> Outline the **A** approach. Compare the **A** approach with the **B** approach. **(16 marks)**

Comparison of approaches is a section on the specification for A Level, and often comes up as part of a 16-mark question. You would probably be asked to outline one approach (**A**), then compare it with another (**B**). The comparison becomes your AO3. Beware: you will not get any marks for evaluating approach **A** by itself. The normal evaluation points are not relevant, unless you can use them as a direct comparison with aspects of approach **B**. The best way to compare is to use the different approaches' positions on issues and debates, as outlined on this spread. You also get no marks for outlining approach **B**. Read the question carefully, and plan your answer:

- Outline approach **A** (e.g. the biological approach).
- DO NOT outline approach **B** (e.g. the humanistic approach).
- DO NOT go straight for normal evaluation points for approach **A** or approach **B**.
- Make comparison points between approach **A** and approach **B** based on basic assumptions, positions on the free will/determinism debate, nature-nurture debate or commitment to scientific method. You could also compare treatments for particular disorders based on the different approaches.
- You need to be clear how the approaches differ in relation to a specific point, using 'whereas', just as you do when answering 'distinguish' questions (see p. 81).
- You need **four** effective AO3 points for 16-mark questions.

REVIEW

Think through each possible comparison of pairs of approaches, looking for points which you can use to show a similarity or a difference with another approach. For example:

1 Identify **one** similarity and **one** difference between:

    a. the psychodynamic and social learning approaches.

    b. the humanistic and behaviourist approaches.

    c. the biological and psychodynamic approaches.

    d. the behaviourist and cognitive approaches.

And so on…

After identifying these similarities and differences, try expanding each to a level where you could use them in an exam answer.

The nervous system

 RECAP

AO1 Description

The central nervous system

- The **central nervous system (CNS)** is comprised of the **brain** and **spinal cord**. It controls behaviour and regulates physiological processes.

- The CNS receives information from the sensory receptors in the sense organs via sensory neurons, and sends messages to the muscles and glands via motor neurons.

- Simple reflexes are relayed via the spinal cord without brain involvement.

- The brain has four main areas: the cerebrum (left and right cerebral hemispheres), the cerebellum (balance and coordination), the diencephalon and the brain stem (regulates autonomic functions like breathing, heartbeat and swallowing).

- The cerebrum is made up of right and left cerebral hemispheres which are connected by the corpus callosum. They have four lobes each, which have specialist functions, e.g.: frontal lobe (thought and speech production), occipital lobe (visual processing).

- The diencephalon is made up of the thalamus (relay of impulses from sensory neurons) and the hypothalamus (regulates body temperature and other homeostatic functions, links to the endocrine system via the pituitary gland).

The peripheral nervous system

- The **peripheral nervous system** consists of all other nerves in the body, including the **somatic nervous system** (sensory neurons and motor neurons), and the **autonomic nervous system** (which controls involuntary bodily functions such as heartbeat and digestion).

- The autonomic nervous system has two branches that tend to have opposite effects on organs: the sympathetic and parasympathetic nervous systems.

- The sympathetic nervous system controls the fight-or-flight emergency responses. Noradrenaline is the main neurotransmitter. It increases heart rate, dilates blood vessels and pupils, and slows down non-emergency processes like digestion.

- The parasympathetic nervous system is concerned with the rest and digest response. Acetylcholine is the main neurotransmitter. It slows heartbeat, reduces blood pressure, and restores digestive processes to normal.

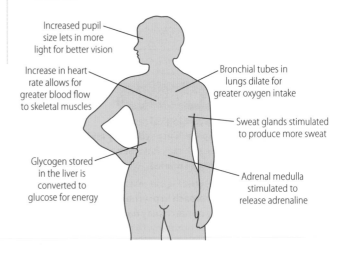

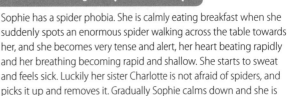

APPLY: Exam skills

AO2: An example

SCENARIO Tasmin loves rollercoasters. She explains that she enjoys the adrenaline rush they give her, the feeling of her heart racing and breathlessness. Once she has ridden the rollercoaster she finds she quickly returns to a 'normal' state and so queues up to ride again and again.

Use your knowledge of the peripheral nervous system to explain Tasmin's experience of riding the rollercoaster. **(3 marks)**

ANSWER When Tasmin is on the ride the sympathetic branch of her autonomic nervous system (ANS) is responding, causing a fight-or-flight response. This explains Tasmin's experience of an 'adrenaline rush', leading to an increase in her heart rate and shallow breathing, which causes her to feel breathless. After the ride is over the parasympathetic branch of her ANS relaxes Tasmin, as the emergency has ended. Her heart rate slows and breathing returns to normal.

AO2: Research methods

Johansson *et al.* studied a group of sawmill 'finishers' who performed repetitive jobs that required high levels of attention and responsibility (i.e. high levels of workload).

Workers who carried out maintenance at the mill or were cleaners were used as a control group.

Adrenaline levels of the workers were measured several times a day, at home and at work. 'Finishers' had higher levels of adrenaline than the control group. Finishers' adrenaline levels were over twice as high at work than at home. In the control group, adrenaline levels were less than 1.5 times higher at work than at home.

a. **Why did Johansson *et al.* measure adrenaline levels in the workers? (2 marks)**

b. **Why did they use a control group? (2 marks)**

c. **What would you conclude from this study about the effect of high workload on workplace stress? (4 marks)**

AO2: One for you to try

Sophie has a spider phobia. She is calmly eating breakfast when she suddenly spots an enormous spider walking across the table towards her, and she becomes very tense and alert, her heart beating rapidly and her breathing becoming rapid and shallow. She starts to sweat and feels sick. Luckily her sister Charlotte is not afraid of spiders, and picks it up and removes it. Gradually Sophie calms down and she is able to continue with her breakfast.

Using your knowledge of the fight-or-flight response explain what is happening in Sophie's body to produce this sequence of responses. (6 marks)

How do I answer... selection (multiple choice) questions?

Which **one** of the following divisions of the nervous system is **not** part of the peripheral nervous system?

A autonomic nervous system

B spinal cord

C parasympathetic nervous system

D somatic nervous system

Although multiple choice questions are generally worth only 1 mark, getting them correct is still important because that 1 mark can be the difference between one grade and another. So, some general advice on answering these:

- Read the question very carefully. Is it asking you to pick the statement that matches or the 'odd one out' that doesn't match? Or does it want you to pick **two** statements?

- Make life easier by crossing out any that are obviously *not* going to be the correct answer, given the specific demands of the question.

- In this question, you can start by crossing out any options which you know **are** part of the peripheral nervous system. If you cross out **A** and **C**, you are left with just two options, which increases your chance of selecting the right answer even if you have to guess. In fact, you should know that the spinal cord is part of the central nervous system, as opposed to the peripheral nervous system, so **B** is the correct answer.

REVIEW

You will need to learn the divisions of the nervous system. These are best learned visually, so keep drawing the branching hierarchy and checking until you are confident about these divisions. You can also map out the brain areas on your own head, by pointing at the position of the four lobes, the cerebellum, the brain stem and the spinal cord, and telling yourself what they do. You will have your body with you in the exam so this may help to prompt your memory. Then try writing some of your own multiple choice questions to check your knowledge.

Neurons and synaptic transmission

 RECAP

AO1 Description

The structure and function of neurons

- Neurons are cells specialised to carry information throughout the body. They consist of a cell body, dendrites and an axon. The axon is covered in an insulating layer called the myelin sheath, which allows nerve impulses to travel along it more rapidly.

- Neurons receive a signal via their dendrites from other neurons or from sensory receptors, and pass it on via their axon. Nerve impulses travel along the axon in the form of an electrical signal called an action potential.

- **Sensory neurons** carry nerve impulses from sensory receptors to the spinal cord and the brain (CNS).

- **Relay neurons** connect sensory and motor neurons, and are found in the CNS. They are also known as interneurons.

- **Motor neurons** are located in the PNS and have long axons which carry nerve impulses to muscles, triggering muscle contraction.

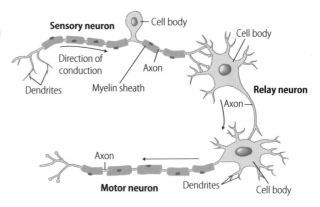

Synaptic transmission

- In **synaptic transmission**, the nerve impulse crosses the **synapse** between the presynaptic and postsynaptic neuron with the help of neurotransmitters.

- The arrival of an action potential at the end of the axon triggers the release of neurotransmitter molecules from synaptic vesicles into the synaptic gap, by exocytosis.

- These neurotransmitter molecules diffuse across the gap and bind to specialised receptors in the membrane of the postsynaptic neuron, where they trigger a new action potential.

- Neurotransmitters are removed from the synaptic gap by reuptake into the presynaptic neuron, for recycling, or they may be broken down by enzymes. Some drugs affect the rate of reuptake or breakdown of neurotransmitters. For example, SSRIs (a type of anti-depressant) affect the reuptake of serotonin.

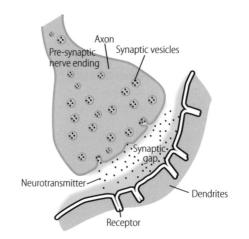

Excitatory and inhibitory neurotransmitters

- Neurotransmitters can have different effects when they bind to the receptor on the postsynaptic neuron. The total effect determines whether an impulse is produced in the next neuron.

- Excitatory neurotransmitters cause an excitatory postsynaptic potential (EPSP), making the postsynaptic neuron more likely to fire. They include acetylcholine and noradrenaline.

- Inhibitory neurotransmitters cause an inhibitory postsynaptic potential (IPSP), making the postsynaptic neuron less likely to fire. They include serotonin and GABA.

- The summation of EPSP and IPSP inputs determines whether or not an action potential is produced, or how frequently the neuron will fire.

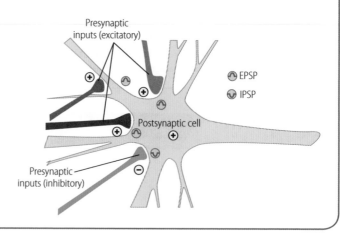

APPLY: Exam skills

AO2: An example

SCENARIO Matt is cooking a meal for his family. He uses a tea towel to take a dish out of the oven. Unfortunately, the towel slips and his hand touches the edge of the dish. It is so hot he instantly relaxes his grip and the dish, along with the food it contains, crashes to the floor.

Use your understanding of neurons to explain why Matt reacted in this way.
(4 marks)

ANSWER *Sensory neurons receive information (heat, pain) from the sensory receptors in the skin on Matt's hand. The sensory neurons carry these nerve impulses to the CNS. Relay neurons in the CNS allow sensory neurons to communicate with motor neurons. Motor neurons form synapses with muscles, enabling Matt to react appropriately to events in the environment, in this case letting go of the dish as it is painful to hold. This seems to be a reflex action and so the sensory neurons involved may terminate in the spinal cord rather than the brain, allowing for a faster reaction without the delay of sending impulses to the brain to be processed.*

AO2: Research methods

Researchers wanted to find out how much oxygen is used during different mental tasks. They used two groups of participants, who each carried out two conditions of the experiment. The first group were Maths A Level students, and the second group had failed Maths GCSE. In the first condition, participants were asked to relax physically and focus on a screen displaying a landscape picture. In the second condition, they were asked to relax physically while performing some complex calculations, which appeared on the screen. The table below shows the mean oxygen consumption (units per hour) during the task by participants in each condition.

	Maths A Level students	**Students who failed Maths GCSE**
Condition 1	55	53
Condition 2	62	76

a. **What does the table show about oxygen consumption during different tasks? (3 marks)**

b. **Why were participants asked to relax physically in each condition? (2 marks)**

c. **How could researchers have found a sample of participants for this study? (2 marks)**

AO2: One for you to try

Researchers tested synaptic transmission in slices of rat brain. They stimulated different combinations of presynaptic neurons, and found that an action potential was sometimes produced, but not always.

Use your knowledge of excitatory and inhibitory neurotransmitters to explain this finding. (6 marks)

 ## How do I answer... label a diagram (AO1) questions?

You could be asked to fill in words in boxes next to a diagram, such as the reflex arc. (Another common diagram you could be asked to label is the working memory model.)

- Take care to see which label is attached to which structure, as the diagram may be presented differently from in your textbook or your notes.
- Ensure that you spell the words correctly.
- Do not leave a blank – if you can't remember the word you want (that tip-of-the-tongue feeling), fill in a word you think may possibly be right. You can't get a mark if you don't write anything, but if you guess you could be correct (and you won't *lose* marks for a wrong answer). Then put a star next to it, so if you have time at the end of the exam you can come back and check.

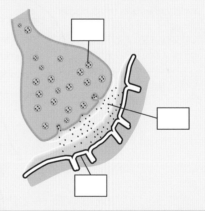

REVIEW

It is vital to be able to tell the story of synaptic transmission fluently, using the correct terminology.

1. Try telling the story of synaptic transmission to a friend. The story should have a beginning (nervous impulse arrives at presynaptic neuron), a middle (neurotransmitters released from vesicles, by exocytosis from axon terminal membrane, diffuse across synaptic cleft), and an end (new action potential triggered in postsynaptic neuron).

2. Try telling your story to a friend who studies Biology, to see if it makes good biological sense. Perhaps your friend could sketch a diagram as you explain the process.

3. Compare the diagram with the diagram on this spread. How accurate is it? How could you improve your story?

The endocrine system

AO1 Description

Glands and hormones

- **Endocrine glands** produce and secrete hormones into the bloodstream. Each gland in the endocrine system produces specific hormones.

- **Hormones** are the body's chemical messengers. They are released by endocrine glands into the bloodstream, where they circulate around the whole body.

  > They bind to specific receptor molecules on the surface of target cells, stimulating a response in the target cells.

Pituitary gland

- The pituitary gland is controlled by the hypothalamus, which regulates many body functions. The pituitary releases hormones which control many other endocrine glands.

  > The anterior pituitary releases adrenocorticotrophic hormone (ACTH) as a response to stress, and also produces luteinising hormone (LH) and follicle-stimulating hormone (FSH).

  > Pituitary hormones have different effects in males and females. In females, LH and FSH stimulate the ovaries to produce oestrogen and progesterone, whereas in males, they stimulate the testes to produce testosterone and sperm.

  > The posterior pituitary releases oxytocin. In females, this stimulates contraction of the uterus in childbirth, and is involved in mother–infant bonding. In males, oxytocin plays a role in sexual behaviour and in the reduction of anxiety.

The adrenal glands

- The **adrenal glands** sit on top of the kidneys. The adrenal cortex produces cortisol, which regulates important cardiovascular functions in the body. The adrenal medulla releases adrenaline and noradrenaline, which prepare the body for fight or flight.

  > Cortisol production is increased in response to stress. If cortisol level is low, the individual has low blood pressure, poor immune function and an inability to deal with stress.

  > Adrenaline helps the body to respond to acute stress by increasing heart rate and blood flow to the muscles and brain, and encouraging the breakdown of glycogen into glucose to provide energy.

  > Noradrenaline constricts the blood vessels, causing blood pressure to increase.

Hormone regulation

- Glands and hormones are self-regulated by negative feedback (homeostasis).

  > For example, the hypothalamus releases corticotrophin releasing hormone (CRH). This stimulates the pituitary to release adrenocorticotrophic hormone (ACTH). This in turn stimulates the release of hormones from the adrenal cortex, such as cortisol. An increase in the blood concentration of cortisol slows down the release of CRH and ACTH. This ensures levels of hormones circulating in the blood are kept stable.

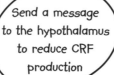

AO3 Evaluation/Discussion

The feedback system may break down in long-term stress…

The hypothalamus and pituitary gland have special receptors that monitor circulating cortisol levels.

Monitoring and controlling cortisol levels limits the potentially damaging effect of this hormone on the body. However, research has found that the longer an individual is exposed to stress, the more adverse the effects are.

This might explain why individuals in stressful jobs or stressful relationships suffer more stress-related illness.

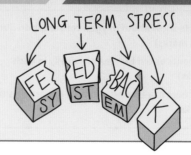

APPLY: Exam skills

AO2: An example

SCENARIO Mr Ray is planning a health and well-being lesson for his Year 7 class. He decides to teach about the effects of hormones, especially as puberty is likely to be a relevant topic to this age group.

Suggest suitable information Mr Ray may wish to focus on in the lesson. **(3 marks)**

ANSWER Mr Ray should explain that glands within the body are responsible for the release of hormones and that these hormones regulate activity of the organs and tissues in the body. He could introduce the class to the pituitary gland as the pituitary, under control of the hypothalamus, influences the release of hormones from other glands. As puberty is likely to be a relevant topic for this age group of students, he may wish to focus on the glands of the reproductive system, explaining that in females the ovaries produce oestrogen and progesterone, while in men the testes produce testosterone.

AO2: Research methods

Malarkey *et al.* studied 90 newlywed couples over a 24-hour period in a laboratory. The couples were asked to discuss marital issues likely to cause conflict between them (e.g. finances). The study found that marital conflict produced significant changes in adrenaline and noradrenaline levels. These changes were associated with lower levels of immune system functioning.

a. **Suggest why conflict increased adrenaline and noradrenaline levels. (2 marks)**

b. **Why might there be issues with validity in this study? (3 marks)**

c. **Explain how the results might have differed if the couples had been studied in their own homes? (3 marks)**

AO2: One for you to try

Sandra has recently been diagnosed with Cushing's disease, which is caused by a tumour in the pituitary gland. Her symptoms include high blood pressure, fatigue and anxiety. She also finds that cuts and insect bites take a long time to heal.

Using your knowledge of the hormones produced by the pituitary gland, explain Sandra's symptoms. (6 marks)

How do I answer... description only (AO1) questions?

There is a fairly simple formula in answering description only questions. For 2 marks, say two things (i.e. two bullet points' worth), for 3 marks say three things and so on.

Work through the sample questions below, using the AO1 material on the opposite page.

Q1: What is a hormone? (2 marks)

Use both of the **two** AO1 points for hormones (see opposite).

Q2: Describe the role of the pituitary gland in regulating other endocrine glands. (3 marks)

Use **three** AO1 points under the AO1 heading for the pituitary gland (i.e. 'The pituitary gland is…', 'The anterior pituitary…', 'Pituitary hormones…').

Q3: Outline the role of **one** endocrine gland and **one** hormone it produces. (4 marks)

You have a choice: use one point for a hormone and one for a gland which produces it; for example the adrenal medulla, located above the kidney, produces adrenaline (explain what the role of adrenaline is). Do the same again for another hormone and gland. This gives 4 marks' worth.

Q4: Outline the role of the endocrine system in behaviour. (6 marks)

There are many possible ways of answering this question, but remember it needs **six** good AO1 points – equivalent to **six** points from the information opposite. Be selective! It makes sense to start generally by outlining the overall function of the endocrine system, then narrow down to illustrate it by choosing two specific endocrine glands.

This approach adds an appropriate level of detail to each answer and gives the examiner a useful way of discriminating between your answer and one that would be worth fewer than the maximum marks for that question.

REVIEW

Make a checklist of the hormones and glands. When you feel you have mastered each of these aspects of the endocrine system, give yourself a tick in the **Got it!** column. Your list should include the topics in this table:

TOPIC	Got it!	Extra detail	Got it!
Endocrine glands generally		Homeostasis	
Hormones generally		Receptors	
Pituitary gland – anterior and posterior		ACTH, LH, FSH Oxytocin	
Adrenal glands – cortex and medulla		Cortisol Adrenaline, noradrenaline	
Ovaries		Oestrogen, progesterone	
Testes		Testosterone	

The fight-or-flight response

RECAP

A01 Description

- The **fight-or-flight response** is a sequence of activity within the body that is triggered in response to stress, enabling us to react quickly to life-threatening situations.

- The stress response is triggered by the amygdala, an area of the brain which associates sensory inputs (sights, sounds and smells) with emotions like fear and anger. The amygdala sends a distress signal to the hypothalamus.

- The hypothalamus activates the sympathetic nervous system (SNS). The SNS activates the adrenal medulla, causing the adrenal medulla to release adrenaline.

- Adrenaline causes an increase in heart rate, breathing and blood pressure, so more oxygen reaches the heart and muscles. It also triggers release of glucose into the blood to supply energy, but inhibits digestion during the emergency.

- When the threat has passed, the parasympathetic nervous system restores heart rate and blood pressure to normal, and allows digestion to restart.

- If the threat is ongoing, the **HPA axis** kicks in:
  - > **'H'** – The **hypothalamus** releases corticotrophin-releasing hormone (CRH) into the bloodstream.
  - > **'P'** – The **pituitary gland** responds to CRH and releases adrenocorticotrophic hormone (ACTH), which is transported to the adrenal glands.
  - > **'A'** – This stimulates the **adrenal** cortex to release cortisol.
  - > Cortisol reduces sensitivity to pain and gives a quick burst of energy.
  - > Special receptors in the hypothalamus and pituitary gland monitor circulating levels of cortisol, releasing CRH and ACTH if levels rise above normal, bringing cortisol levels to normal.

A03 Evaluation/Discussion

Females may show a 'tend and befriend' response rather than fight or flight...

This involves protecting themselves and their young through nurturing behaviours (tending) and forming protective alliances with other women (befriending).	Women's responses evolved in the context of being the primary caregiver of their children. Fleeing at any sign of danger would put a female's offspring at risk.	*This finding suggests that previous research, which has mainly focused on males, has obscured patterns of stress response in females.*

Issues/Debates
Gender bias

The first response may be a 'freeze response'...

Gray (1988) argues that the first phase of reaction to a threat is not to fight or flee, but to avoid confrontation.	This initial freeze response is essentially a 'stop, look and listen' response, where the animal is hyper-vigilant, alert to the slightest sign of danger.	*The adaptive advantages of this response for humans are that 'freezing' focuses attention and makes them look for new information in order to make the best response for that particular threat.*

Acute stress can lead to cooperative behaviour in men and women...

Von Dawans et al. (2012) challenge the classic view that, under stress, men respond only with 'fight or flight', whereas women are more prone to 'tend and befriend'.	This could explain the human connection that happens during times of crises such as the 9/11 terrorist attacks in New York.	*This makes sense as human beings are fundamentally social animals and it is the protective nature of human social relationships that has allowed our species to thrive.*

A genetic basis to sex differences in the fight-or-flight response...

A03 PLUS

The *SRY* gene, found exclusively on the male Y chromosome, directs male development, promoting aggression and resulting in the fight-or-flight response.	The *SRY* gene may prime males to respond to stress in this way by the release of adrenaline and through increased blood flow to organs involved in the fight-or-flight response.	*In contrast, the absence of the SRY gene in females (who do not have a Y chromosome) may prevent this response to stress, leading instead to 'tend and befriend' behaviours.*

 APPLY: Exam skills

AO2: An example

SCENARIO Mikala, Daniella and Lucy are about to give a presentation to the class. They are all feeling very nervous as they want to perform well in front of their classmates. As they stand in front of the class, Lucy whispers to Mikala, 'My mind has gone blank, I can't remember anything!'. Mikala responds by reassuring her she is going to be fine and reminds her she can use her flash cards as a prompt. Daniella said she would sit behind the laptop to manage the slideshow as, 'There was no way she would be able to talk to the class'.

Using your knowledge of the fight-or-flight response explain the students' different responses to the stress of giving a presentation in class. **(3 marks)**

ANSWER *Daniella seems to be fleeing the situation as she has almost removed herself from the threat of giving a presentation by sitting behind the laptop, changing slides. Rather than fight or flight, Lucy is showing the freeze response – a kind of stop, look and listen behaviour that is preventing her acting in the situation as she is unable to begin the presentation. Mikala is showing 'tend and befriend' as her response to Lucy is nurturing and supportive.*

AO2: Research methods

Researchers were interested in how the fight-or-flight experience applied to combat. To do this, they decided to interview a volunteer sample of 30 army combat veterans who had seen action in Iraq or Afghanistan. The interviewer would ask a series of open questions to probe their experiences when involved in life-threatening close combat. From these interviews, researchers identified two further types of response in addition to the fight-and-flight responses. These were 'freeze' (a stop, look and listen response), and 'tonic immobility' (playing dead). The number of participants mentioning these different responses is shown in the graph.

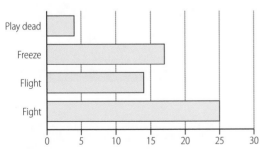

Number of participants mentioning each response

a. **Briefly explain why using a volunteer sample might pose problems for any conclusions drawn from this study. (2 marks)**

b. **What can you conclude from the graph about the relative importance of the different responses in combat situations? (4 marks)**

c. **Identify two possible ethical issues in this study and explain how the researcher might deal with each of these. (6 marks)**

AO2: One for you to try

Karl and Karla are walking down the street on a Saturday night when they come face to face with a large, aggressive-looking group of teenagers. Karl's muscles tense, and he approaches them, making a loud, challenging statement and raising his fists. Karla, on the other hand, stops very still and becomes pale and starts shaking uncontrollably.

Using your knowledge of the fight-or-flight response, discuss Karl and Karla's behaviour in this threatening situation. (12 marks)

How do I answer... essay questions with an AO2 component?

Essay questions with an AO2 (application) component are essentially the same as a straightforward essay (see p.113) *but* some of the marks available are diverted for your ability to explain the scenario outlined in the question in the context of the material you are discussing.

For example, for the 12-mark question about Karl and Karla (above), there would be 6 marks' worth of AO1, 2 marks of AO2 and 4 marks of AO3.

If you meet this as a 16-marker (at A Level), you should write 6 marks' worth of AO1, 6 marks' worth of AO3 and 4 marks' worth of AO2.

It's worth taking time to plan your answer before you begin, to make sure you link your AO1 to the stem, explaining how the link works to get the AO2 marks.

For example, you could include a point about Karla's response: 'Karla stops very still and shakes. This seems to be a freeze response rather than fight or flight. Gray argues that this initial freeze response is very common, and allows an individual to assess the situation before reacting.'

REVIEW

As well as application essays, you could be asked straightforward AO1 questions or AO1/AO3 outline and evaluate questions on this topic.

1 Try writing a plan for 4-mark and 6-mark 'outline' questions on the fight-or-flight response.

2 Create a plan for a 12-mark (AS) or 16-mark (A Level) essay.

Test yourself on the key points by covering up your plan and writing it out again. It's useful to have a supply of cheap paper for this, or a mini whiteboard, as the more times you practise retrieving the information, the better you will remember it.

Spaced practice is also very effective: come back to the same topic tomorrow and start your revision by seeing how many of the points you can remember before you look at your essay plan.

Localisation of function

AO1 Description

- **Localisation of function** refers to the belief that specific areas of the brain are associated with specific cognitive processes.

Motor and somatosensory areas

- **Motor cortex:** responsible for the generation of voluntary movements. Located along the precentral gyrus of the frontal lobe. It sends nerve impulses to the muscles. The right hemisphere controls the left half of the body and vice versa.

- **Somatosensory cortex:** located in the postcentral gyrus and it processes sensory information from the skin. The information relating to each half of the body is processed in the opposite hemisphere of the brain.

Visual and auditory centres

- **Visual centres:** a nerve impulse from the retina is transmitted via the optic nerve to the thalamus, which relays it to the visual cortex in the occipital lobes. Input from the left of the visual field transfers to the visual cortex in the right hemisphere, and vice versa.

- **Auditory centres:** nerve impulses from the cochlea travel via the auditory nerve to the brain stem for basic decoding, then continue via the thalamus to the auditory cortex, where the sound is interpreted.

Language centres

- **Broca's area** is located in the posterior part of the left frontal lobe, near to the motor region which controls the mouth and vocal cords. It is involved in speech production.

- **Wernicke's area** is near the auditory cortex. It is involved with speech comprehension.

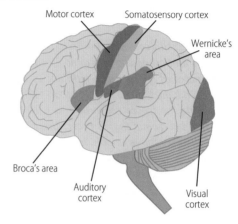

AO3 Evaluation/Discussion

Damage to Broca's and Wernicke's areas results in different types of aphasia...

Expressive aphasia (also known as Broca's aphasia) is an impaired ability to produce language. In most cases, this is caused by brain damage in Broca's area.	Receptive aphasia (also known as Wernicke's aphasia) is an impaired ability to extract meaning from spoken or written words. This form of aphasia is usually the result of damage in Wernicke's area.	*This demonstrates the important role played by these brain regions in different aspects of language.*

However, there are individual differences in language areas...

There is considerable variability in patterns of brain activation when reading, with activity in the right temporal lobe as well as in the left frontal, temporal and occipital lobes.	In addition, Harasty *et al.* (1997) found that women have proportionally larger Broca's and Wernicke's areas than men.	*These anatomical differences may well explain the superior language skills often found in females.*

Language production may not be confined to Broca's area alone...

Dronkers *et al.* (2007) re-examined the preserved brains of two of Broca's aphasic patients using high-resolution brain MRI imaging. They showed damage in other areas besides Broca's area.	This finding is significant because, although lesions to Broca's area alone can cause temporary speech disruption, they do not usually result in severe disruption of spoken language.	*This study suggests that language and cognition are far more complicated than once thought and involve networks of brain regions rather than being localised to specific areas.*

Communication between brain areas may be more important than localisation...

Wernicke claimed that, although different regions of the brain have different specialist functions, they are interdependent and in order to work they must interact with each other.	For example, in 1892 a neurologist, Joseph Dejerine, described a case in which the loss of an ability to read resulted from damage to the connection between the visual cortex and Wernicke's area.	*This suggests that complex behaviours, like reading, involve impulses being passed around the brain through a network of neurons.*

APPLY: Exam skills

AO2: An example

SCENARIO Dr Suresh is researching the effects of head injury in patients displaying speech difficulties. She has arranged for each patient to undergo functional magnetic resonance imaging (fMRI) to identify which regions of the brain are active when completing different cognitive tasks. She plans to compare the activity recorded to a control group of adults with no known head injury.

What activities could Dr Suresh ask the sample to attempt during the fMRI? What differences might she find between the patients and the control group? **(5 marks)**

ANSWER *While in the fMRI participants' ability to understand speech could be tested. This could be done by asking patients to hold up a certain number of digits, for example, 'hold up three fingers': if they understand speech they should hold up three fingers for the researcher to see. A control group following this instruction should show brain activity in the area known as Wernicke's area which is located in the posterior portion of the left temporal lobe. In comparison, if the patients with head injuries are unable to understand the instructions then this area of the brain may be damaged and so activation in this area may be greatly reduced or non-existent. She plans to compare the activity recorded to a control group of adults with no known head injury.*

AO2: Research methods

A neurologist was investigating a very frustrated patient who had lost his ability to speak after a stroke. The neurologist decided she would like to publish the details in a case study.

Identify one ethical issue the neurologist should consider in publishing this case study. Suggest how she could deal with this ethical issue. (3 marks)

AO2: One for you to try

A neurologist observed that her patient, Lionel, seemed to be experiencing a familiar pattern of difficulties. He appeared to be able to understand speech, and could make vocal sounds, but could not express any intelligible words. He was also unable to write down what he wanted to say.

Using your knowledge of localisation of function in the brain, suggest which area(s) of the brain may have been damaged by this patient's stroke. (6 marks)

How do I answer... evaluation (AO3) questions?

AO3 questions come in all sorts of shapes and sizes. Terms like 'Evaluate', 'Discuss', 'Explain', 'Criticism', 'Strength' and 'Limitation' all indicate that AO3 is required.

Q1: Briefly explain one criticism of the theory of localisation of function in the brain. (2 marks)

For **Q1:** you need to use one brief AO3 point which could support or challenge localisation. This could be the 'lead-in phrase' followed by the first two columns of the point *or* a brief summary of all three columns.

Q2: Explain **one** limitation of the theory of localisation of function in the brain. (3 marks)

For **Q2:** you need to concentrate on just one *limitation* of the idea of localisation of function (e.g. that communication between brain areas may be more important than localisation). For 3 marks, you would use all three columns to make an effective point.

Q3: Paul Broca studied patients with language deficits and concluded that brain functions are localised in specific areas of the brain. Evaluate localisation of function in the brain. (6 marks)

Although there is a contextual quote in **Q3:**, you are not being asked to do anything with it, so you can safely ignore it. This is not always the case, so read the question carefully. For a 6-mark question, you would choose two of the AO3 points opposite and use all three columns for each.

 ## REVIEW

You are likely to be asked questions requiring AO1 knowledge of localisation of function, so practise these too. And don't forget you might also need to apply this knowledge to a stem (AO2).

You could make a large labelled diagram of the brain, adding the functions on to the names of the areas. Then plan which points you would use to answer a 4-mark, 6-mark, 8-mark, 12-mark and 16-mark question on localisation of function. Remember that you never need more than 6 marks of AO1.

Lateralisation and split-brain research

RECAP

A01 Description

Hemispheric lateralisation

- **Hemispheric lateralisation:** The left hemisphere is dominant for language and speech. The right hemisphere specialises in visuomotor tasks.

- Broca (1861) reported that damage in a particular area of the left hemisphere led to language deficits, yet damage to the equivalent area of the right hemisphere did not.

- The two hemispheres are connected by bundles of nerve fibres such as the corpus callosum, and exchange information. This means that we can talk about things perceived by the right hemisphere (e.g. face recognition).

Split-brain research

- **Split-brain research:** To treat severe epilepsy and prevent seizures from affecting both halves of the brain, surgeons would sometimes cut the nerve fibres of the corpus callosum. These 'split-brain' patients were researched to explore how each hemisphere responded separately to visual inputs.

- Sperry and Gazzaniga (1967): If a picture is shown to the left visual field of a split-brain patient, this information is processed by the right hemisphere, but it cannot respond verbally as it has no language centre.

- The left hemisphere does not receive the information and therefore cannot talk about it, despite having a language centre.

A03 Evaluation / Discussion

Lateralisation is related to increased neural processing capacity...

By using only one hemisphere to engage in a particular task (e.g. language or mathematical ability), this would leave the other hemisphere free to engage in another function.	In chickens, brain lateralisation is associated with an enhanced ability to perform two tasks simultaneously – finding food and being vigilant for predators.	*This finding provides some evidence that brain lateralisation enhances brain efficiency in cognitive tasks that demand the simultaneous but different use of both hemispheres.*

Lateralisation changes with age...

Lateralised patterns found in younger individuals tend to switch to bilateral patterns in healthy older adults.	For example, Szaflarski *et al.* (2006) found that language became more lateralised to the left hemisphere with increasing age in children and adolescents, but after the age of 25, lateralisation decreased with each decade of life.	*This may be because using the extra processing resources of the other hemisphere may compensate for age-related declines in function.*

Some findings of early split-brain research have been disconfirmed more recently...

A major claim of split-brain research was that damage to the left hemisphere leads to a loss of language function.	However, case studies have demonstrated that this was not necessarily the case. One patient, known as J.W., developed the capacity to speak about information presented to the left or to the right brain (Turk *et al.,* 2002).	*This challenges the claim that the right hemisphere is unable to handle even the most rudimentary language.*

Limitations of split-brain research...

The split-brain procedure is rarely carried out nowadays, and many studies only included a few participants, or even just one.	These patients may have had underlying physical disorders that made the split-brain procedure necessary, or there may have been some intact nerve fibres remaining.	*This means the results of studies are not always replicated, and it may be unwise to draw general conclusions from them.*

Issues/Debates
Idiographic and nomothetic approaches to research

APPLY: Exam skills

AO2: An example

SCENARIO In an attempt to treat his severe epileptic seizures, patient X underwent a surgical procedure to cut the nerve fibres forming the corpus callosum. A psychologist decided to test the effect of splitting the two hemispheres. Patient X was asked to focus on a central dot while the psychologist presented an image in either the left or right visual field. Each time the psychologist asked patient X whether they could see anything.

Use your knowledge of split-brain research to predict and explain what patient X would answer when an image was presented in their left visual field and on a second trial, when an image was presented in their right visual field. **(4 marks)**

ANSWER When the image is presented in patient X's right visual field the patient would be able to say they had seen the image. This is because information from the right visual field is processed in the left hemisphere which also contains the language centres so patient X is able to give a verbal response. However, when the image is presented in the left visual field the patient would say they cannot see the image. Information from the left visual field is processed by the right hemisphere which can see the image but has no language centre to respond.

AO2: Research methods

In a study of hemispheric dominance, normal participants were played recordings of different word lists through headphones, so that each ear received a different list of ten words. They were then asked to recall as many words as possible.

The table shows how many words from each list were accurately recalled by the participants.

Participant	1	2	3	4	5	6	7	8	9	10
Words heard by left ear	3	9	6	8	5	0	2	10	7	3
Words heard by right ear	7	2	4	0	1	7	6	1	2	4

a. **Give an appropriate directional hypothesis suitable for this study. (2 marks)**

b. **Identify the experimental design used in this study and briefly explain one limitation of this design. (3 marks)**

c. **What percentage of participants remembered more words heard in their left ear? (1 mark)**

d. **Calculate the median number of words recalled when presented to the left ear. (1 mark)**

e. **Calculate the mean number of words recalled when presented to the right ear. (1 mark)**

AO2: One for you to try

B.L. is a split-brain patient, whose corpus callosum was severed surgically in order to treat her severe epilepsy. When a picture of a cat is presented to her left visual field, and a lion to her right visual field, she says she has seen a lion. However, when she is asked to pick a matching card using her left hand, she picks the picture of the cat.

Explain this using your knowledge of lateralisation of function in the brain. (8 marks)

How do I answer... short essay (8-mark) questions?

Q1: Discuss the findings of research involving split-brain patients. (8 marks)

Not all essays follow the 12-mark or 16-mark format. Some have a slightly lower tariff. Of these lower tariff essay questions, the 8-marker is the most common. It does pay to know what you are dealing with, however, as they are not always straightforward.

For example, **Q1:** if it were on an AS paper, would be worth 4 marks for AO1 (4 points) and 4 marks for AO3 (one effective, fully elaborated point and one briefer one). In fact, it is simply two thirds of a 12-mark question, so two thirds of the marks for each skill. However, it is *half* of a 16-mark question at A Level, so that would lead to a different mark division of 3 marks for AO1 and 5 marks for AO3 (two effective AO3 points).

AO2: One for you to try: includes a scenario and makes reference to that scenario in the question. This is an indication that there is an additional AO2 requirement in the question, so this question would be 3 marks of AO1 (first three points), 3 marks of AO3 (one complete AO3 point) and 2 marks' worth of AO2. The best strategy is to link your knowledge to the stem at every stage – see p.91 for advice on how to write AO2 answers.

REVIEW

You will remember the key information better if you process it in different ways:

- Write out key terms.
- Write answers to 4-mark, 6-mark, 8-mark and 16-mark questions about lateralisation and split-brain research.
- Draw a diagram.
- Talk to a friend about it or explain it to a relative.
- Watch a video about it. There are some excellent short videos on the Internet showing split-brain patients being tested. Watching these will help you understand the procedure and findings of this research.

Plasticity and functional recovery of the brain

AO1 Description

Plasticity

- **Brain plasticity** refers to the brain's ability to modify its own structure, creating new neural pathways and pruning away weak connections as a result of experience.

- For example, playing video games results in new synaptic connections in brain areas involved in spatial recognition, strategic planning, working memory and motor performance.

- There is a gradual decline in cognitive function with age, but even 60-year-olds still have brain plasticity, and can increase their grey matter in the visual cortex when taught a new skill, such as juggling.

- Davidson *et al.* (2004) found that experienced meditators (Tibetan monks) produced more gamma brainwaves than student volunteers, indicating that meditation causes permanent changes.

Functional recovery

- **Functional recovery** refers to the recovery of abilities and mental processes that have been compromised as a result of trauma. When brain cells are damaged, as they are during a stroke, other parts sometimes take over their functions.

- This can happen by neural unmasking, in which dormant synapses can be reactivated when they receive more neural input than previously.

- Stem cells implanted into the brain may help to treat brain damage, by directly replacing damaged cells.

- Stem cells secrete growth factors that 'rescue' injured cells, or they form a neural network linking uninjured areas with the damaged brain region.

AO3 Evaluation / Discussion

In rats, an enriched environment increases the number of neurons in the brain...

Kempermann *et al.* (1998) found that rats housed in complex environments developed more neurons than rats housed in lab cages.	In particular, they showed an increase in neurons in the hippocampus, which is associated with the formation of new memories and the ability to navigate.	*This shows clear evidence of the brain's ability to change as a result of experience, i.e. it demonstrates plasticity.*

Research support from a study of taxi drivers...

Maguire *et al.* (2000) discovered that changes in the brain could be detected as a result of taxi drivers' extensive experience of spatial navigation.	MRI scans showed the posterior hippocampi of taxi drivers were significantly larger than those of control participants. Posterior hippocampal volume was positively correlated with the amount of time they had spent as a taxi driver.	*This shows that the highest levels of plasticity were evident in those with more extensive experience.*

Age differences in functional recovery...

It is a commonly accepted view that functional plasticity reduces with age, and that adults with brain trauma require social support or must develop strategies to deal with cognitive deficits.	However, studies have suggested that even abilities commonly thought to be fixed in childhood can still be modified in adults with intense retraining.	*The capacity for neural reorganisation is still much greater in children than in adults, as demonstrated by the extended practice that adults require in order to produce changes.*

Educational attainment and functional recovery...

A retrospective study by Schneider *et al.* (2014) examined data on traumatic brain injuries (TBI) from a US TBI database.	This showed that nearly 40 per cent of patients with college-level education achieved disability-free recovery after a year, compared to less than 10 per cent of patients who left school early.	*The researchers concluded that 'cognitive reserve' (associated with greater educational attainment) was an important factor in neural adaptation during recovery from traumatic brain injury.*

A LEVEL ONLY ZONE

 # APPLY: Exam skills

AO2: An example

SCENARIO At the age of 48 Simon, a university lecturer, suffered a major stroke in the left side of his brain. Damage to the language centres found in the left hemisphere meant he was unable to form words and found it very difficult to communicate with others. When Simon was physically well he began a therapeutic programme involving bi-weekly speech therapy, which was supported by family and friends helping Simon practise the activities set by his therapist on a daily basis. After a year Simon was able to utter a short sentence. Four years later, Simon is able to use a wide range of simple sentences and is overjoyed to have regained his ability to talk.

How might psychologists explain the progress Simon has made following his brain injury? **(4 marks)**

ANSWER *Brain plasticity can be used to explain the recovery of function shown by Simon following his stroke. Life experiences, such as repeatedly practising speech techniques, have changed Simon's neuronal structure and function, meaning he is able to regain functions, such as speech, that were previously lost. Increased rates of input to dormant synapses in Simon's brain 'unmasks' these synapses, opening connections to the previously inactive areas of the brain. Before his stroke Simon was a university lecturer, which may have increased his likelihood of experiencing functional recovery. For example, Schneider et al. (2014) found patients with the equivalent of a college education were more likely to show rapid recovery than those whose level of education did not reach the end of high school.*

AO2: One for you to try

Nick's grandfather has had a stroke, and Nick's mum thinks he will never be able to walk again or look after himself.

What could Nick say to his mum about his grandfather's possible recovery? (4 marks)

How do I answer... application (AO2) questions?

Let's look at the question in **AO2: One for you to try** above.

Nick's grandfather has had a stroke, and Nick's mum thinks he will never be able to walk again or look after himself.

What could Nick say to his mum about his grandfather's possible recovery? (4 marks)

One way of answering questions such as this is to remember the 'Say one thing for 1 mark' and 'Say four things for 4 marks' strategy.

1. **Find a bit of appropriate psychology** (e.g. 'When brain cells are damaged by a stroke, other parts of the brain can take over their functions, by neural unmasking.').

2. **Use this to explain some aspect of the scenario** (e.g. 'Nick's grandfather's brain may be able to reactivate dormant synapses, especially if he gives them extra input during physiotherapy.').

3. **Find a second bit of psychology** (e.g. 'Functional recovery is possible even in older adults, although they may take longer to recover than children.').

4. **Use this to explain the scenario** (e.g. 'Nick's grandfather may take some time to recover, but his abilities may gradually return with plenty of practice.').

AO2: Research methods

Below is some data from the US Traumatic Brain Injury systems database.

Total no. of patients	Patients with DFR*
769	214

*DFR = disability-free recovery after one year

a. **What percentage of the total number of patients achieved DFR? Show your workings. (2 marks)**

The table below shows the relationship between DFR and years of education.

Years of education	≥16	12–15	≤12
% DFR	39.2	30.8	9.7

b. **Display these findings on an appropriate graph. (4 marks)**

c. **What do they show about the relationship between educational attainment and functional recovery? (3 marks)**

REVIEW

If the question asked you to 'Discuss' functional recovery, you would also need to include AO3 evaluation. Again, link points to the stem as much as possible.

Practise linking the AO3 points to the scenario above:

AO3 point	Link to Nick's grandfather
Age differences in functional recovery	
Educational attainment and functional recovery	

Ways of studying the brain

A01 Description

Post-mortem examinations

- If a researcher suspects that a patient's behavioural changes were caused by brain damage, they may look for abnormalities after the person dies. For example, Broca observed patients' speech difficulties, and found lesions in the brain post-mortem.

- Henry Molaison (HM)'s brain has been extensively investigated post-mortem, confirming damage to his hippocampus related to his inability to store new memories (see p.24). Post-mortem studies have also identified brain abnormalities in schizophrenia and depression.

Scanning techniques

- **Functional magnetic resonance imaging (fMRI)** measures changes in blood oxygenation and flow, indicating increased neural activity, in particular brain areas.

  > fMRI images are useful for identifying which areas of the brain are involved in particular mental activities.

- **Electroencephalograms (EEG)** measure electrical activity in the brain via electrodes placed on the scalp. EEGs show brainwaves over time.

  > EEG patterns in patients with epilepsy show spikes of electrical activity. Alzheimer's patients often show overall slowing of electrical activity.

- **Event-related potentials (ERPs)** are very small voltage changes triggered by specific stimuli or cognitive events.

  > Sensory ERPs occur in the first 100 milliseconds after the stimulus is presented; cognitive ERPs are generated later, and demonstrate information processing.

A03 Evaluation/Discussion

fMRI is a non-invasive way of scanning the brain without exposure to harmful radiation…

fMRI offers a more objective and reliable measure of psychological processes than is possible with verbal reports.	However, fMRI measures changes in blood flow in the brain, so it is not a direct measure of neural activity in particular brain areas.	Critics also argue that fMRI overlooks the networked nature of brain activity, as it focuses only on localised activity in the brain.

EEG is useful in clinical diagnosis of epilepsy, as seizures show as characteristic spikes…

One strength of the EEG technique is that it provides a recording of the brain's activity in real time rather than a still image of the passive brain.	However, EEG can only detect the activity in superficial brain regions, so it cannot reveal what is going on in the deeper regions such as the hypothalamus or hippocampus.	Also neighbouring electrodes pick up electrical activity from overlapping areas, so EEG can't pinpoint the exact source of activity.

ERPs can be used to measure the response to a specific stimulus…

An ERP can measure the processing of stimuli even in the absence of a behavioural response, making it possible to monitor brain processes without requiring the person to respond verbally.	However, ERPs are very small and difficult to pick out from other electrical activity in the brain, so it takes many trials to gain meaningful data.	Another limitation of the ERP technique is that, similarly to EEG, electrical activities occurring deep in the brain are not recorded.

Post-mortem examinations can examine brain structures in more detail than fMRI and EEG…

For example, post-mortem studies of the brain have enabled researchers to discover structural abnormalities and neurochemical changes in schizophrenia.	However, diverse causes of death, use of drugs and age at death may affect the brain tissue, so there are many confounding variables.	Another problem is that data can only be collected retrospectively, when it is too late to test hypotheses about cognitive function relating to abnormalities.

APPLY: Exam skills

A02: An example

SCENARIO Roberta and Jamal are discussing their research projects. Roberta has been gathering recordings of brain activity in head trauma patients to identify differences in brainwaves between patients and normal patterns of activity. Jamal shows Roberta recordings of blood flow in particular areas of the brain gathered as participants performed visual tasks.

Identify the different scanning techniques used and suggest one limitation that may be faced when using each technique. **(6 marks)**

ANSWER *Roberta is using an EEG. One problem Roberta may face when using an EEG is that she is only able to detect activity on the brain's surface. This means that she is unable to determine any effects experienced in deeper regions of the brain as a result of the patients' trauma. Jamal is using fMRI. However, this technique only shows localised activity and ignores the neural networks involved in responding to stimuli. As a result, any conclusions Jamal might draw about the effects of head trauma may not be a complete explanation of neural activity in particular brain regions in response to a stimulus.*

A02: Research methods

Identify one ethical issue with the use of HM's brain after death, and explain how this issue might have been dealt with. (4 marks)

A02: Two for you to try

1. **Flora has been experiencing seizures, which started with short blank periods, but recently she has become unconscious and fallen to the ground during a seizure. Her GP referred her to a neurologist for investigation.**

   a. What technique would be most appropriate for examining Flora's brain, and why? **(4 marks)**

   b. What limitations might there be to this method of investigation? **(4 marks)**

2. **Match up the technique with its advantages:**

   1 fMRI

   2 EEG

   3 ERP

   4 Post-mortem examinations

   A Measures brain's response to a stimulus

   B Detailed examination of brain tissue, anatomy and neurochemistry

   C Non-invasive, no radiation, measure pattern of activity of living brain

   D Records brain activity over time; can detect epilepsy

How do I answer... 'Distinguish between' questions?

If you are asked to 'Distinguish between…','Compare…' or 'Explain the difference between…', then these rules apply:

1 Don't just *describe* the two things you are being asked to distinguish between.

2 Pick a characteristic that applies to both but which is different for each (e.g. measuring brain regions in a functioning brain).

3 Use words like 'whereas','however','on the other hand' to point out this difference.

4 One point of difference is usually enough for 2 marks.

So… how might we distinguish between fMRI and EEG as ways of studying the brain, using these rules?

EEG and fMRI both measure activity in functioning brains, but EEG only detects activity in superficial areas as it is measured using electrodes on the scalp, whereas fMRI can detect activity in deeper areas such as the hypothalamus, as it scans 'slices' through the entire brain.

EEG has poor spatial resolution as the electrodes pick up electrical activity from neighbouring areas, whereas fMRI shows changes in blood flow in particular brain regions, indicating the activity of the neurons in that area.

 REVIEW

There are many ways you can distinguish between the four ways of studying the brain, using AO1 or AO3 points from the opposite page. Select random pairs and think of two characteristics you could choose to distinguish between them. Make sure they are equivalent and comparable points, and be clear how the techniques differ on each point.

Circadian rhythms

A01 Description

- Biological rhythms lasting about 24 hours adapt the body to meet the demands of the day/night cycle. These are called **circadian rhythms**.

- The **sleep–wake cycle** refers to alternating states of sleep and waking that are dependent on the 24-hour circadian cycle, controlled by the suprachiasmatic nucleus (SCN) in the hypothalamus.

- The strongest sleep drive is usually from 2 am to 4 am and from 1 pm to 3 pm. This sleepiness is more intense if we are sleep deprived.

- The homeostatic drive for sleep increases gradually throughout the day, as we use up energy in activity.

- This 'free-running' internal circadian 'clock' maintains a cycle of 24–25 hours even in the absence of external cues. It is disrupted by major changes in sleep schedules, such as jet travel or shift work.

- Environmental light levels cause neural signals to be sent to the SCN, so that the circadian rhythm can be synchronised with daylight hours. This is photoentrainment.

- Core body temperature is lowest (about 36°C) around 4.30 am, and highest (about 38°C) around 6 pm. It also dips between 2 pm and 4 pm.

- Hormone production also follows a circadian rhythm. For example, melatonin production by the pineal gland peaks during the hours of darkness, promoting sleepiness.

A03 Evaluation / Discussion

Evidence for a 'free-running' circadian rhythm…

The French cave explorer Michel Siffre spent six months in a cave in Texas with no daylight, clocks or radio, and his circadian rhythm settled to just over 24 hours, but with some dramatic variations.	When he stayed underground at age 60, his circadian rhythm had slowed down, sometimes stretching to 48 hours.	*This shows that the circadian rhythm is not wholly dependent on light or social cues and can vary with age.*

There are individual differences in circadian rhythms…

One is the cycle length; research has found that circadian cycles can vary from 13 to 65 hours.	The other type of individual difference relates to cycle onset – individuals appear to be innately different in terms of when their circadian rhythms reach their peak.	*This would explain why some people prefer to rise early and go to bed early (about 6 am and 10 pm), whereas others prefer to wake and go to bed later (10 am and 1 am).*

Methodological flaws in early research studies…

In most studies, participants were isolated from variables that might affect their circadian rhythms, such as clocks, radios and daylight.	However, they were not isolated from artificial light because it was believed that dim artificial light, in contrast to daylight, would not affect their circadian rhythms.	*Czeisler et al. (1999) altered participants' circadian rhythms down to 22 hours and up to 28 hours by using dim artificial lighting alone. This weakens the evidence of earlier studies.*

Temperature may be more important than light in setting the body clock…

It seems that the SCN transforms information about light levels into neural messages that set the body's temperature.	Buhr et al. found that fluctuations in body temperature over the 24-hour period cause tissues to become active or inactive.	*So, although the SCN responds to light, the circadian fluctuation of body temperature may actually control the other biological rhythms.*

APPLY: Exam skills

AO2: An example

SCENARIO Tina has begun a new career as a nurse working in the Accident and Emergency centre of a local hospital. By her own admission she has found working night shifts a challenge. She feels extremely sleepy at work and finds it difficult to sleep during the daytime. She is concerned that this is affecting her performance at work as well as her ability to drive safely to and from the hospital.

Using your knowledge of circadian rhythms explain the problems Tina is facing. What advice could you offer her to reduce these difficulties? **(6 marks)**

ANSWER *Tina's internal body clock has become out of balance with external cues. Melatonin production is increased during periods of darkness, leading to feelings of sleepiness. This means Tina will find it difficult to feel alert while working the night shift. Furthermore, attempts to sleep during the daytime are hindered by a decrease in melatonin and so Tina will feel too alert to sleep. If these problems continue then over time Tina will become sleep deprived and she will feel an increasing need to sleep, which could lead to accidents either at work or when driving. Tina could consider using artificial lights to alter her circadian cycle. Turning lights on as soon as she wakes could help her feel more alert. She should also reduce the amount of light when she is trying to sleep during the day. An eye mask or blackout blinds on her windows may help to increase melatonin production, leading to feelings of sleepiness.*

AO2: One for you to try

Katie and Jack have moved in together, and found that they have very different sleep patterns. Katie likes to go to sleep by 10 pm and wakes about 6 am, often going for a run before breakfast. Jack, however, prefers to stay up until 1 or 2 am, and sleeps until 10 am.

Referring to psychological research, how can you explain this difference? What advice would you give Katie and Jack if they want to see more of each other? (6 marks)

AO2: Research methods

Researchers measured body temperatures of a group of participants at 2-hourly intervals during a 24-hour period. The table below shows the means and standard deviations of these measurements.

Mean	00:00	2:00	4:00	6:00	8:00	10:00	12:00	14:00	16:00	18:00	20:00	22:00	24:00
Mean body temperature °C	36.5	36.6	36.0	36.9	37.2	37.3	37.7	36.8	37.5	38.1	37.9	37.1	36.5
Standard deviation	0.7	0.3	0.6	1.5	1.8	0.4	0.2	0.5	0.7	1.1	1.9	1.7	0.8

a. **Using the data in the table draw an appropriate graph. Fully label your display. (4 marks)**

b. **Comment on what the findings show about the circadian rhythm for body temperature. (4 marks)**

 How do I answer... 'Describe and evaluate' (AO1 + AO3) questions?

Q1: Outline and evaluate research into circadian rhythms. (6 marks)

Q2: Discuss the sleep–wake cycle. (6 marks)

- **Step 1** in answering mixed AO1 + AO3 questions is recognising that this is what you are being asked to do! Having two different command words, e.g. 'Outline' (an AO1 term) and 'evaluate' (an AO3 term) is usually a good clue.
- **Step 2** is planning how much you should write for each. In mixed AO1 + AO3 questions up to 6 marks, the division is half and half (it is different with mark totals higher than this as we will see on p.113).
- **Step 3** is deciding *what* to write. For **Q1:**, remember that 'research' can mean research studies or their findings. You could use the first bullet point, plus two of the AO3 points fully elaborated.
- For **Q2:** 'discuss' means 'outline and evaluate'. You will need the second, third and fourth bullet points for AO1 and one of the AO3 points fully elaborated.

REVIEW

What else could be asked about this topic? Thinking of questions can help you process the information and be ready to use it in different ways.

1 What question would have each of the bullet points as its answer?

2 Looking at the AO3 points one by one, what question could you be asked that you could use this point to answer?

Ultradian and infradian rhythms

 **RECAP**

AO1 Description

Ultradian rhythms

- **Ultradian rhythms** are cycles lasting less than 24 hours, such as the sleep stages. Sleep involves a repeating cycle of 90–100 minutes, with five stages including REM (rapid eye movement) sleep.

- Each of the five sleep stages shows a characteristic EEG pattern. During deep sleep, brainwaves slow and breathing and heart rate decrease. During REM sleep the EEG pattern resembles waking brainwaves and dreams occur.

- This 90-minute rhythm continues during the day as the Basic Rest Activity Cycle (BRAC). The BRAC involves periods of alertness alternating with periods of physiological fatigue and low concentration.

Infradian rhythms

- **Infradian rhythms** are cycles with a duration longer than 24 hours, for example the female menstrual cycle. This can vary between 23 and 36 days, but averages 28 days. It is regulated by hormones and ovulation takes place roughly half way through the cycle.

- There may also be weekly infradian rhythms, with changes in hormone levels and blood pressure at weekends.

- Annual rhythms can be seen in seasonal variations in mood, increased rates of heart attacks in winter, and a peak of deaths in January.

AO3 Evaluation/Discussion

Individual difference in sleep patterns may be genetic in origin...

Tucker *et al.* (2007) studied participants over 11 days and nights in a sleep lab. They assessed sleep duration, time to fall asleep and the amount of time in each sleep stage.	They found large, consistent individual differences in each of these characteristics. For deep sleep (stages 3 and 4), the individual differences were particularly significant.	*This meant that differences between individuals may not be caused just by circumstances, but are at least partially biologically determined.*

Research support for the BRAC in elite performers...

Ericsson *et al.* (2006) found that elite violinists generally practise for no more than 90 minutes at a time, several times a day.	The violinists frequently napped to recover from practice, with the very best violinists napping more than their teachers.	*Consistent with the predictions of the BRAC, Ericsson discovered the same pattern among other musicians, athletes, chess players and writers.*

The menstrual cycle is affected by exogenous cues...

When several women of childbearing age live together and do not take oral contraceptives, their menstrual cycles tend to synchronise.	Russell *et al.* (1980) applied daily samples of sweat from one group of women onto the upper lips of women in a separate group. Their menstrual cycles became synchronised.	*This suggests that a woman's menstrual cycle can be affected by pheromones from other women as well as her own pituitary hormones.*

The menstrual cycle influences mate choice...

Women generally prefer 'slightly feminised' male faces, representing kindness and cooperation, when picking a partner for a long-term relationship.	However, around ovulation, women showed a preference for more masculinised faces, representing 'good genes' for short-term liaisons with more likelihood of conception.	*This shows how a hormonally controlled rhythm may also impact behaviour.*

 APPLY: Exam skills

AO2: An example

SCENARIO Ali has volunteered to take part in a sleep study. She will be spending one night in a sleep laboratory during which an EEG will measure electrical activity in her brain. Ali is interested to learn what is happening in her brain while she is sleeping.

Explain what Ali is likely to learn from the EEG readings. **(3 marks)**

ANSWER *Ali's EEG will show that she experiences an ultradian rhythm while asleep, with cycles repeating every 90 to 100 minutes. During each cycle her brain activity will show periods of NREM and REM sleep. In her first cycle Ali would move from light stage 1 sleep, through to stage 2 sleep and into the deeper sleep stages (3 and 4) before returning to stage 2 and then entering a period of REM. During REM sleep Ali's EEG recordings would be similar to the EEG recordings of a person awake.*

AO2: One for you to try

Mr Walker, the Principal of Moody College, is considering changing the college timetable to benefit students' concentration levels.

What advice would you give him, based on your knowledge of ultradian rhythms? (4 marks)

AO2: Research methods

Many midwives believe that more babies are born during a full moon than during a new moon. Arliss *et al.* (2005) collected data to examine this belief across 62 lunar cycles, and the table below shows their findings.

Phase of moon	Average number of births
New moon	320.0
Full moon	321.3

Statistical testing of these results found that the difference was not significant at $p<0.05$.

a. **Explain what the statement 'not significant at $p<0.05$' means in the context of this study. (3 marks)**

b. **Psychological research such as this must go through a peer review process prior to publication. Explain the purpose of such a review. (3 marks)**

How do I answer... longer (12-mark or 16-mark) essay questions?

In A Level, a 16-mark question needs 6 marks of AO1 and 10 marks of AO3, so you should aim to write almost twice as much AO3 as AO1. We have given you enough AO1 points for 6 marks of AO1. Practise writing this in 7 ½ minutes.

For your AO3, you need to write three effective points for 6 marks, or four effective points for 10 marks.

Q1: Outline and evaluate the role of infradian and/or ultradian rhythms in human behaviour. (16 marks)

For **Q1:** you would probably opt to include both infradian and ultradian rhythms in your answer. Fully discussing both would be overkill, but one may not give you enough AO3. The best idea is to aim for 1 ½ rhythms. This strategy applies to any topic where there are two explanations, two treatments etc. We call it the 'One and a half rule'. This means, for a 16-mark A Level essay:

- Outline one in detail (three points of AO1) and the other briefly (1 point).
- Present four effective evaluation points (from the opposite page).

A 16-mark question on *just* infradian rhythms or *just* ultradian rhythms would be unlikely (not impossible, but unlikely), although you could get a shorter 8-mark or 10-mark essay question on these (see **How do I answer... ?** on p.105 for advice about answering these shorter essay questions).

Q2: Discuss research into biological rhythms affecting human behaviour. (16 marks)

For **Q2:** you could use any combination of rhythms, i.e. infradian and ultradian, ultradian and circadian, circadian and infradian. It is wise to stick to just two as trying to do all three would make your coverage too superficial. Remember that 'research' means theory (built on research) or studies. You should include some methodological evaluation in this case, and you could comment on validity issues in a lab study of sleep patterns, or the support of Ericsson's findings from a variety of samples of different elite performers.

Watch out also for the command word 'Discuss', which is looking for a more balanced and wide-ranging discussion, not just a list of strengths or limitations of a theory. This could include applications, implications, counterevidence, and alternative explanations, as well as issues and debates (biological determinism is relevant here).

REVIEW

To practise retrieving the relevant points from your memory, make a table and insert key terms to represent each of the points you need to elaborate. Then you can imagine elaborating them while testing yourself. Work towards remembering all the points without having to peep.

For example:

AO1 Ultradian < 24 hrs e.g. Sleep stages			AO1 Infradian > 24 hrs		
AO1 EEG patterns			AO1 Weekly – hormones, blood pressure		
AO1 BRAC = 90 mins			AO1 Annual – mood, heart attacks		
AO3 Tucker sleep lab	Large indiv diffs in deep sleep	Bio det?	AO3 Ericsson elite performers	Naps	Supports BRAC
AO3 Menstrual cycles synchronise	Russell – sweat upper lip	Pheromones	AO3 Menstrual cycle, mate choice	Feminised = LTR, masculinised at ovulation	Hormones affect behaviour

 **RECAP**

AO1 Description

Endogenous pacemakers

- **Endogenous pacemakers** are internal biological clocks in the brain.
- The suprachiasmatic nucleus (SCN) in the hypothalamus acts as the 'master clock', controlling other pacemakers in the body. It receives information about light levels via the optic nerve which keeps the SCN's circadian rhythm synchronised with daylight.
- The SCN sends signals to the pineal gland, which produces the hormone melatonin at night. Melatonin inhibits brain mechanisms that promote wakefulness, and so induces sleep.
- Neurons in the SCN spontaneously synchronise with each other. They have links with other brain regions controlling sleep and arousal, with peripheral pacemakers, and with the pineal gland.

Exogenous zeitgebers

- **Exogenous zeitgebers** are environmental events which affect the biological clock.
- Light resets the biological clock each day, keeping it on a 24-hour cycle. Specialised light-detecting cells in the retina contain melanopsin. They gauge brightness and send signals to the SCN to set the daily clock.
- This system works in most blind people too, even in the absence of rods and cones or visual perception.
- We are also influenced by social cues (e.g. mealtimes, bedtime, etc.) from the activity of people around us.

AO3 Evaluation/Discussion

The role of the SCN as an endogenous pacemaker was shown with hamsters...

Morgan (1995) bred hamsters with abnormally short circadian rhythms (20 hours), and transplanted some of their SCN neurons into normal hamsters, which then displayed the abnormal rhythm too.	Further confirmation came in the reverse experiment, when SCN neurons from normal hamsters were transplanted into the abnormal hamsters. They then changed to a normal 24-hour circadian pattern.	*This supports the importance of the SCN in regulating the 24-hour circadian rhythm.*

Artificial light at night can disrupt the circadian rhythm...

Touitou *et al.* (2017) showed that teenagers spend increasing amounts of time on electronic media at night. The LED bulbs of these devices are enriched with a blue light.	This leads to suppression of melatonin secretion and circadian disruption. As a result, adolescent sleep becomes irregular, shortened and delayed.	*In the long run, sleep deprivation can lead to increased rates of cardiovascular disorders and mood disorders such as depression.*

Support for the role of melanopsin...

The important role played by melanopsin in setting the circadian rhythm is demonstrated in studies of blind people who lack any visual perception.	Skene and Arendt (2007) estimate that most blind people who still have some light perception have normally entrained circadian rhythms. People without light perception show abnormal circadian entrainment.	*This suggests that when the pathway from retinal cells containing melanopsin to the SCN is still intact, light can still act as an exogenous zeitgeber.*

Light exposure can be used to avoid jet lag...

Burgess *et al.* exposed volunteers to light treatments in order to shift their sleep–wake cycles. Participants' sleep patterns and melatonin levels were monitored in a lab.	Participants who had been exposed to bright light felt sleepy two hours earlier in the evening and woke two hours earlier in the morning.	*This shows that circadian rhythms can be shifted by light exposure, which could be useful for air travellers.*

APPLY: Exam skills

AO2: An example

SCENARIO On returning to England, following a holiday in the USA, Eric finds his sleep–wake pattern has been disrupted. He feels sleepy during the day but wakes up in the middle of the night.

Using your knowledge of endogenous pacemakers and exogenous zeitgebers, explain Eric's experiences. **(3 marks)**

ANSWER *Eric has jet lag because his internal sleep–wake cycle, originating from the SCN, has become out of sync with environmental cues (exogenous zeitgebers). Light usually entrains the sleep–wake cycle to a 24-hour pattern of sleeping during darkness and wakefulness during the day, which offers an adaptive advantage. But we are not able to adapt to rapid changes in zeitgebers resulting from flying across time zones. Eric is experiencing the effects of increased melatonin during daylight so feels sleepy when he should feel awake.*

AO2: Research methods

A researcher wanted to investigate children's sleep patterns and their sensitivity to light. She decided to carry out a field experiment, monitoring the children's sleep in their own homes using an electronic activity monitor worn on the wrist. Half of the children were given thin curtains which let the daylight in, and the other half were given blackout blinds. The children were asked to follow normal bedtime routines and were monitored for a week.

a. **Briefly explain what is meant by a 'field experiment' and why it was appropriate in this study. (4 marks)**

b. **Give one strength and one limitation of field experiments as they might apply to this study. (4 marks)**

c. **Identify one ethical issue the researcher should consider in this research. Suggest how the researcher could deal with this ethical issue. (3 marks)**

d. **Explain one problem with the design of this study and suggest ways of dealing with this problem. (4 marks)**

AO2: One for you to try

Jade lives in the UK, but has to travel to Chicago for a week every three months for her work. When she returns home, the six-hour time difference makes it hard for her to get to sleep at night, and it generally takes her a week to recover normal sleep patterns.

What advice could you give Jade to help her adjust to the time changes more quickly? (4 marks)

How do I answer... research methods questions?

Questions requiring research methods knowledge can appear in any section of any paper in the AS or A Level exams. They could include any aspect of research methods, data analysis or ethical issues. Here are a few tips:

- Take time to think – remember the relevant research methods key terms.
- When you are interpreting data, make comparisons between different values such as 'higher', 'lower' or 'similar', but don't quote the numbers as this will not get you marks.
- Research methods questions require you to link your knowledge to the stem information. They use phrases like 'in this study', and you must link explicitly or give relevant examples from the study.

For example, in the **AO2: Research methods** question on the left, you must refer to an ethical issue that is relevant to this study. You must then suggest how the researcher could deal with this issue again in a way that would work in this particular study. You could pick informed consent, which has particular issues when researching children. The researcher should deal with it by informing the parents and getting their consent, but also by letting the parents know it's OK to stop the experiment if the child is distressed.

In the second part of this question you can refer to experimental design, as this is an independent groups design, so individual differences will affect the findings, especially if it uses a small sample. 'How this problem could be dealt with' must be **relevant** and **practical**. You could suggest repeated measures with counterbalancing to deal with this, but you need to explain specifically how that works: 'Use the same children in each condition, with half sleeping for a week with thin curtains and a week with blackout blinds, and the other half doing the two conditions in the other order'.

REVIEW

You should think about research methods issues with every study you learn. Ask yourself:

- What kind of study is it? (lab experiment, field experiment, observation, self-report etc)
- If it's an experiment, what experimental design was used? (then think about confounding variables relating to that design, and how they affect internal validity)
- What kind of sample? (then think about population validity)
- What kind of task is involved? (think about mundane realism)
- What about ethics? (think how it could be improved)

Try applying these questions to the studies on this page. This deep processing will help you remember the study details, as well as being a way of practising your research methods skills.

RECAP

AOI Description

- Psychological investigations begin with an **aim**, which may be an intention, e.g. 'to investigate the effect of TV on the work a student produces', or a research question, e.g., 'Does noise affect the quality of work?'

- The **independent variable (IV)** is directly manipulated by the experimenter. The different values of the IV are known as the experimental conditions.

- The **dependent variable (DV)** is measured to see how the change in the IV has affected it. In an **experiment**, the IV is deliberately changed to see if there is any effect on the DV. This permits us to draw causal conclusions – conclusions about cause and effect.

> **Issues/Debates**
> Determinism. Scientific determinism allows researchers to draw conclusions from experiments.

- This leads to a **hypothesis**: a testable statement of what you expect to find. A good hypothesis includes the two (or more) levels of the IV, e.g. 'Students who do a memory task with the TV on produce work that gets fewer marks than those who do the same task without the TV on.'

- The hypothesis should be fully **operationalised**, i.e. the variables should be defined in a way that they can easily be measured or tested. A concept such as 'educational attainment' needs to be specified more clearly if we are going to investigate it. For example, it might be operationalised as 'GCSE grade in Maths'.

- **Standardised procedures** ensure that each participant does exactly the same thing within each condition in order that the study can be repeated. They may include standardised instructions – the instructions given to participants to tell them how to perform the task.

- **Extraneous variables** (EVs) should be identified and controlled before the experiment begins. These are any variable, other than the IV itself, which may potentially affect the DV. If EVs are not controlled they may become confounding variables, which affect the validity of the findings.

- The procedure should also include consideration of **ethical issues** and how to deal with them (see p.128–129).

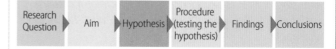

Research Question → Aim → Hypothesis → Procedure (testing the hypothesis) → Findings → Conclusions

APPLY: Exam skills

AO2: One for you to try

A researcher becomes interested in the effects of simple rewards on children's ability to do well on school tests. The researcher intends to conduct a laboratory experiment to investigate this. He invites 30 children to his laboratory and gives them a general knowledge test. Beforehand he tells half of the children that he will give them £1 as a reward for doing the test. Afterwards he compares the children's scores on the test.

a. What is the aim of this study? (2 marks)

b. Identify the operationalised independent variable and the operationalised dependent variable in this study. (2 marks + 2 marks)

c. Write a hypothesis for this study. (2 marks)

d. Is your hypothesis directional or non-directional? (1 mark)

e. Identify one possible extraneous variable in this study. Explain how this extraneous variable could have affected the results of this experiment. (1 mark + 3 marks)

f. With reference to this study, explain one strength and one limitation of lab experiments. (2 marks + 2 marks)

AO2: A marking exercise

Read the student answers, given below, to the following exam question.

> An experiment was conducted in which participants completed a test in a very hot room or a cool room to demonstrate the effect of temperature on aggression levels. Aggressiveness was assessed by a researcher and each participant was given an aggression score.
>
> Identify the operationalised independent variable and the operationalised dependent variable in this study. (2 marks + 2 marks)

Kerry's answer

The operationalised independent variable is room temperature and the operationalised dependent variable is aggression.

Megan's answer

The operationalised independent variable is temperature and the operationalised dependent variable is the difference in aggression between the participants.

Rohan's answer

The operationalised independent variable is the room temperature (hot or cool) and the operationalised dependent variable is the aggression score.

For each answer there are 2 marks available. Write the marks you would give each answer in the table below.

	Mark for IV out of 2	Mark for DV out of 2
Kerry		
Megan		
Rohan		

Control of variables

RECAP

AO1 Description

- There is a trade-off between control and realism in psychological research.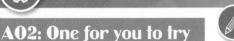

- Laboratory experiments have the greatest **control**, and allow conclusions about cause-and-effect relationships, but findings in this artificial context may not be generalisable to real-life situations. They may lack **mundane realism**, so the results may not apply to behaviour in the real world.

- However, studies in everyday settings lack control of **extraneous variables**, so the findings may be meaningless. Uncontrolled extraneous variables may affect the DV in an experiment, becoming **confounding variables**. These could include factors like time of day, noise and distractions.

- Researchers hope to be able to **generalise** the findings of a study beyond the research setting. Generalisability may be limited if aspects of the study lack realism, for example: the materials used in the study; the environment of the study, particularly if participants are aware they are being studied; the sample of participants.

- **Validity** refers to whether an observed effect is a genuine one.

- **Internal validity** is the degree to which an observed effect was due to experimental manipulation rather than factors such as the confounding/extraneous variables.

- **External validity** is the extent to which the findings from particular research participants can be generalised to other people and situations.

  > **Ecological validity** Can the research findings be generalised to everyday life?

  > **Population validity** Can the findings from this sample of participants be generalised to all people?

  > **Historical validity** Can the results of an old study be generalised to people's behaviour today?

APPLY: Exam skills

AO2: One for you to try

Match the experiment to the validity issue.

1. I test some drinks on ten five-year olds then conclude that 'Nine out of ten people prefer hot chocolate to coffee.'

2. I give a class a memory test using a word list, with half the class sitting and half standing, then say 'People remember things better when they are sitting down than standing up.'

3. I want to compare males' and females' memories, so I get them to listen to a story and write it down, and I count how many words they have written as a measure of memory.

4. I read some classic research about women's colour preferences and make recommendations to a paint company based on these findings.

A Internal validity   **C** Ecological validity
B Historical validity   **D** Population validity

How do I answer... 'Write an aim' questions?

Q1: A researcher wanted to find out whether girls watch more television than boys, and asked 100 children to complete a questionnaire about their viewing habits for a week. What was the aim of this study? (2 marks)

The 'aim' of a study is, as we stated on p.116, the researcher's intention, i.e. what they want to find out about the things they are investigating. Unlike hypotheses, the aim can be stated as a general statement and is either explicit (as here) or implicit in the details you are given about the study. For example, in this study the aim is helpfully incorporated into the description you are given in the scenario: *'The aim of this study was to find out whether girls watch more television than boys.'* However, it is more likely you will need to work it out from the information given.

Have a go at working out an appropriate aim in the following two studies, and then develop each of these into a 2-mark answer.

a. Relationship breakdown can be a major stressor in people's lives. Researchers interviewed a number of recently divorced couples, asking them questions about their mental health and general well-being following their divorce.

In the first example, the researchers were asking questions about mental health and well-being after divorce, so the aim is simply to find out about mental health and well-being after divorce.

b. A researcher measured aggression scores in two groups of children, one group who regularly played violent video games and another group who did not play violent video games.

In the second example, they are comparing two groups, so they must be trying to find out if there is a difference between aggression scores between the two groups. The aim can be worded quite generally, without operationalising the variables. Start with 'To find out…' e.g. To find out whether playing video games affects children's aggression.

REVIEW

There are over 100 key terms you need to know for **Research methods**. You could make flash cards or put them into an app on your phone so you can keep testing yourself on these terms. You need to be able to define them or to pick the right term to match a definition. Key terms are highlighted in **bold** throughout this **Revision Guide** to help you.

Return to hypotheses and other things

 RECAP

A01 Description

Directional and non-directional hypotheses

- A **directional hypothesis** states the expected direction of the results. For example:
  > *People who get an average of eight hours or more of sleep per night achieve higher marks in class tests than those who get fewer than eight hours of sleep.*

- A directional hypothesis can be used when past research (theory or studies) suggests that the findings will go in a particular direction. If there is no relevant past research, or findings are contradictory, then a non-directional hypothesis should be used. A **non-directional hypothesis** states that there is a difference between the two conditions, but does not state the direction of the difference.
  > *Lack of sleep affects performance in class tests.*

- To fully operationalise these hypotheses, an operationalised IV and DV should be used in each case, e.g.
  > *'... an average of eight hours or more sleep per night (IV)... higher marks in class tests (DV).'*

A few other things

- A **pilot study** is a small-scale trial run of a research design, to check all aspects of the procedure and change some if necessary. These could include:
  > the instructions to participants. (Are they clear? Did participants understand what they had to do?)
  > the timings. (Too long or too short?)
  > the materials used. (Did participants have any difficulties understanding them? Were there too many tasks or questions, leading to boredom or fatigue?)
  > whether participants had guessed the purpose of the study.

- If a researcher tries out the research design using a few typical participants, they can see what needs to be adjusted without having invested a large amount of time and money in a full-scale study.

- The results of a pilot study are irrelevant. However, carrying out a pilot study and making appropriate changes to the procedure can improve the validity and reliability of the main study's findings.

- Sometimes a researcher has to use another person to play a role in an investigation. They are part of the research set-up rather than being a participant. For example, Milgram's study on obedience used **confederates** to play the roles of the experimenter and the learner. In Asch's study on conformity the confederates pretended to be other participants.

APPLY: Exam skills

A02: Five for you to try

1. **Read the item below and then answer the questions that follow.**

   A psychologist wants to compare the effectiveness of different memory improvement strategies in learning French vocabulary. The participants are children from a local school. One group of students use strategy A and the other group use strategy B. They are asked to learn lists of French words, and are tested on their recall the next day. The results are shown in the table.

	Mean number of words remembered correctly	Standard deviation
Strategy A	12	1.9
Strategy B	14	3.8

   a. Write a non-directional hypothesis for this experiment. **(2 marks)**

   b. Why is a non-directional hypothesis suitable in this study? **(1 mark)**

   c. Explain two reasons why the results from this study may lack validity. **(4 marks)**

2. **Which two of the following are directional hypotheses? (2 marks)**

   Tick **two** boxes only.

   A People who feel hot are more aggressive than people who feel cold. ☐

   B To investigate the effect of temperature on aggression. ☐

   C Men and women are different in terms of their aggression scores. ☐

   D Drinking through a straw is better than not drinking through a straw. ☐

3. **Match the examples on the left with the related key terms.**

   1 Younger people have better memories than older people.

   2 To see if blondes have more fun than brunettes.

   3 Do people who sleep with a teddy bear sleep longer than people who don't?

   4 Positive expectations lead to differences in performance.

   5 Men with beards are more attractive.

   6 Lack of sleep may affect schoolwork.

   A Research question

   B Aim

   C Directional hypothesis

   D Directional hypothesis

   E Non-directional hypothesis

   F Non-directional hypothesis

APPLY: Exam skills

4. **If researchers do not have evidence of previous research findings in the area they wish to study, they should use:**

   A a pilot study. ☐

   B a directional hypothesis. ☐

   C a correlational analysis. ☐

   D a non-directional hypothesis. ☐

5. **Read the student answers to the following exam question, given below:**

   > A researcher is investigating the hypothesis that people given a list of emotionally charged words recall fewer correctly than participants given a list of emotionally neutral words.
   >
   > Suggest why the researcher might carry out a pilot study for this investigation. (2 marks)

   A *The researcher would select all of the participants for the experiment, and give them a few words to try to learn first. They would then decide how many words should be included in the actual experiment.*

   B *The researcher wants to save time and money by checking the procedure before carrying it out on all his participants.*

   C *The researcher wants to check that the participants understand all the words. If they don't, then the word lists can be changed before the actual experiment is carried out.*

   How many marks would you give each answer, A, B and C?

How do I answer... 'Write a hypothesis' questions?

On p.117, we looked at writing aims for a study. Now we can look at how we generate hypotheses for the same study.

> A researcher wanted to find out whether girls watch more television than boys, and asked 100 children to complete a questionnaire about their viewing habits for a week. Write a suitable hypothesis for this study. (3 marks)

There will undoubtedly be at least one question asking you to write a hypothesis, and surprisingly few students get full marks for this. It's not difficult if you ask yourself these questions:

- Should it be directional or non-directional? (See rules on opposite page.)
  - > In the question, there is no mention of previous research so it must be non-directional.
- What is the IV?
  - > The researcher is comparing boys and girls so gender is the IV, and to operationalise it you must mention the two groups, boys and girls.
- What is the DV?
  - > The research question is about how much TV children watch, but it is a self-report questionnaire so the DV is 'how much TV the children report they have watched in a week'.

Now put this together into a hypothesis, which should be a statement in the present tense:

  - > Girls and boys report they have watched different amounts of TV in a week.

REVIEW

Practise writing hypotheses whenever you can. There are plenty of examples throughout this book and in *The Complete Companions* Year 1 and AS Student Book (p.183), as well as in past papers on the AQA website. Check carefully against mark schemes to make sure you have all the required elements.

Experimental design

AO1 Description

- In a **repeated measures design**, every participant carries out each condition of the experiment (all levels of the IV). The performance (DV) of each participant on the two tests can be compared.

  > To deal with **order effects** in a repeated measures design, researchers can use counterbalancing to ensure that each condition is tested first or second in equal amounts.

  > For example, half of the participants carry out condition A then B, and the other half do B then A. Alternatively, all participants take part in each condition twice: ABBA.

- In an **independent groups design**, each group of participants does one condition of the experiment, and the performance of the two groups is compared.

  > Participants should be **randomly allocated** to the conditions, in order to distribute participant variables evenly so they do not become confounding. In a **matched pairs design**, two groups of participants are used, but pairs are matched on key characteristics believed to affect performance on the DV. For example, age or gender may be relevant to some studies, but this decision must be based on evidence.

- For each matched pair, one member is randomly allocated to each condition.

GROUP 1   GROUP 2

AO3 Evaluation / Discussion

Limitations of repeated measures design...

| Order effects, such as practice (that may improve performance), boredom or fatigue effects (that may worsen performance). | Participants may also guess the purpose of the experiment, affecting their performance in the second condition. | *Researchers may use two different but equivalent tests to reduce practice effects. Counterbalancing is the main way of dealing with order effects. A cover story can help to prevent participants guessing the aims of the study.* |

Limitations of independent groups design...

| Participant variables (individual differences) cannot be controlled, and are a confounding variable. | In addition, more participants are required than a repeated measures design. | *Randomly allocating participants to conditions helps to distribute participant variables evenly (in theory).* |

Limitations of matched pairs design...

| It is very time consuming and difficult to match people on key variables, and requires participants to be selected from a large pool. | Also, only known variables can be matched, and there are likely to be other relevant variables that were not known about but still affect the DV. | *Restricting the number of variables to match would make it easier. Researchers could conduct a pilot study to explore which key variables may be important to match.* |

Strengths of each design...

| The limitations of one design are often the strengths of another. | For example, one limitation of repeated measures is that participants do better in the second condition because of a practice effect. | *Therefore, one strength of independent measures and matched pairs designs is that they avoid order effects because each participant does only one condition.* |

 APPLY: Exam skills

AO2: Three for you to try

1. **A researcher wants to conduct an experiment to investigate differences between people who are left- and right-handed. One area they are particularly interested in is how this affects creativity. The researcher intends to assess creativity using a test.**

   Answer the following questions:

   a. Explain why this is an independent groups design. **(2 marks)**

   b. Explain why a repeated measures design would be unsuitable to use in this experiment. **(3 marks)**

   c. Explain one strength and one limitation of using an independent groups design. **(4 marks)**

   d. Write a non-directional hypothesis for this experiment. **(2 marks)**

2. **Match the key term with the definition.**

1	Participant variable	A	Same participants in both conditions
2	Repeated measures	B	Two groups, unpaired participants
3	Independent groups	C	Used in independent groups design
4	Order effect	D	Two groups where participants are paired
5	Matched pairs	E	A problem in independent groups design
6	Random allocation	F	A problem in repeated measures design

3. **A study investigates the effect of coffee on reaction time by testing each participant twice – at the start of the experiment and again after they have drunk a cup of coffee.**

   Explain two reasons why it was more appropriate to use a repeated measures design than an independent groups design. (4 marks)

 REVIEW

Look up studies from any topic and identify the experimental design used. Why did researchers choose this design? Think about the advantages and limitations of the design they used, and whether there were practical or ethical reasons for doing it the way they did.

For this Research Methods chapter you could create a grid of all the Key Studies you have covered with the columns labelled: Research method, design, sample, type of data, methodological evaluation and ethical issues.

How do I answer... experimental design questions?

Q1: Reaction time is tested before and after a training activity to see if test scores improve with training.

  a. Identify the design used in this experiment. (1 mark)
  b. Evaluate the use of this design in this study, and suggest how it could be improved. (3 marks)

Q2: Two groups of participants are given different word lists to remember, in order to find out whether nouns or verbs are easier to recall.

  a. Identify the design used in this experiment. (1 mark)
  b. Suggest how the experiment could be improved by changing the design. (2 marks)

When you are asked to identify the design used in an experiment, the answer is one of three things:

- repeated measures
- independent groups
- matched pairs.

Ask yourself two questions:

1. Would you analyse the findings by comparing the scores from the same person, or by comparing scores of two (or more) different groups of people?

2. If they are different groups, have the people in the two groups been matched? (Don't forget twins studies are using matched pairs.)

You may then be asked to suggest how the experiment could be improved by changing the design. To answer this, think of the limitation of the current design, and suggest how that would be dealt with by using a different design.

So in **Q1:a**, you just need to write 'repeated measures'. For **Q1:b**, it would have to be repeated measures as it is a 'before and after' type of experiment, but there is the limitation that participants may get better anyway, without training. To improve it, there should be a control group who didn't get the training.

For **Q2:a**, the answer is 'independent groups'. For **Q2:b**, you can comment that individual differences are a confounding factor as some people may just be better at learning words than others. To improve it you could use repeated measures with counterbalancing, so half the participants learn verbs first then nouns, and half do the conditions the other way round.

Laboratory and field experiments

 **RECAP**

A01 Description

- All experiments involve the manipulation of the IV while trying to keep all other variables constant, so that the IV's effect on the DV can be measured. We can then conclude that the change in the IV has caused the change in the DV.
- **Laboratory experiments** are carried out in a special environment where variables can be controlled.
  - > Participants are aware that they are taking part in a study, so they may alter their behaviour.
  - > In addition, the laboratory environment and the materials used may be quite unlike everyday life.
  - > Not all laboratory studies are laboratory experiments; they could be observations, natural experiments or quasi-experiments.
- **Field experiments** are carried out in a more natural environment. The IV is still deliberately manipulated by the researcher.
  - > Participants are usually unaware that they are participating in an experiment, so their behaviour may be more natural.
  - > Not all field studies are experiments; the IV must be manipulated by the experimenter.
  - > Some experiments may be carried out in a laboratory environment, but the purpose of the study is so well concealed that participants behave quite naturally, so the study is more like a field experiment.

- There is a balancing act between control and ecological validity, as lab experiments have better control at the expense of mundane realism, and field experiments may be more like everyday life, but lose control of variables.

A03 Evaluation/Discussion

Strengths and limitations of laboratory experiments...

They are high in internal validity, because variables are tightly controlled, so we can be more certain that any change in the DV is due to the IV.	However, they have poor ecological validity. This is because the setting is low in mundane realism and the IV or DV may be operationalised in ways that don't represent everyday life.	*In addition, the participants know they are in a study so may alter their behaviour (demand characteristics).*

Strengths and limitations of field experiments...

They are in a more natural setting so participants are less likely to respond to cues in their environment.	However, there is less control of extraneous variables. This means they may be lower in internal validity than a laboratory experiment.	*Also, participants may be unaware that they are being studied and it is difficult to debrief them afterwards, which presents an ethical issue.*

APPLY: Exam skills

A02: Two for you to try

1. **Which one of the following statements is not true of field experiments? Tick one box only.**

   A They tend to have lower internal validity than a laboratory experiment. ☐

   B They tend to have higher ecological validity than a laboratory experiment. ☐

   C The IV is naturally occurring. ☐

   D They are carried out in a natural environment. ☐

2. **A group of pupils were given information about how their peers had performed on a Maths task. They were told that their peers had either done well (condition 1) or done poorly on the test (condition 2). The children were later given a Maths test in class, to see whether their expectations affected their performance.**

   a. What type of experiment was this? **(1 mark)**

   b. What experimental design was used? **(1 mark)**

   c. Write a suitable hypothesis for this experiment. **(3 marks)**

Natural and quasi-experiments

 RECAP

AO1 Description

- A **natural experiment** is conducted when it is not possible, for ethical or practical reasons, to deliberately manipulate an IV – the IV is naturally occurring. It may take place in a laboratory or in the natural environment.

    > The DV is measured, but only tentative conclusions can be drawn about the IV's effect on the DV, as the IV was not deliberately manipulated and participants were not randomly allocated to conditions.

    > An example is a study of the effect of institutionalisation on children, in which the two groups were adopted before or after six months of age. The DV could be measured in a lab, e.g. IQ or behaviour in the Strange Situation.

- In a **quasi-experiment** the IV is also naturally occurring – it is a naturally existing difference between people, for example gender. Again, causal conclusions must be tentative.

    > The IV could be measured by psychological testing, for example groups of people with internal or external locus of control. This is a personal attribute of the individuals, not something that was manipulated by researchers.

    > Participants' responses in a situation would then be the DV measured in the quasi-experiment.

AO3 Evaluation / Discussion

Strengths of natural and quasi-experiments…

| Natural experiments allow psychologists to research 'real' problems. | For example, the effects of a disaster on health, where the IV already exists. | *This gives high levels of mundane realism and ecological validity.* |

Limitations of natural and quasi-experiments…

| The IV is not directly manipulated, so we can't be sure that any change in the DV is caused by the IV. | Also, participants are not randomly allocated to conditions, so there may be differences between groups of participants, giving a confounding variable. | *Finally, the sample may be unique, so the findings can't be generalised to other groups and the study has low population validity.* |

 APPLY: Exam skills

AO2: One for you to try

1. **A study investigates the antisocial effects of TV by monitoring whether people who watch a lot of TV (more than five hours a day) are more aggressive than those who don't. Their aggression levels are measured by asking friends and family to rate them on a scale.**

    a. Identify the IV and DV. **(2 marks)**

    b. Identify whether it is a laboratory, field, natural or quasi-experiment. **(1 mark)**

    c. Explain your decision. **(2 marks)**

    d. Explain why you think the study would have high or low validity. **(2 marks)**.

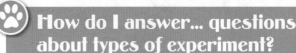

How do I answer... questions about types of experiment?

> **Q1:** People who score high on the Authoritarian Personality scale are compared with people low on the scale in terms of how willing they are to obey orders in a Milgram-type study.
>
> **What type of experiment is being used in this research? (2 marks)**

It can be difficult to decide which of the four types an experiment falls into. Sometimes it can be two different types. In this the IV is the high or low score on the Authoritarian Personality scale, which is a characteristic of the individuals. Therefore, this is a quasi-experiment. They have been brought into a special situation and given a special task to do, and the standardised procedure is controlling other variables, so it is also a lab experiment.

 REVIEW

Identify which type of experiment is being used in any piece of experimental research you come across.

To practise this, find key experimental studies in each chapter of this book, and answer the following questions:

1. What were the IV and DV?

2. Was the setting high or low in mundane realism?

3. What relevant variables might not have been controlled?

4. Do you think this was a lab, field, natural or quasi- experiment?

More problems with experiments

A01 Description

Demand Characteristics

- Participant effects refer to the behaviour of participants in response to an experimental situation.

- **Demand characteristics** are cues that make participants unconsciously aware of the aims of a study or help them work out what the researcher expects to find. The situation creates expectations and participants do not behave as they would usually.

- Participants generally want to be helpful, and can therefore behave over-cooperatively. However, some participants deliberately try to spoil an experiment – the 'screw you' effect. Thus, demand characteristics may act as a confounding variable.

Investigator effects

- **Investigator effects** are any cues from an investigator that encourage certain behaviours in the participant, and which might lead to a fulfilment of the investigator's expectations.

  > For example, investigators may be more encouraging to one group of participants, or may ask leading questions.

  > Investigator effects may act as a confounding variable. These may include direct effects (as a result of the investigator interacting with the participant) and indirect effects (as a consequence of the way the investigator designed the study).

- **Participant variables** are the characteristics of individual participants, which act as extraneous variables in an independent groups design, such as age, intelligence and motivation. These variables can be controlled by a repeated measures or matched pairs design (matching for relevant characteristics). These are not the same as participant effects.

- **Situational variables** are features of the research situation which may influence participants' behaviour. They become confounding variables if they vary systematically with the IV, for example all members of one group are tested in the morning, and the second group in the afternoon.

A03 Evaluation/Discussion

Single blind designs can help to deal with demand characteristics...

| In a single blind design, the participant is not aware of the research aims or which condition of the experiment they are in. | This prevents the participant from responding to cues about the aims or expectations of the experiment. | *This means they should behave more naturally, improving the validity of the study.* |

Double blind designs are even better at reducing demand characteristics...

| In a double blind design, both the participant and the person conducting the experiment are 'blind' to the aims or hypotheses in the study. | Ideally, the person conducting the experiment will also be unaware of which participants are in which group or condition. | *This means that the investigator is less likely to produce cues linked to their expectations of what will happen in the study.* |

Experimental realism also helps to reduce demand characteristics...

| If the events appear natural and realistic the participant will behave more naturally. | If the participant is sufficiently engaged in the task, they are not paying attention to the fact that they are being observed. | *This means they are less likely to change their behaviour to fit the expectations of the experimenter.* |

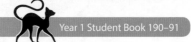

APPLY: Exam skills

A02: Three for you to try

1. **A study into teachers' expectations was carried out by Rosenthal in the 1960s. He randomly allocated children to two groups, and told their teachers that one group had been found to score high for 'intellectual blooming', and should be expected to show great increases in intelligence during the coming year. Children's IQ scores (a measure of intelligence) were tested at the beginning and the end of the year. The findings are shown in the table below.**

School Year	Mean gains in IQ during the year	
	'normal' group	'high score for intellectual blooming potential' group
1	12	27.4
2	7	16.5
3	5	5

   a. Draw a fully labelled bar chart to display these findings. **(4 marks)**

   b. What conclusions can you draw about the effect of teachers' expectations on the children's learning? **(3 marks)**

2. **In a pilot study, Orne and his colleagues asked a number of casual acquaintances whether they would do the experimenter a favour; when they agreed, they were asked to perform five push-ups. Their response tended to be amazement, incredulity and the question, 'Why?' Another similar group of individuals were asked whether they would take part in an experiment of brief duration. When they agreed to do so, they too were asked to perform five push-ups. Their typical response was, 'Where?'**

   Using your knowledge of demand characteristics, explain why this different reaction from the two groups might have occurred. (4 marks)

3. **Which one of the following is an effect of demand characteristics? Choose one box.**

   a. Participants may be harmed by the experiment ☐

   b. The experimenter makes unreasonable demands on the participants ☐

   c. Participants may change their behaviour to match what they think is expected ☐

   d. The experimenter may behave differently towards participants with particular characteristics ☐

REVIEW

Many of the key studies you have met in this course have been criticised for demand characteristics. Identify the demand characteristics in:

- Asch's study
- Milgram's study
- Zimbardo's study
- Godden and Baddeley's context-dependent recall study
- Ainsworth's Strange Situation research
- any other studies you meet!

Sampling

A01 Description

- The population is the wider group of individuals the researcher is interested in. From this population they select a smaller sample to study, e.g. 20–30 participants. Ideally the sample will be representative of the population so that generalisations can be made.
- **Opportunity sample** People are recruited based on convenience or availability.
- **Random sample** Each person in the population has an equal chance of being selected.
  - > The lottery method – all names are written on slips of paper, put in a hat, and the number of names required are selected.
  - > Random number generators – everyone is given a number, and the computer picks numbers randomly.

I'm trying to sleep in here

- **Stratified sample** Subgroups within the population are identified (e.g. age groups or genders). Participants are obtained from each group in proportion to their occurrence in the population, using random selection.
- **Systematic sample** Uses a predetermined system to select participants, such as every twentieth person on a list.
- **Volunteer sample** Advertisements are placed on the Internet or on a noticeboard or in a newspaper and the study uses those who respond to this request.
- **Bias** is a distortion in the data. Biases in psychological research include: experimenter bias, interviewer bias, observer bias, social desirability bias, and sampling biases.
  - > Sample bias – a sample inevitably differs from the population and does not perfectly represent it.
  - > Volunteer bias occurs because volunteers are likely to differ from the population, as they are willing and available to take part.

A03 Evaluation/Discussion

Most studies use opportunity or volunteer sampling...

| These are the easiest methods, and so take less time to find a sample than other methods. | However, an opportunity sample is inevitably biased by who happened to be available at the time. | Volunteer bias can also be a problem, as participants may be highly motivated to take part, and therefore differ from a typical member of the population. |

Random sampling is theoretically the least biased method...

| All members of the population have an equal chance of being selected. | However, it requires a list of names of all members of the population, from which a random selection is recruited. | This is time consuming, and some randomly selected people may refuse to take part, resulting in a biased sample. |

Stratified sampling can be more representative than some methods...

| This is because there is a proportional representation of subgroups. | However, subgroups must be identified and and, participants randomly selected from subgroups, then contacted. | This is very time consuming, and people may not agree to participate, giving a biased sample. |

 APPLY: Exam skills

AO2: Three for you to try

1. **A psychologist plans to study the use of mobile phones by adults. The psychologist selects 30 participants for the study and divides them into two groups: heavy users (more than three calls per day) and light users (three calls or fewer per day). All participants are rated for friendliness to test the hypothesis that heavy users are more friendly than light users.**

   Answer the following questions:

   a. Identify a suitable method to use for selecting the sample and explain how this sample would be obtained. **(3 marks)**

   b. Identify one strength of using this sampling technique in this study. **(2 marks)**

   c. Identify the experimental design. **(1 mark)**

   d. Identify the operationalised independent variable (IV) in this study. **(2 marks)**

   e. Explain why this is a natural experiment. **(2 marks)**

2. **Student answers to the following question are given below.**

   > A study used opportunity sampling. Evaluate the choice of this sampling technique. (3 marks)

   What marks would you give the following answers?

   Dylan's answer

   Opportunity sampling can create a bias as the types of people who are available will vary depending on the time and place. However, opportunity sampling is often good because it doesn't involve a long process or special criteria for how to choose participants.

   Carrie's answer

   Opportunity sampling allows you to take advantage of whoever is available to the researcher at the time. This means there is a high chance of bias and low population validity therefore this may not be representative data.

   Charlotte's answer

   Opportunity sampling is a good technique because everyone has an equal chance of being in the research. However, it may be biased and participants may not be aware that they are being studied.

Student	Mark
Dylan	
Carrie	
Charlotte	

3. **The table below lists the three main methods used to select participants. Underneath the table are descriptions of the sampling methods used in various studies.**

   Place the letters A–F next to the appropriate sampling method.

Sampling method	Matching description
Opportunity sample	
Volunteer sample	
Random sample	

   A A study is conducted in a primary school. Only ten participants are needed. All the names in the school are put in a hat and ten names are drawn out.

   B Some psychology students advertise for participants by putting a notice on the school noticeboard.

   C A psychology class do an experiment in class and the participants are the class members.

   D Opinions on smoking are collected by interviewing people in a town centre.

   E People fill in a questionnaire in a magazine and the data is used in a psychology study.

   F Participants for a child health study are selected by using computer-generated numbers to pick 100 names from a list of the babies born in the UK in the week beginning 1 January 2013.

How do I answer... questions about sampling?

When you are asked to suggest a suitable method of sampling, it must be one that is practical and appropriate for the study described. There are usually several possible options, but opportunity or volunteer samples can be used for most types of research, and in fact they generally are!

> Suggest a suitable method of selecting participants for this study, and explain how the researcher could select this sample. (4 marks)

In this example, there would be 1 mark for naming a sampling method that is appropriate for the study. The other 3 marks are for explaining **how** the researcher actually goes about selecting the participants. You need to give step-by-step instructions. For example, for random sampling, say three things for 3 marks:

- Write names of all possible participants (your population) on pieces of paper.
- Put them in a bowl.
- Take out an appropriate number (you need to suggest how many, e.g. 20) – this is your sample.

 REVIEW

How were samples chosen in key studies that you have learned about? What are the evaluation points relating to these methods of sampling in those studies? Think through how you would explain specifically how the sampling affects the population validity of the conclusions. For example, 'Asch's study was carried out on male students, so may not apply to females as they may have different rates of conformity. This gives his conclusions low population validity.'

Ethical issues

RECAP

A01 Description

- Ethical issues are conflicts between what the researcher wants to do in order to conduct useful and meaningful research, and the rights of participants. All research must be conducted in an ethically appropriate way, including student research.

- The British Psychological Society (BPS) identifies four ethical principles for researchers:

  1. Respect for the dignity of people.
  2. Competence – high standards of professional work.
  3. Responsibility – to clients and the public.
  4. Integrity – honest research and reporting.

- **Informed consent** means telling participants the true aim of a study and what is going to happen, so they can make an informed decision about participating.

  > They should be aware of any potential risks or benefits, although researchers cannot always predict the risks or benefits of taking part in a study.

  > Researchers may not want to reveal the true aims of a study because it could change the way the participants behave.

- **Deception** can be necessary to avoid demand characteristics. There is a difference between withholding some details of the research aims (acceptable) and deliberately giving false information (less acceptable).

  > The issue is that deception can lead people to see psychologists as untrustworthy, and contravenes the right to informed consent.

  > However, much of the deception in research is minor and harmless, and participants would have little reason to refuse to take part.

- **The right to withdraw** is important if participants feel distressed during a study, particularly if they were not fully informed.

  > Participants should not lose any payments or rewards by withdrawing.

  > The problem is that if participants do leave during the study the sample will become biased, as those who remain may be more compliant or hardy.

- **Protection from harm** Research is considered acceptable if the risk of harm (physical or psychological) is no greater than a participant would be likely to experience in ordinary life, and they leave the study in the same state in which they arrived.

  > However, this is difficult to guarantee as studies addressing some important questions may involve a degree of distress or embarrassment, and outcomes may be hard to predict.

- **Confidentiality** is a legal right for participants. Personal data can only be recorded in such a way that the participants cannot be identified.

  > This can be difficult to protect, as researchers wish to publish the findings. They can guarantee anonymity, but it may be possible to identify details of participants from their particular characteristics in a small target population.

- **Privacy** People would not expect to be observed by others in certain situations, such as in their own homes, whereas in public places (a park, for example), being observed would not feel so invasive.

  > Researchers may need to study participants without their awareness, which could be seen as an invasion of privacy.

APPLY: Exam skills

A02: Two for you to try

1. **In the Stanford Prison Experiment the researchers took great care to gain informed consent. However, the participants did not know the amount of psychological distress that would be caused by participating.**

   Discuss how the issue of psychological harm could have been dealt with more effectively in this study. (6 marks)

2. **Which one of the ethical principles in psychological research can be an issue for researchers, because it can result in a biased sample? Tick one box.**

   A The right to confidentiality. ☐

   B The right to withdraw. ☐

   C The right to protection from harm. ☐

   D Informed consent. ☐

How do I answer... questions about ethical issues?

A patient with brain damage, known as JJ, has been researched for a case study. Identify **one** ethical issue associated with this case study, and suggest how psychologists could deal with it. (4 marks)

There are often questions asking you to outline ethical issues a researcher should have considered, and how they should be dealt with. Remember that an ethical issue is a potential conflict between the rights of the participant and the aims of the researcher.

- First identify an issue that is likely to be relevant to this study, e.g. 'informed consent'.
- Then explain why it is an issue, e.g. 'JJ may not fully understand what he is being asked, or may not remember consenting.'
- Then suggest how it should be dealt with. This suggestion must be relevant to the particular study, and be reasonably practical, e.g. 'Consent should be obtained from a carer and the researcher should take care to stop the research if JJ becomes distressed.'

Dealing with ethical issues

RECAP

AO1 Description

- The **BPS 'Code of Ethics and Conduct'** gives **ethical guidelines** on which behaviours are acceptable and how to deal with ethical dilemmas. If a psychologist conducts unacceptable research, the BPS may bar them from practising.

- **Ethics committees** in research institutions must approve any study before it can go ahead, after considering how researchers intend to deal with ethical issues.

Dealing with specific ethical issues

- **Deception** Any deception must be approved by an ethics committee after a **cost–benefit analysis**, which attempts to judge the research in terms of its costs and benefits to the participants themselves and to society as a whole. However, cost–benefit decisions are flawed because the outcomes are not evident until after the study.

- **Informed consent** Participants sign a consent form and are offered the right to withdraw. However, if participants are given full information this may invalidate the study. Even if they have been fully informed, do they really understand what they have agreed to?

- **Presumptive consent** could be used instead. However, presumptive consent assumes that people can imagine the scenario and their responses accurately, which may not be the case.

- **Debriefing** Participants must be fully **debriefed** and have the opportunity to discuss any concerns and withdraw their data. A problem could be that debriefing can't undo any harm to participants.

- **Right to withdraw** Participants should be informed at the beginning of the study that they can withdraw at any time without losing any benefits. However, participants may feel they shouldn't withdraw because it might spoil the study.

- **Protection from harm** The study should be stopped if harm is suspected. However, harm may only become apparent later.

- **Confidentiality** Researchers should use numbers or false names to protect participants' confidentiality. However, it may be possible to identify participants via details of location, etc.

- **Privacy** To protect privacy, researchers should not study anyone without their informed consent, unless it is public behaviour in a public place. A limitation is that it is not universally agreed what constitutes a public place.

AO3 Evaluation/Discussion

Ethical guidelines...

The 'rules and sanctions' approach has limitations, as it is impossible to cover every situation that might arise in research.

The Canadian approach instead encourages debate around hypothetical dilemmas.

This encourages psychologists to engage deeply with ethical issues, rather than just following rules.

Limitations of a cost-benefit approach...

It is difficult to predict the costs and benefits before a study, or to quantify them afterwards.

Diana Baumrind argued that cost-benefit analysis can legitimise unethical practices, such as deception and harm, if the benefits are seen to be great enough.

This means that cost-benefit analysis simply exchanges one set of dilemmas for another.

APPLY: Exam skills

 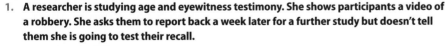

AO2: One for you to try

1. **A researcher is studying age and eyewitness testimony. She shows participants a video of a robbery. She asks them to report back a week later for a further study but doesn't tell them she is going to test their recall.**

   At this second session she shows participants some photographs and asks them to identify the robber and one of the victims. There are two groups of participants: children aged 6–10 years and adults aged 30–40 years.

   Answer the following questions:

   a. Identify two ethical issues associated with this study. Suggest how psychologists could deal with each of these issues. **(8 marks)**

   b. Aside from ethical issues, explain one potential problem with this study. **(2 marks)**

   c. Explain the purpose of the BPS Code of Ethics. **(3 marks)**

REVIEW

Get into the practice of analysing the ethical issues associated with any study you learn about, and how the researcher dealt with them (or should have). When you make a mind-map to revise a key study, think about ethical issues and how they were (or should have been) dealt with. Check through your revision notes or mind-maps and add the ethical issues on if necessary.

Observational techniques

 RECAP

AO1 Description

- In a **naturalistic observation**, behaviour is studied in a natural situation, and the researcher does not interfere with what is happening.

- In a **controlled observation**, some aspects of the environment are organised by the researcher, enabling them to investigate the effects of particular objects or situations on behaviour. For example, Ainsworth's Strange Situation.

- In an **overt observation**, participants are aware that they are being observed. Researchers carrying out overt observation try to be as unobtrusive as possible, and may be hidden behind a one-way mirror.

- A **covert observation** takes place without participants' awareness. Knowing that behaviour is being observed is likely to alter the participants' behaviour.

- In **non-participant observation**, the observer watches from a distance and does not interact with participants.

- In **participant observation**, the observer joins the group being observed, either overtly or covertly.

- If two or more observers record behaviour, then **inter-observer reliability** can be calculated. More than 80 per cent consistency between their data indicates a high level of reliability.

Overt and covert observations

AO3 Evaluation / Discussion

Observational studies may have high validity…

They record people's actual behaviour, including any unexpected behaviour.	However, it is difficult for observers to be objective; what they observe can be distorted by their expectations. Only observable behaviours are recorded, not thoughts or motivations.	*This means that observer bias and interpretation of behaviour can affect the internal validity of the findings.*

Naturalistic versus controlled observations…

Naturalistic observations are high in ecological validity, especially if participants are unaware that they are being observed.	However, other variables are not controlled, so may influence behaviour. On the other hand, controlled observations enable control of the environment so observers can focus on specific behaviours.	*However, this is at the cost of ecological validity as the situation may feel unnatural to participants. This leads to a trade-off between ecological validity and control.*

Ethical issues arise in covert observations…

As participants are unaware they are being observed, they cannot give or withhold consent.	In addition, the researcher must take care not to invade people's privacy while observing them.	*The observer can sometimes seek retrospective consent, but it is not always possible to follow up people who have been observed in a public place.*

 APPLY: Exam skills

AO2: One for you to try

In each of the studies described below, decide whether the study involved observations that were:

a. naturalistic or controlled **(1 mark)**

b. overt or covert **(1 mark)**

c. participant or non-participant **(1 mark)**

Study A Ainsworth studied infant attachment patterns using the Strange Situation (see p.50). Infants and a caregiver were placed in a room with a predetermined and fixed set of toys.

They were observed through a one-way mirror so that the infants wouldn't be disturbed by the observer's presence. Caregivers gave informed consent.

Study B Ainsworth also studied 26 mothers and their infants who lived in six villages in Uganda. She observed the mothers in their own homes interacting as they normally would with their infants.

Study C One study observed boys and girls aged three to five years during their free-play periods at nursery school, without the children's awareness. The researchers classified activities as male, female or neutral and recorded how playmates responded.

Study D Moore spent weeks walking round New York, writing down everything he heard and uncovering some interesting exchanges between people he observed.

Study E Rosenhan conducted a classic study on insanity. Sane individuals pretended to hear voices and were admitted to mental hospitals. While in hospital they noted down the behaviour of the staff in the institution and the patients.

Observational design

RECAP

A01 Description

- In **unstructured observations**, the researcher records all relevant behaviour, but without an observational system. This may be useful in a novel situation to decide what behaviours could be more systematically recorded.

- Once researchers have decided which behaviours are relevant and observable, they can plan a **structured observation** using behavioural categories and sampling procedures.

- **Behavioural categories** Behaviours must be operationalised by breaking them down into categories which are:

  > Objective – not requiring interpretation, just recording explicit actions.

  > Comprehensive – covering all possible component behaviours, without an 'other' box.

  > Mutually exclusive – each behaviour must fit in only one category .

- **Sampling** procedures. The observer should ideally record every instance of a behaviour. However, if the behaviours are very frequent this becomes impossible so sampling enables observers to calculate an estimate of the frequency of the behaviour.

  > **Event sampling** Counting the number of times a certain behaviour occurs in a target individual in a period of time. For example, counting how many times a person smiles in ten minutes.

  > **Time sampling** Noting what a target individual is doing every 30 seconds (or an appropriate time interval), by ticking behavioural categories on a checklist.

APPLY: Exam skills

A02: Three for you to try

1. **A psychologist observed ten infants using the Strange Situation technique.**

   Answer the following questions:

   a. Identify two behavioural categories used in this technique. **(2 marks)**

   b. Identify one limitation of using observational techniques. **(2 marks)**

   c. Give one strength of conducting an observational study in a laboratory setting. **(2 marks)**

2. **A researcher decided to observe a sloth at the zoo over a two-hour period, and record all of its behaviour.**

   What kind of observation was the researcher using?

   A Time sampling. ☐

   B Event sampling. ☐

   C Structured observation. ☐

   D Unstructured observation. ☐

3. **A researcher is interested in what young people talk about. He sits in a pub and records the conversations he hears.**

   Identify one ethical issue the researcher would need to consider in this research, and suggest how the researcher could deal with this ethical issue. (3 marks).

How do I answer... questions about observational design?

Q1: A research team investigated peer relations in children. They planned to observe children in their day-care environment and assess their social development. To conduct the observations they selected behavioural categories, one of which was 'argues with other children'.

a. Suggest one other relevant behavioural category the researcher could select in this study. (1 mark)

b. How could the researchers use time sampling to collect their data? (3 marks)

You may be asked questions about aspects of observational research, like the question above, or you may be asked to design an observational study. In either case, you need to choose some behavioural categories and make decisions about sampling.

For **Q1:a** the behavioural category must be clearly observable and relevant to the research question, e.g. 'playing with other children'.

For **Q1:b** you need to describe the process of time sampling, and decide what is a sensible length of time for the observation, and how often behaviours should be tallied. For example, the children's behaviour could be recorded on video for one hour. Then the researchers could watch the video and record behaviours every 30 seconds by ticking the behavioural categories on a tally chart.

REVIEW

If you carry out the two types of sampling yourself, you will remember the process better. Try observing your friends or family, or a pet, going about their normal lives. (Overt or covert? Participant or non-participant?)

First you will need to do some unstructured observation to identify some suitable behavioural categories. Then, for your structured observation, decide on your sampling method, make a tally sheet, and collect some data.

Try both sampling methods to see which is easier and which seems to give a better representation of behaviour. For example, if your cat sleeps for the entire 30 minutes of your observation, that behaviour would only be tallied once with event sampling, but 30 times with time sampling at one-minute intervals! Don't forget ethical issues: respect your participants' privacy, informed consent and right to withdraw (unless it's your cat of course…).

Self-report techniques

 RECAP

A01 Description

- **Questionnaires** are a predetermined set of written questions which can permit a researcher to find out what people think and feel.
  - > They can be used to collect quantitative data which is then analysed using statistical tests, or qualitative data which gives deeper insight into individuals' experiences.
  - > The questionnaire may provide data directly to answer a research question. Alternatively, it may be part of an experimental study, for example to identify two groups of participants with different beliefs (the IV) in order to explore their responses (the DV).

- **Structured interviews** also have predetermined questions. The interviewer reads out the questions and the interviewee replies. There is no deviation from the written questions.
- In an **unstructured interview**, the interviewer may begin with general aims and a few starting questions, but the conversation develops depending on the answers given.

A03 Evaluation/Discussion

Self-report techniques may lack validity…

| Researchers are trying to gain access to people's thoughts, feelings and attitudes. | However, people may not be able to express their thoughts clearly, or may not be truthful. | This leads to a **social desirability bias** in the findings, as people answer in a way which presents them in a good light. |

Questionnaires and interviews can both give biased data…

| Questionnaires can be used to collect data from a large sample of people, and people may be more honest in them than in an interview. | However, people who complete questionnaires may not be representative of the population as they have to have time and motivation. | On the other hand, interviewers can influence the answers people give, by unconscious non-verbal signals, giving interviewer bias. |

Data from structured interviews is easier to analyse than from unstructured interviews…

| Unstructured interviews are similar to questionnaires, and data from standardised questions can be analysed quite simply. | However, in an unstructured interview the interviewer tailors the questions to specific responses, so answers are harder to analyse. | But unstructured interviews allow researchers to obtain more detailed information and deeper insights into individuals' feelings, thoughts and experiences. |

 APPLY: Exam skills

A02: Two for you to try

1. **A psychologist conducted a study of day care experiences of children, using a questionnaire with children aged 10–18 who had attended day care before they started school.**
   a. Explain why the psychologist might want to carry out a pilot study before the main study. **(2 marks)**
   b. For this study, explain one strength of collecting information using a questionnaire. **(3 marks)**
   c. The researcher wonders if it might be better to use an interview instead of a questionnaire. Explain why an interview might be better. **(3 marks)**

2. **Which of the following does not affect data collected using self-report techniques? (1 mark)**
   A Social desirability bias.
   B Observer bias.
   C Interviewer bias.
   D Sample bias.

 **REVIEW**

Make sure you can distinguish between interviews and questionnaires, structured and unstructured interviews, closed and open questions, qualitative and quantitative data, and be able to explain the advantages and disadvantages of each. Test yourself by making a table, and ticking off the row when you know it.

	What is it?	Advantages	Disadvantages	Done?
Interviews				
Questionnaires				

Self-report design

RECAP

A01 Description

Questionnaire construction

- Questions should be clear (avoiding ambiguity, double negatives and double-barrelled questions) and unbiased (avoiding leading questions).

- **Closed questions** have a limited range of responses. They can include Likert scales, forced choice questions, or other tick-box questions. They can be used in questionnaires or interviews. They produce **quantitative data**, which can be summarised and analysed using graphs and statistics.

- **Open questions** allow respondents to elaborate on their answers. They give **qualitative data**, which can be rich, detailed and sometimes unexpected, but is more difficult to analyse.

Closed questions often use boxes

Design of interviews

- The same factors should be considered in designing an interview schedule. In addition, the interview must be recorded, by note-taking or audio or video recording. The interviewer should use listening skills, such as non-verbal communication, warmth and encouragement.

- Psychological tests often involve completing questionnaires, and include IQ tests, personality tests, mood scales, attitude scales and aptitude scales. The data is then analysed by a psychologist to produce a profile or score. They are not really self-report techniques, but many of the same considerations are relevant.

- If all the questions in a test are too easy, then everyone will do well. This is called a ceiling effect. Conversely, if all the questions are too hard, most people will score very low – a floor effect. It is important, therefore, to include a range of questions of different difficulties, and to test out the questions in a pilot study.

> **Issues/Debates**
> See Idiographic and nomothetic research. Nomothetic research often uses closed questions and quantitative data, whereas idiographic research is more likely to use qualitative data collected from semi-structured or unstructured interviews, using open questions.

A03 Evaluation/Discussion

Closed and open questions both have disadvantages...

| Closed questions can force people to choose answers which may not represent their true beliefs, affecting validity. | Open questions, however, may be time-consuming to answer, so many people only give brief answers, particularly in writing. | *An interview allows clarifying questions or deeper exploration of issues, giving a clearer idea of people's individual lived experiences.* |

APPLY: Exam skills

A02: One for you to try

1. **You have been asked to construct questions for an interview about people's attitudes towards smoking.**

   a. Write one closed question and one open question for this interview. **(2 marks + 2 marks)**

   b. When asking questions about smoking attitudes, what factors might be important in an interviewer's behaviour? **(4 marks)**

   c. An interviewer should avoid using leading questions. Give an example of a leading question that the interviewer should avoid in this interview. **(1 mark)**

How do I answer... questions about self-report design?

Q1: You have been asked to research 16-year-olds' attitudes to alcohol, using a questionnaire.

    a. Briefly discuss the benefits for researchers of including both open and closed questions in this questionnaire. **(4 marks)**

    b. Write one question suitable for this questionnaire. Explain which type of question it is and why you think it would be suitable. **(5 marks)**

To answer this question, you need to apply your knowledge to the particular research area (AO2).

You need four points for **Q1:a**. Think of a point about closed or open questions, and make sure it is relevant to this research topic. Make sure your points are all benefits, not limitations.

You could explain how closed questions give quantitative data, which is easier to collate and display. They limit the answers participants can give, which can make sure the researchers find out about the particular aspects of attitudes to alcohol they are interested in. On the other hand, open questions allow the teenagers to elaborate their answers, which gives rich, qualitative data about attitudes to alcohol. They also allow the teenagers to say things that the researchers hadn't anticipated.

For **Q1:b**, you could choose to write an open or a closed question. If you write an open question, make sure it is not possible to answer it with 'yes' or 'no' or any other single word. A good way to start is, 'Explain why...' or 'Describe how...'.

If you write a closed question, make sure you give the answer options, with tick boxes. For example, 'Do you ever consume alcoholic drinks at home with your family? Yes ☐ No ☐'

Correlations

📖 RECAP

AO1 Description

- A **correlation** is a systematic association between two **continuous variables**. A continuous variable can take on any value within a certain range, and can be displayed on a regular numbered scale on a graph.

- Studies using correlational analysis are known as correlational studies. The results can be displayed on a **scattergram**, where each point plotted shows the values of the two variables for one individual.

- A correlational hypothesis states the expected association between the **co-variables**. This could be:

  > a **positive correlation** – as one increases, the other increases.

  > a **negative correlation** – as one increases, the other decreases.

  > **zero correlation** – no association.

- A non-directional correlational hypothesis states that there is a relationship between the two variables, without specifying the direction of the relationship.

- A **correlation coefficient** is a number between -1 and +1 which tells us how closely the co-variables are related. A perfect positive correlation would be +1, and a perfect negative correlation would be -1. A strong correlation has a correlation coefficient closer to +1 or -1 and a weak correlation is nearer to zero.

- The statistical **significance** of the correlation depends on the number of participants. This can be analysed using tables of significance. (See **A Level Year 2 Student Book** p.30–31.)

−0.9	0	+0.5
Strong negative	No correlation	Moderate correlation

AO3 Evaluation / Discussion

Correlation can be used when it is not possible to manipulate a variable…

This contrasts with an experiment, where the investigator manipulates the IV in order to observe the effect on the DV.

Correlations can therefore be used to investigate trends in data that may have been collected for another purpose.

However, this means that no conclusion can be made about one co-variable causing a change in another in a correlational study.

Correlation does not imply causation…

There may be **intervening variables** that explain the association between the co-variables. Alternatively, the causal relationship may be the opposite of what it seems (i.e. B causes A rather than A causes B).

For example, a correlation between attendance and exam results may have other explanations, such as personal circumstances or motivation to succeed. We cannot conclude that increasing attendance would improve results.

This means that further investigation would need to be carried out to find out if the relationship is causal.

Validity should still be considered in a correlational study…

Issues such as the generalisability of the sample or the operationalisation of variables would affect external (population) validity and internal validity.

However, correlational studies can often be easily replicated, so findings can be confirmed.

In addition, causality can be explored further using experimental or longitudinal methods.

Correlations are not always linear…

AO3 PLUS

Linear correlations produce a scattergram with values lying on a straight line. However, a curvilinear correlation is also possible.

This is a consistent relationship between two variables, the nature of which changes as one variable increases, for example the relationship between anxiety and accuracy of eyewitness testimony.

This requires a different sort of statistical significance testing, to see how closely the data fits a curve rather than a straight line.

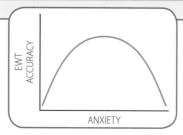

APPLY: Exam skills

AO2: Three for you to try

1. **A research study looks at the relationship between hours spent in day care per week and aggressiveness. The study finds a positive correlation.**

   Answer the following questions:

   a. Suggest how you might operationalise aggressiveness. **(2 marks)**

   b. Write an appropriate non-directional hypothesis for this study. **(2 marks)**

   c. One newspaper claimed that the results showed time in day care caused aggressiveness. Explain why this claim may be untrue. **(3 marks)**

   d. Explain one strength of using a correlational analysis in this study. **(3 marks)**

2. **Explain why it would be appropriate for the researcher to use a pilot study in this research above. (4 marks)**

   Hint: When a question includes the phrase 'in this study' or 'in this research', you must refer to details of the study in your answer.

3. **Match up the terms with their descriptions.**

1	Positive correlation	**A**	Bottom left to top right.
2	Negative correlation	**B**	A number that expresses the strength of a correlation.
3	Zero correlation	**C**	All dots close together in a line.
4	Correlation coefficient	**D**	Random scatter.
5	Scattergram	**E**	Top left to bottom right.
6	Strong correlation	**F**	Graph showing correlational data.

REVIEW

Remember – a 'relationship' between two variables means a correlation, and is represented on a scattergram, or with a correlation coefficient. Can you write a correlational hypothesis? Are you clear how it differs from an experimental hypothesis?

How do I answer... questions about correlation?

> **Q1:** A researcher used standardised tests to measure children's intelligence and happiness. Analysis of the scores from the two tests gave a correlation coefficient of 0.31.
>
> a. Write a hypothesis for this study. (2 marks)
>
> b. What do these findings show about the relationship between intelligence and happiness? (3 marks)

For **Q1:a** the hypothesis must be in the form, 'There is a (positive/negative) relationship between . . . '. Be careful to express it correctly, so it is not an experimental hypothesis (variable A *affects* variable B, OR there is a *difference* between condition A and condition B).

As you have not been told about previous research, it must be non-directional. So, for this example, you would write *There is a relationship between children's intelligence as measured on a standardised test and their happiness scores.*

A null hypothesis would also be fine:

There is no relationship between children's intelligence as measured on a standardised test and their happiness scores.

If you were given information about previous research you could have written a directional hypothesis. There are two possibilities for this, depending on the direction of the relationship: 'There is a positive correlation between...' or 'There is a negative relationship between . . .'.

Just make sure you don't use the words 'effects' or 'difference' as these would express an experimental hypothesis, not a correlational one.

For **Q1:b**, describe the **strength** and **direction** of the relationship: 'It is a weak positive correlation'. Then elaborate, using the names of the variables, 'so as happiness scores increase, intelligence scores also increase'.

Generally, a correlation of 0 to +0.4 can be described as 'weak positive', between +0.4 and +0.6 is 'moderate', and above +0.6 is 'strong'. For negative correlations the same rough guide applies: weak negative is 0 to -0.4, moderate negative is -0.4 to -0.6, and strong negative is -0.6 to -1.0.

However, be aware that a weak correlation can still be statistically significant, if there is a very large sample size! (See A Level Year 1 Student Book p.206.)

Other research methods

AO1 Description

- Some studies don't neatly fit any category of research methods, but are simply investigations of particular situations: for example, Milgram's study of obedience.

- Many published studies use a combination of research methods. For example, Schaffer and Emerson's study of attachment (see p.42) used naturalistic observation, interviews and rating scales, but also included an experimental element.

- **Systematic review** studies use databases of published research to search for studies addressing a particular aim or hypothesis.

- A **meta-analysis** then assesses trends in the data and evaluates the **effect size** across all of the studies, using statistical analysis.

- Other research methods:
  - > A longitudinal study of an individual or group can observe long-term effects such as treatments or ageing.
  - > A cross-sectional study compares groups at the same point in time, for example 20-year-olds and 50-year-olds in 2015.
  - > In cross-cultural studies, researchers compare samples from different cultures in a kind of natural experiment. For example, the IV could be childrearing practices in different cultures, and the DV could be a particular behaviour such as attachment.
  - > Role play (such as Zimbardo's prison simulation study) is a form of controlled observation.

AO3 Evaluation/Discussion

Meta-analysis can increase the validity of conclusions...

Conclusions are based on a wider sample of participants, so an overall conclusion can be drawn, even if the original studies produced contradictory results.

However, the research designs of the original studies may vary considerably, so they may not be truly comparable.

This means that conclusions should still be examined carefully for validity.

Case studies

- **Case studies** are the detailed study of a single individual, institution or event.
  - > Many research methods may be used, such as observation, interview (of the person themselves or their family and friends), psychological tests or experiments.
  - > Case studies are often longitudinal, following an individual over an extended period of time.

Content analysis

- **Content analysis** is a form of indirect observation by analysing a sample of artefacts produced by people, such as TV programmes, articles, adverts, songs, paintings, etc.
  - > It aims to systematically describe the content, often tallying coding units (themes or behavioural categories) to transform qualitative into quantitative data.

> **Issues/Debates**
> Idiographic and nomothetic research

AO3 Evaluation/Discussion

Case studies provide rich, in-depth data relating to an individual or an event...

AO3 PLUS

They are also valuable for investigating rare cases or situations that could not be generated experimentally for ethical reasons.

However, case studies are often unique, and data is gathered retrospectively (e.g. after brain damage), so we do not know what abnormalities were already present.

This makes the findings difficult to generalise to other populations and other situations.

Content analysis is based on observations of material produced by people in real life...

AO3 PLUS

If these sources can also be accessed by other researchers then findings can be replicated.

But different observers may interpret the meanings of material and the behavioural categories or coding systems differently, due to observer bias.

Therefore, content analysis has high ecological validity, but may lack reliability and internal validity.

APPLY: Exam skills

AO2: Three for you to try

1. The effects of privation were investigated by looking at one institution in Eastern Europe where orphaned children were looked after.

Answer the following questions:

a. Aside from interviewing the staff at the institution, describe one other technique that might be used as part of this case study. **(2 marks)**

b. In order to conduct this study the researchers had to select just one institution in Eastern Europe. Describe a sampling method they might have used to select this institution. **(2 marks)**

2. A university psychology department is asked to conduct a case study of the 2011 riots in London.

a. Psychologists use a range of techniques to gather information in case studies. Outline one technique that the psychologists could use in this case study. **(2 marks)**

b. Apart from ethical issues, explain one or more limitations that may be a problem in this case study. **(4 marks)**

c. Explain one strength of studying this behaviour by using a case study. **(2 marks)**

3. Match up the terms with their definitions.

1 Lab experiment	**A** The relationship between continuous variables is analysed.
2 Field experiment	**B** A study where the researcher does not interfere in any way.
3 Natural experiment	
4 Study using correlational analysis	**C** Experiment conducted in an everyday setting where the experimenter controls the IV.
5 Observation	**D** Using observations of behaviour made indirectly.
6 Naturalistic observation	**E** Study with IV and DV, in a contrived environment with high level of control.
7 Controlled observation	
8 Content analysis	**F** A study where behaviour is recorded by watching or listening to what people do.
9 Questionnaire	**G** A self-report technique with a predetermined set of questions in written form.
10 Interview	
11 Case study	**H** A detailed study of one individual, group or event.

I Study with an IV and DV, where researcher makes use of an IV that is not controlled by the researcher.

J A self-report technique where questions are delivered by another person who may respond if needed.

K A study using observational techniques where the researcher controls some aspects of the environment.

How do I answer... 'Design a study' questions?

Q1: Research has shown that pet ownership can benefit the mental health of elderly people with dementia. Design an experiment to investigate the effect of cats on the mood of elderly patients with dementia. You should provide details of:
- Design – including the experimental design, a research hypothesis and controls.
- Data analysis – including reference to suitable descriptive and inferential statistics.
- Ethical issues and how these could be dealt with.

(12 marks)

You may be asked to design a study to answer a particular research question. You will then be given bullet points to tell you what you must include in your answer, such as sampling, design, analysis of data, how to establish reliability, ethical issues, a consent or debrief form, etc.

1 Start by imagining how the research could work. Is it an observation, an experiment, self-report, or something else? You need a simple, fairly practical and ethical idea. In this example you also need to make sure that you would collect data you know how to analyse (see the A Level Year 2 Student Book for inferential statistical tests).

2 You do need to include some explanation of your methodology, but just an outline, so that you can explain your decisions about the different aspects of the research you have been asked about. If a bullet point asks you to describe the procedure, you would need to provide more detail.

3 Think about the bullet points in the question. Use them as side headings to organise your answer, and don't write about aspects of research that you're not asked for. (In this example you would get no credit for describing the sampling, for instance.) Use the bullet points as a checklist, and cross off each part as you complete it. They will probably get roughly equal weighting in terms of marks, so divide your answer equally between the points.

REVIEW

For any research method you meet in an exam question, you may need to be able to describe how it works, and evaluate it. What are the strengths and limitations of each? Use the checklist in the **AO2: Three for you to try Q3** (matching terms and definitions exercise) to think this through.

Meta-analyses are often based on a more varied sample of participants

Mathematical skills

AO1 Description

Mathematical requirements in the specification

- Ten per cent of the marks in the AS and A Level exams are related to mathematical skills. These include arithmetic, handling data, simple algebra and graphs.

Some basic mathematical concepts

- A **fraction** expresses part of a whole number. For example, if there are 120 participants in a study and 40 are in condition A, this is $\frac{40}{120}$. This can be simplified to $\frac{1}{3}$ as the top and bottom of the fraction can be divided by 40.

- A **percentage** is a fraction out of 100, so 5% means $\frac{5}{100}$ or $\frac{1}{20}$.

- As a **decimal** this would be 0.05.

- To change a fraction to a percentage, first divide the top by the bottom using a calculator to make a decimal. Then multiply by 100.

  > For example, in an EWT experiment 13 participants matched a face correctly, and 27 did not. What percentage chose the correct face?

  > The total number of participants is 13 + 27 = 40.

  > 13 ÷ 40 = 0.325 = 32.5%.

- **Ratios** show how much there is of one thing compared to another thing.

  > For example, if the ratio of insecurely (type A) to securely (type B) attached infants is 2:3, that means out of every 5 children, 2 are type A and 3 are type B.

  > So out of 50 children there will be 20 type A and 30 type B.

- It is a good idea to **estimate** the result of a calculation, to check your answer makes sense. You can do this by rounding and by checking whether a result should be smaller (if you have divided) or larger (if you have multiplied) than the starting numbers.

  > However, if you multiply by a number less than 1, the result will be smaller.

  > For example, 24 × 0.5 = 12.

- You may be asked to round a number to 2 or 3 **significant figures**. The rest of the digits are then replaced by zeros. You must consider whether to round up or down.

  > So, for example, the fraction $\frac{19}{36}$ is 52.7777778% as a percentage.

  > This can be rounded to 52.8% to 3 significant figures (sf), or 53% to 2 sf, or even 50% to 1 sf.

- With very large or very small numbers we can put them into **standard form**. This enables us to compare their **order of magnitude**.

  > For example, 8,600,000,000 is 8.6 x 10^9. The 9 represents how many places the number has moved in relation to the decimal point (we have divided by 10^9 or 1000,000,000).

  > 0.0045 is 4.5×10^{23} (as we have multiplied by 10^3 or 1000).

  > 5.8×10^3 is less than 2.1×10^4 because it is a lower order of magnitude. ($5.8 \times 10^3 = 5,800$ and $2.1 \times 10^4 = 21,000$)

Useful mathematical symbols:

= and ~	< and <<	> and >>	≤	∝
Equal and approximately equal	Less than and much less than	More than and much more than	Less than or equal to	Proportional to

 # APPLY: Exam skills

A02: Three for you to try

1. **A psychologist carried out an observation of baby monkeys with their mothers and aunts. She filmed a baby interacting with each adult separately for ten minutes. She then used a time sampling technique to record the frequencies of different behaviours by the baby. Her findings are shown in the table below.**

	Gripping adult	Suckling	Being groomed by adult	Total
Mother	11	8	1	20
Aunt	5	0	15	20
Total	16	8	16	40

   a. In what percentage of the total observations was the baby suckling? Show your calculations. **(2 marks)**

   b. In what fraction of total observations was the baby being groomed? **(2 marks)**

   c. What was the frequency of time sampling used by the researcher? **(1 mark)**

2. a. Give $\frac{3}{8}$ as a percentage. Give your answer to two significant figures. **(2 marks)**

   b. Explain what the following expression means, where n is the number of girls, and m is the number of boys: $n < m$. **(1 mark)**

   c. Express 0.02 as a fraction. **(1 mark)**

   d. A researcher wants to divide 4,526 by 42. Estimate what the result would be, explaining how you arrived at your answer. **(2 marks)**

   e. If there are 36 participants divided into four groups, how many will be in each group? **(1 mark)**

   f. In the AS Psychology exam, there are two exam papers of 72 marks each. At least 25% of the marks will relate to Research Methods. How many marks will this be altogether? **(2 marks)**

   g. In the A Level Psychology exam, there are three exam papers of 96 marks each. At least 10% of the marks will require mathematical skills. How many marks will this be altogether? Give your answer to two significant figures. **(2 marks)**

3. **Match up the fraction with the correct decimal and percentage.**

$\frac{1}{10}$	0.1875	4%
$\frac{1}{25}$	0.125	50%
$\frac{3}{16}$	0.1	18.75%
$\frac{1}{8}$	0.5	12.5%
$\frac{1}{2}$	0.55 (to 2 sf)	55% (to 2 sf)
$\frac{83}{150}$	0.04	10%

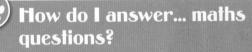 ## How do I answer... maths questions?

- You will be allowed to use a calculator in the exam – just make sure you have one.
- Make sure you show all the stages of your working as there will be marks for this as well as for the correct answer.

↻ REVIEW

If you know that you struggle with the maths needed in psychology exams, such as percentages and fractions or standard form, remember that these questions use only GCSE-level maths skills. Find some online GCSE maths questions to practise, preferably self-marking ones so you can get instant feedback. Your school or college may have access to a maths website with lots of these questions – ask a maths teacher.

Measures of central tendency and dispersion

A01 Description

- **Quantitative data** is numerical and can be summarised in terms of its central tendency and dispersion, to identify trends in the data. These are descriptive statistics.

Measures of central tendency

- **Measures of central tendency** are averages, which describe the centre of a set of data.
  - > **Mean** Add up all the values and divide by the number of items.
  - > **Median** The middle value in an ordered list. For an even number of items, the median is the mean of the central two.
  - > **Mode** The most common data item or category. A data set may be bi-modal.

Measures of dispersion

- **Measures of dispersion** describe the spread of the data.
  - > The **range** is the difference between the top and bottom values in a data set, plus one.
  - > The **standard deviation** is the average distance of each data item from the mean.

- Levels of measurement (**NOIR**):
  - > **N**ominal data is in categories that do not have any particular order, e.g. grouping people by their favourite pet.
  - > **O**rdinal data can be ranked in order but is not on a regular scale, e.g. the order of preference of pets.
  - > **I**nterval data is measured using units of equal intervals, e.g. temperature. Psychological scales can also be treated as interval data.
  - > **R**atio data relate to a true zero point, e.g. age. You don't need to be able to identify this level (as interval data includes ratio data).

A03 Evaluation/Discussion

The mean is the most sensitive measure of central tendency…

| It takes into account all the data values. | However, it can be distorted by extreme values, so may not represent the data in a skewed distribution. | In addition, the mean can only be used with ratio and interval level data. |

The median and the mode are less sensitive than the mean…

| The median is not as sensitive as the mean because it ignores all the data except the middle. | However, the median is not affected by extreme scores and can be used for ordinal data and skewed distributions. | The mode is only used for nominal data and is therefore limited in its application to different forms of data. |

The standard deviation is a very sensitive measure of dispersion…

| Like the mean, it takes into account all the data values, but is also affected by extreme scores. | It is used with the mean as a way of describing the characteristics of interval data that are normally distributed. | The range has to be used if data is skewed or ordinal. |

The modal group here is the first one, as there are 8 puppies in that group.

Nominal data counts the number in each category

APPLY: Exam skills

AO2: Two for you to try

1. **The data from a laboratory experiment is shown in the table below.**

   A student is given a series of similar puzzles to solve, and the time taken to solve the puzzle is measured in seconds.

Attempt	Time taken for student to solve a puzzle
1	72
2	67
3	61
4	55
5	56
6	34
7	39
8	43

   a. Calculate the mean time taken for the student to solve the puzzle. Show your calculations. Give your answer to 3 significant figures. **(2 marks)**

   b. Choose a suitable measure of dispersion for this data, and explain your choice. **(2 marks)**

   c. Draw a fully labelled graph of this data. **(4 marks)**

   d. What conclusions can you draw about how this student's ability to solve the puzzle changed? Suggest reasons for this change. **(3 marks)**

2. **A cognitive psychologist investigating how memory works gave participants the same word list to recall in one of two conditions. All the words were of equal difficulty.**

   Condition 1: Twenty participants recalled the words in the same room in which they had learned the words.

   Condition 2: Twenty different participants recalled the words in a different room to the one in which they had learned the words.

   Results:

Number of words recalled	Condition 1	Condition 2
Mean	16.3	11.2
Standard deviation	5.4	2.6

   What do the results in the table above show? Refer to both the mean and standard deviation in your answer. (4 marks)

How do I answer... questions about means and standard deviations?

See **AO2: Two for you to try Q2** below left. You will often be asked what the results in a table show, and instructed to refer to means and standard deviations, for 4 marks in total. The requirement is very simple:

- 2 marks for comparing the means:
  - > Make the comparison. (Which is higher than which?)
  - > Say what this tells you about the two conditions.
- 2 marks for comparing the standard deviations:
  - > Make the comparison. (Which is bigger than which? Or are they similar?)
  - > Say what this tells you about the dispersion of results in the two groups.

Remember, don't quote actual numbers, just make a comparison. And when you're comparing, you must mention both groups or conditions (e.g. The mean number of words recalled in Condition 1 is higher than the mean number of words recalled in Condition 2). You can use bullet points in answers to Research Methods questions. In this example answer, each bullet point represents one mark's worth.

So, in **AO2: Two for you to try Q2** on the left:

- The mean number of words recalled in Condition 1 is higher than that in Condition 2.
- This shows that people generally recalled the words better in the room in which they had learned the words than in a different room.
- However, the standard deviation is also much bigger in Condition 1 than in Condition 2.
- This shows that the results are more dispersed in Condition 1 than in Condition 2: some participants recalled words much better in the same room than in a different room, others didn't.

REVIEW

Practise calculating and comparing means. You won't be asked to calculate standard deviations, but you do need to be able to interpret them, and check you know how to calculate the range, the mode and the median as well.

You must also know how to choose an appropriate measure of central tendency or dispersion for a particular set of data, and justify your choice.

RECAP

A01 Description

Display of quantitative data

- Tables and graphs should have a short but informative title. Use operationalised variables as titles for columns (in a table) or axes (on a graph).

- Tables can display raw data, but they usually display summaries – measures of central tendency and dispersion for the groups or conditions.

- **Bar charts** display discrete (data that can take only certain values) or nominal (category) data. The spaces between the bars indicate the lack of continuity of the IV, which is on the horizontal axis. The vertical axis is for scores (the DV) or frequencies.

- **Histograms** are used for continuous data (data can be any measurement within a range), and the bars should therefore be touching. The vertical axis should start from zero.

- Frequency polygons display the same data as frequency histograms, but are better for comparing two or more sets of data as the bars are replaced by dots that are joined with a line.

- Line graphs have continuous data on both axes, and can be used for time series.

- Scattergrams are used for correlational analysis (p.134)

Data distributions

- The **normal distribution** is a symmetrical bell-shaped curve. Many human characteristics are normally distributed, such as height and intelligence.

  > Mean, median and mode are all at the exact mid-point.

  > The dispersion of data follows a predictable pattern, so that 68.26% of people fall within one standard deviation of the mean (half each side). Only 4.56% are more than 2 standard deviations from the mean. This distribution underlies the concept of the statistical infrequency model of abnormality (see page 60).

- In a **skewed distribution** the scores are not distributed symmetrically around the mean.

- In a **positive skewed distribution**, a few high extreme high scores have a strong effect on the mean, which will therefore be higher than the median and mode.

- In a **negative skewed distribution**, the bulk of the scores are high, e.g. if an exam was too easy (a ceiling effect) but a few extreme low scores skew the mean to the left of the median and mode.

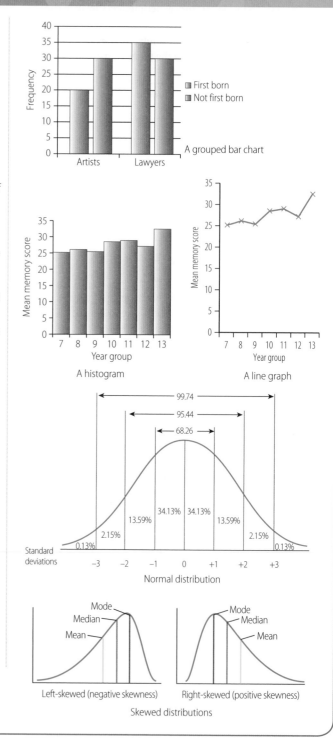

A grouped bar chart

A histogram

A line graph

Normal distribution

Left-skewed (negative skewness)

Right-skewed (positive skewness)

Skewed distributions

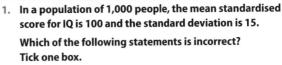

APPLY: Exam skills

A02: An example

1. *Explain why the mean is always lower than the mode in a negative skew.* **(2 marks)**

2. *What kind of skew would result if a test was too easy, so many participants got full marks?* **(1 mark)**

1. Calculation of the mean involves using all the scores in a data set so it will be drawn down by the few atypically low scores in a negatively skewed distribution. The mode is unaffected by extreme scores.

2. A ceiling effect occurs if a test is too easy for participants and most of them obtain high marks, therefore the skew would be negative (with a few low scores).

A02: One for you to try

A day care study followed children over a period of ten years, testing each child's social development every two years. The mean social development scores for children in day care and home care are shown in the graph below.

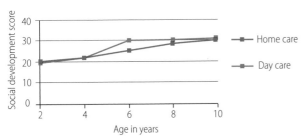

What does the graph show about the effects of day care on social development? (4 marks)

REVIEW

Can you remember which skewed distribution is which? Practise sketching them and labelling the mean, median and mode. The way to remember is: Negative skew or left skew has a long tail to the left. Positive skew or right skew has a long tail to the right.

A02: Three for you to try

1. **In a population of 1,000 people, the mean standardised score for IQ is 100 and the standard deviation is 15.**

   Which of the following statements is incorrect?
   Tick one box.

   A   All of the scores are between 85 and 115.   ☐

   B   Less than five people are likely to have an IQ above 145.   ☐

   C   Half of the population have scores above 100.   ☐

   D   The most common score (mode) is 100.   ☐

2. **Identify which type of graph is appropriate for each of these data sets:**

Data representing:	Appropriate graph
A Mean number of words recalled in each condition in a memory experiment.	
B Frequency of behaviours in each category in a naturalistic observation (e.g. children playing).	
C Participants' stress scores and illness scores obtained from questionnaires.	
D The number of participants who score 0–5, 6–10, 11–15, and 16–20 in a recall test.	
E Data comparing the number of male and female students who spend 1 hour, 2 hours, 3 hours, etc. on private study each week.	

3. **Match up the graphs with their purposes.**

1	Bar chart	**A**	Can be used to display a series of results over a period of time
2	Histogram	**B**	A distribution in which the mode is to the right of the mean
3	Frequency polygon	**C**	Graph to display frequencies of continuous data, useful for comparing two sets of data
4	Line graph	**D**	A distribution with most values to the left and a long tail to the right
5	Scattergram	**E**	Graph to display frequencies of continuous data, with touching bars
6	Normal distribution	**F**	A symmetrical bell-shaped frequency distribution
7	Positively skewed distribution	**G**	Graph to display category data
8	Negatively skewed distribution	**H**	Displays findings of a correlational study

Types of data

AO1 Description

Quantitative and qualitative data

- **Quantitative data** measures behaviour numerically.
  - > It can be collected from measurement of the DV in an experiment, or from closed questions in questionnaires and interviews.

- **Qualitative data** is non-numerical data, such as words, pictures or videos.
  - > It comes from open questions, descriptions of behaviour, and collected material such as articles, books, photos, and web forum discussions.
  - > Qualitative data can be turned into quantitative data by tallying behavioural categories in an observational study, or coding categories in a content analysis.

> **Issues/Debates**
> Idiographic and nomothetic approaches to research

How did the film make you feel?

QUAL

How frightened were you on a scale of 1-10?

QUANT

Primary and secondary data

- **Primary data** is collected directly, first-hand, by the researcher, specifically to address the aims and hypothesis of the study.
  - > Primary data can be collected using a research method such as an experiment, observation or questionnaire.
  - > The researcher designs the study, gains ethical approval, pilots the study, recruits and tests participants, analyses the data and draws conclusions.

- **Secondary data** is information gathered for a different purpose or by another researcher.
  - > It could include government statistics or health records.
  - > Secondary data is used in review studies and meta-analyses, and often in correlational studies.

AO3 Evaluation/Discussion

Quantitative data…

| Quantitative data is easy to analyse using descriptive statistics and statistical testing. | However, this may oversimplify reality, leading to meaningless conclusions. | Overall, quantitative data allows researchers to collect reliable, numerical data which can be presented in charts, graphs and statistical summaries. |

Qualitative data…

| Qualitative data provides rich, detailed description of people's lived experiences. | However, the complexity makes it more difficult to analyse the data and draw conclusions. | Qualitative data is powerful in helping researchers to explore underlying meanings of behaviour. |

Primary data…

| The researcher has high control over the type, quality and quantity of primary data they collect to test a specific hypothesis. | However, data collection is time-consuming and often expensive. | Despite these difficulties, most psychological research aims to collect primary data. |

Secondary data …

| Secondary data is easier and cheaper to access than primary data, and is valuable for meta-analyses and correlational studies. | However, it may not exactly fit the needs of a new study. | This means there may be validity issues in comparing data collected or operationalised in different ways. |

APPLY: Exam skills

AO2: An example

In each of the following examples, identify whether primary data or secondary data would be involved, or both. Explain your answers. (2 marks each)

a. Zimbardo's study of social roles (p.8).

b. Study of HM (p.24).

c. Schaffer and Emerson's study of infants (p.42).

 **ANSWER**

a. Primary data because it involved direct observations of participants.

b. Both. There were direct observations of HM (primary data) and also examination of medical records (secondary data).

c. Secondary data, as both the observations and the mothers' recall of infants' behaviour were collected directly for the purpose of this study.

AO2: Three for you to try

1. **A researcher is analysing data from a mental health database to investigate the effectiveness of treatments for depression. The data gives symptom scores obtained from patients' responses to a questionnaire survey.**

   Which type of data is this? Tick two boxes.

   A Primary data. ☐

   B Secondary data. ☐

   C Quantitative data. ☐

   D Qualitative data. ☐

2. **A researcher wishes to investigate children's aggressive behaviour when playing together in small groups, using an observational technique.**

   Her hypothesis is that boys play more aggressively than girls. She obtains ten-minute video recordings of the children playing.

   a. Suggest how she could use this material to obtain:

      (i) Qualitative data. **(3 marks)**

      (ii) Quantitative data. **(3 marks)**

   b. Evaluate the use of each type of data in this study, and suggest which will best address her hypothesis. **(6 marks)**

3. **Identify the type of data collected or used in the following key studies. Is it quantitative or qualitative? Primary or secondary?**

   a. Lorenz's study on imprinting in geese.

   b. Harlow's monkey study.

   c. Ainsworth's Strange Situation research.

   d. van Ijzendoorn and Kroonenburg's cross-cultural study of attachment.

   e. Bowlby's theory of maternal deprivation.

   f. Asch's study of conformity.

   g. Milgram's study of obedience.

   h. Loftus and Palmer's hit/smash traffic accident study.

   i. Sperry and Gazzaniga's split brain research.

How do I answer... questions about types of data?

Q1: Researchers asked one group of participants to write a love story and another group to solve maths problems, with a bowl of jelly babies on their desk. The researchers counted how many jelly babies each participant ate.

Identify the type of data in this experiment, and explain your answer. (2 marks)

The first mark here is for identifying the type of data, and you could write 'quantitative' or 'primary'. (It would also be OK to write 'interval' – see the **A Level Year 2 Student Book** section on 'Levels of measurement'.)

The second mark requires an explanation, and this must relate to the type of data you identified. So, if you chose 'quantitative' you could say, 'it is numerical data' or you could be more specific, 'the data is the number of jelly babies they each ate'. If you chose 'primary', you could say, 'it is collected first-hand from participants', or you could say, 'it is collected for this specific study, to answer a research question'. So there are various options for getting 2 marks, but you need to word the explanation correctly.

 **REVIEW**

Can you identify and evaluate the type of data used in a study? Flick through this book, or your notes, find a key study, and decide if it uses primary/secondary and quantitative/qualitative data. Then think of some relevant evaluation points.

Introduction to statistical testing

AO1 Description

- Inferential statistics test the **probability (p)** that a particular set of data could have occurred by chance.

- They establish **significance**: whether the differences or associations we have observed in our sample are likely to be true in the population as a whole.

- At a level of significance of $(p) < 0.05$, there is less than 5% probability that the results are due to chance and so not a real effect.

- At a level of significance of $(p) < 0.01$ there is a 1% chance of this happening. This would be a more stringent test, which would be suitable for testing drug treatments.

The sign test

- The **sign test** can be used to test significance in paired or related data (repeated measures or matched pairs design).

1. State the hypothesis.

2. For each pair of data, add a sign column (+ or − depending on which item in the pair is greater). If there is no difference between a pair of scores, leave blank.

3. Find the **calculated value** of the **test statistic**, S, which is the frequency of the less frequent sign.

4. Find the **critical value** of S from the **table of critical values**, where N = total number of scores (ignoring blank rows), and choosing a **one- or two-tailed test** (a directional hypothesis requires a one-tailed test, a non-directional hypothesis requires a two-tailed test) and a level of significance of $(p) < 0.05$ $(p) < 0.01$.

5. Compare the calculated value with the critical value, following the instruction below the table, to see if the difference is significant. Then decide whether the result is in the expected direction, so whether the hypothesis can be accepted.

One-tailed and two-tailed.

When looking up critical values a 'one-tailed test' is used for a directional hypothesis – when you look at a one-tailed cat you know which direction it is going. A two-tailed cat goes in both directions (non-directional hypothesis).

Table of critical values of S.

Level of significance for a one-tailed test	0.05	0.01
Level of significance for a two-tailed test	0.10	0.02
N		
5	0	
6	0	0
7	0	0
8	1	0
9	1	1
10	1	1
11	2	1
12	2	2
13	3	2
14	3	2
15	3	3
16	4	3
17	4	4
18	5	4
19	5	4
20	5	5
25	7	7
30	10	9
35	12	11

Calculated value of S must be EQUAL TO or LESS THAN the critical value in this table for significance to be shown.

 # APPLY: Exam skills

AO2: An example

SCENARIO Do people's happiness scores improve after they go on holiday? To compare happiness ratings before and after a holiday, the sign test has been partially calculated in the following table.

Table of results

Participant	Happiness score before	Happiness score after	Difference (after–before)	Sign
1	6	7	1	+
2	3	4	1	+
3	4	6	2	+
4	8	6	−2	−
5	7	5	2	+
6	5	7	−2	−
7	7	5	2	+
8	5	8	3	+
9	4	7	3	+
10	8	5	−3	−
11	4	4	0	
12	8	9	1	+
13	6	7	1	+
14	5	6	1	+

a. *Use the table of critical values of S on the opposite page to decide whether there is a significant effect. (The hypothesis is directional.)* **(2 marks)**

b. *What can be concluded about the effect of holidays on happiness ratings?* **(2 marks)**

ANSWER
a. This is directional, so a one-tailed test is needed.

- The calculated value of S = 3
- N = 13 (1 score omitted).
- The critical value of S = 3 as well, so the result is significant at the p < 0.05 level.

b. The conclusion is: The null hypothesis can be rejected and the experimental hypothesis can be accepted. There is a significant improvement in happiness after a holiday compared to before.

Not everyone enjoys holidays

AO2: One for you to try

A slimming club wanted to find out whether their programme worked. They recorded the weights of ten members of the club when they first joined, and after three months.

Use the sign test to work out whether the programme was effective for these members. (4 marks)

Slimming club member	Starting weight	Weight after three months	Difference	Sign
Jan	80	74		
Julie	125	102		
Jess	113	114		
Josie	108	87		
Jodie	96	82		
Jenny	78	78		
Joe	102	94		
Jeff	124	125		
June	97	75		
Jade	122	94		

a. Write a directional hypothesis for this study.

b. Complete the sign column.

c. Calculated value of S =

d. *N* =

Use the table of critical values of S on the opposite page.

e. Critical value of S =

f. Is this significant?

g. Does the difference go in the expected direction?

h. Can the hypothesis be accepted on the basis of this test?

How do I answer... questions about statistical significance?

You may need to carry out the sign test in an AS or A Level exam. You don't need to learn a formula for this, you just need to count up the number of positive and negative cases in a set of data. This means how many people's results go up, and how many go down. You ignore any that didn't change. The result of the sign test (S) is simply the frequency of the least frequent sign. In the exam, you would then be given the relevant part of the table of critical values, as in the examples above. All you have to do is follow the instruction under the table to know how to compare your calculated value of S with the critical value from the table. Then know how to state the conclusion:

The difference *is / is not* significant.

This means the hypothesis *is supported / must be rejected*.

REVIEW

Practise as many examples as you can, until you are confident of the process. Remember, the only maths involved is: comparing two numbers to decide which is bigger; and counting how many have gone up or down. Other than that, it's just a matter of using the right wording for your conclusion.

The scientific process and peer review

RECAP

AO1 Description

- The scientific process has developed to ensure that scientific discoveries are reliable, and includes the requirement for peer review of articles before publication.
- **Peer review** (also called 'refereeing') is the assessment of scientific work by others who are experts in the same field.
- The process comprises:
  > The academic paper is sent to a journal editor by the author.
  > The editor sends it to several experts in the field, the academic referees.
  > The referees comment on the research and recommend acceptance, acceptance with some changes, or rejection.
  > The editor makes a decision to publish the paper as it is, or to return it to the author with a request for changes and resubmission, or to reject it.

- The aim is to ensure that published research is of high quality. Referees comment on:
  > validity
  > originality
  > quality
  > importance.
- The purposes of peer review are:
  > Responsible allocation of research funding by government and charitable bodies.
  > Preventing incorrect data entering the public domain via publication.
  > Assessing the research quality rating of university departments.

AO3 Evaluation/Discussion

Peer review in psychology is essential to establish the validity of published research…

In the 1950s Burt published research into IQs in twins. This now appears to have been fraudulent, which is a problem as educational policy was based on his findings.

In addition, a recent anonymous survey of psychologists indicated that the majority have used questionable research practices, and one per cent admitted to falsifying data (John *et al.*, 2012).

These practices result in a lack of trust for published research. Peer review aims to stop this happening, to the benefit of scientists and society.

Finding an expert peer reviewer may be difficult in a narrow field of research…

This means that the reviewers don't really understand the research, and may accept poor quality research, or may be biased towards prestigious researchers.

This also means it may be difficult to find a journal to publish controversial findings or theories that contradict existing ideas.

So, peer review may actually be assessing the acceptability rather than the validity of a new finding.

Publication bias is a problem…

Journals are more likely to publish positive results, and avoid publishing replications, although these are essential for establishing reliability of findings.

This can lead to the 'file drawer' phenomenon, where non-significant findings remain unpublished in the researcher's filing cabinet.

This means that reviews and meta-analyses also become biased as they can only examine published data.

Once research is published it remains in the public domain…

AO3 PLUS

If errors or fraud are subsequently found, the journal may publish a retraction, but the faulty data is still found in searches, and may still be used.

For example, Brooks (2010) points to peer-reviewed research that was subsequently debunked but nevertheless continued to be used in a debate in Parliament.

This underlines the importance of vigilance by scientists to ensure their work is high quality, and to communicate clearly with the public and policymakers. The public should also remain critical of published material.

Important things can end up left in the file drawer

 APPLY: Exam skills

AO2: An example

SCENARIO A psychologist wishes to publish his research in a mainstream psychology journal.

Explain why it is desirable for this research study to be peer reviewed before publication. **(3 marks)**

ANSWER *Peer review is a form of quality control for research which should ensure that only well-designed, well-conducted, well-reported and worthwhile studies are made public. It helps to ensure that flawed or fraudulent research, with possibly damaging practical applications, does not proceed. Research that passes peer review may lead to more funding and higher research status for the organisation concerned.*

AO2: Three for you to try

1. **a.** Suggest three reasons why a research paper might be rejected for publication after peer review. **(3 marks)**

   b. A future researcher decides to undertake a review of existing research in an area. How could her meta-analysis be affected by the rejection of some research in the area? **(3 marks)**

2. **A researcher sends her article to a journal for publication, and before making a decision about publication, the journal sends it to referees for peer review.**

   Which of these is not a purpose of peer review? Tick one box.

   A To ensure that the research methodology is clear and unambiguous. ☐

   B To check the conclusions are valid, based on the statistical analysis of the findings. ☐

   C To decide whether the findings are novel, important and add to knowledge of a field. ☐

   D To ensure that ethical procedures were followed in the study. ☐

3. **Imagine that you have been sent Zimbardo's research (p.8) to peer review.**

   a. What issues might you comment on?

   b. Why would they be a problem for publication?

   c. What suggestions might you have made to Zimbardo to improve his research?

How do I answer... questions about the process or purpose of peer review?

Q1: Discuss the purpose of peer review. (6 marks)

First check whether you are being asked about the **process** or the **purpose** of peer review. This question asks you to discuss the purpose, so you need to focus on AO3 evaluation, rather than a description of the process. For 6 marks, include two well-elaborated points, or three briefer ones.

Don't mention ethical issues – these are not relevant at this stage, as they would have been addressed by an ethics committee before the research was carried out.

Q2: A psychologist was researching how social media networks can help and harm young people. He gave a talk to fellow researchers and included new data which has not yet been published. He described finding a predictive relationship between activity on Facebook and symptoms of psychological disorders, including alcohol dependence. He also described psychological benefits of social media. He was dismayed to find, within a few days, online news media headlines such as 'Facebook making kids dumb' and 'Facebook harmful to kids'.

With reference to this psychologist's experience, discuss the process and purpose of peer review. (8 marks)

This scenario describes what goes wrong when findings are released to the media before publication in a peer-reviewed journal. To answer this question, you need to describe the process of peer review, and you can use bullet points for this. Make sure you include the final bullet point from the opposite page about the process, giving the three potential outcomes. You must link this to the stem, for example, 'The editor will send the paper to experts in the field of social media and adolescent mental health…'.

Then make points about the purpose, again linking them to the stem. For example, 'This aims to ensure that the findings are published in full and not oversimplified by news media, who in this case ignored half the story, about the benefits of social media.'

Your answer should be balanced between 'process' and 'purpose'. Assume the marks are equally divided between the two parts of your answer.

As you are asked to 'discuss', you must, again, include some evaluation. In an 8-mark answer this is a lot to try to cover, but choose a relevant evaluation point and again link it to the stem if you can. For example, 'A difficulty in the peer review process is that peer reviewers may be biased towards particular theories or researchers; for example, they may know this researcher or may be working on some competing research in the area of social media which they hope to publish, so they may not be objective in their decision. This means that some high quality research may be rejected.'

REVIEW

You can imagine yourself as a peer reviewer for any of our key studies. **Originality** and **importance** are clearly fine, as the research has become famous within psychology and beyond. But what issues of **validity** would you criticise? Would you recommend a larger, or more varied, sample of participants? Do you think there would be confounding variables in the design or methods used? What about demand characteristics?

Thinking through these aspects of the research will help you to remember what peer reviewers are looking for, and also help you practise applying the concepts of validity.

Psychology and the economy

AO1 Description

- Economic psychology is also called 'behavioural economics'.
- Researchers investigate the social, cognitive and emotional factors in economic decisions.
- Irrational thinking has been extensively researched by Kahneman, who was awarded the Nobel prize for economics in 2002. For example:
  - > The availability heuristic – people overestimate the likelihood of events such as a plane accident, because these events are more easily remembered when making a probability judgement, due to media stories.
  - > The framing effect – people's decisions differ depending on whether a choice is presented as a gain or a loss.

- These insights have changed many aspects of life, e.g. juries, business and tax collection.
- The UK government Behavioural Insights Team, also called the 'Nudge Unit', uses psychological research to plan policy. For example, simpler and more personalised letters to non-payers of car tax led to a tripling of payments made.
- People are also influenced by reciprocity, or the idea of fairness. For example, the message on a government website, 'If you needed an organ transplant, would you have one?' led to an increase in donors.

'The framing effect'

AO3 Evaluation/Discussion

Social psychology has been used to influence behaviour positively...

| For example, a campaign to reduce drink-driving used social norms to change people's attitudes. | Similar ideas have been used to reduce social stereotypes and smoking, with benefits to society. | A consequence is that the costs of unhealthy behaviours (e.g. smoking, drink-driving) to the NHS, and to society generally, are reduced. |

Memory research has led to improvements in accuracy of eyewitness testimony...

| Use of the cognitive interview has improved the amount of accurate information collected. | This ensures that police and court times is used efficiently. | This results in economic benefits as it reduces the expense of wrongful arrests. |

Attachment theory has influenced childcare policy...

| We now understand the importance of emotional care in early childhood development. | UNICEF has stated that 'deprivation that stems from lack of care and nurture… can have just as detrimental an effect on brain development as lack of food.' | This has led to healthcare policies that improve children's chances, helping them to become more economically independent. |

Mental health policies have economic implications...

| AO3 PLUS | | |
| Mental health care costs around £22.5 billion a year in England, and there are also huge indirect costs via the impact on the criminal justice system, lost employment, etc. | Treatments vary in their cost implications; for example, drug treatments may be much more cost-effective than psychotherapy for some disorders. | Therefore, evidence-based decisions help to reduce the costs associated with these treatments. |

APPLY: Exam skills

A02: An example

SCENARIO In 2008 Thaler and Sunstein published a book called *Nudge: Improving decisions about health, wealth and happiness* based on the research by Kahneman and others stating that human thinking is not rational. They reasoned that a kind of 'soft paternalism' could be used to nudge people into making better decisions (for themselves and for society) without taking away their freedom of choice. For example, sweets and junk food might be placed on supermarket shelves above eye level.

Suggest an individual and societal cost and benefit of product placement designed to discourage people from eating junk food. **(4 marks)**

ANSWER *At an individual level, people may spend less on 'sweet treats' and other junk foods, leaving them more to spend on healthier options. They may consequently find it easier to control their weight and thus reduce their risk of tooth decay and obesity-related health problems such as hypertension and Type 2 diabetes. At a societal level, the cost to the NHS in the UK of treating these increasingly widespread problems should decrease. The savings made could reduce the overall cost to the country of the health service or allow for more investment into prevention and treatment of other conditions, such as Alzheimer's Disease, which is currently on the increase.*

A02: Two for you to try

1. **The Nudge Unit has successfully increased the payment of car taxes, increased attendance at adult literacy classes, and improved police diversity by using behavioural insights. These changes have economic benefits to society.**

   Discuss ethical issues associated with appointing psychologists and economists to influence citizens in this way. (5 marks)

2. **Tverksy and Kahneman tested the framing effect experimentally, asking participants to select a treatment for a deadly disease affecting 600 people. Two groups were told different facts about the treatments:**

	Treatment	Told:	Choice:
Group 1	A	200 saved	72%
	B	1/3 chance all saved, 2/3 chance no one saved	28%
Group 2	C	400 deaths	22%
	D	1/3 chance no one dies, 2/3 chance all die	78%

   a. Draw a fully labelled bar chart of the findings of Tversky and Kahneman's study into framing effects. **(4 marks)**

   b. What conclusion can be drawn from these findings? **(2 marks)**

 ## How do I answer... questions about psychology and the economy?

Q1: Explain possible implications for the economy of research relating to attachment. (2 marks)

When you are thinking about economic implications, you need to ask yourself:

- How might it enable people to: be more effective members of society; work harder; earn more; pay more taxes; keep mentally healthy; deal better with stress; look after their children better; need less support from social services or the benefit system?
- How might this reduce costs to the NHS / taxpayers / the criminal justice system?

For this question, you could say, 'Recent evidence shows that high quality childcare in nurseries is just as good for children's development as maternal care, so mothers can be recommended to go back to work after having children and keep earning a living.'

Q2: Discuss the implications of psychological research for the economy, referring to topic areas you have studied. (12 marks)

This is an extended answer question, which you should plan with a balance of AO1 Description and AO3 Discussion points. You need to take some time to plan, as you have to retrieve suitable research from your memory. Carrying out the 'Review' task will help you to identify these and be prepared to bring them into an extended answer like this one. These applications to specific topics count as AO3, and you need to be really explicit about the implications for the economy. For example, you could include a paragraph about Loftus' eyewitness testimony research, as it is often referred to during trials. Don't go into too much detail about particular experiments, but summarise findings and their implications for the economy. For example, 'Loftus found that people can develop false memories if they are asked leading questions. This research has led on to the development of the cognitive interview, in which interviewers are careful not to ask leading questions. Due to this, the police get better evidence and this reduces wrongful convictions, so it is better use of police time, and we are not imprisoning the wrong people and then having to pay compensation.'

Another example would be from the area of psychopathology. 'Researchers collect evidence about the effectiveness of different treatments, so the NHS can spend its money on the treatments that are most cost effective. That is why the government has been investing in CBT to try to get depressed people back to work so they aren't taking up time and resources from the health service, and they aren't claiming benefits for being off sick with depression. Instead they are able to go back to work and pay taxes, which helps the economy.'

 ## REVIEW

Other topics with obvious economic implications include:

- psychopathology (cost / effectiveness of different treatments)
- memory (eyewitness testimony)
- biopsychology (stress and sleep).

Think through how you would answer a similar question, replacing 'attachment' with these topics.

There are also many relevant topics in the Year 2 course, such as **Forensic psychology**, **Cognition and development**, and others.

Activities: suggested answers

Chapter 1 Social influence
Types of conformity and explanations for conformity p.4–5

One for you to try: (a) Normative social influence is conforming in order to gain approval or avoid disapproval. Even though he doesn't want to throw a stone, Dave doesn't want to be excluded from his group of friends. By throwing a stone, he will avoid their disapproval (and/or gain their approval), and so he conforms to the majority behaviour.
(b) Pete doesn't know which tube train to get on, and so is guided by the behaviour of others, because he thinks they are right. In informational social influence, we go along with a group because we accept that their perceptions and beliefs are accurate. Presumably, Pete believes the others are going to the match and follows them because he accepts that they must know how to get to Wembley.
(c) A stratified sample could be used. Because there may be a difference in the vulnerability of males and females to taking up smoking, the sample should represent the number of males and females in the Year 10 population in each school.

Research methods: (a) This is an independent groups design because it involved two independent groups of 14–18 year olds from two schools in the same catchment area.
(b) Strength – It allows the researcher to use a larger number of Year 10 pupils than would have been possible with a repeated measures design. Limitation – Participant variables cannot be controlled and so may act as a confounding variable. It is possible that one of the schools may have had more of a culture of smoking among the pupils than the other school.

Variables affecting conformity p.6–7

Two for you to try: In part (a), Mark is being affected by the group's unanimity. When one of the team suggests 'Kathmandu', the other team members agree, and the group is unanimous that this is the correct answer. Research shows that people conform more when the group is unanimous. Mark is probably being affected by this, and perhaps does not want to give a different answer for fear of disapproval from the unanimous group members.
In part (b), the group's unanimity is broken by the appearance of a team member who suggests the same (correct) answer as Mark's.
This increases Mark's confidence that he is correct and breaks the unanimity of the group. There is now less pressure for him to conform.

Research methods: (a) IV = Number of confederates DV = Percentage of errors
(b) There is a positive correlation between the number of confederates all giving the same wrong answer in a conformity task and the percentage of errors made by participants.

(c)

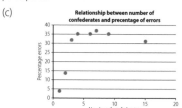

Relationship between number of confederates and precentage of errors

(d) There is a strong positive correlation between the number of confederates and the percentage of errors made, but only to a certain point (4 confederates), after which the relationship does not get any stronger.

Conformity to social roles p.8–9

One for you to try: Mike has been given a position of authority. His social role as a steward is associated with patterns of expected behaviour which he has adopted. He has a visible sign of that authority in the form of a bright yellow high-visibility jacket. In a way, this is similar to the uniform worn by the guards in Zimbardo's study. Mike's 'Aviator' sunglasses make eye contact with him impossible which, again, is similar to the dark shades worn by the guards in Zimbardo's study. Although Mike's job is to ensure that people are safe, he seems to have forgotten that, and has started to behave in an abusive and 'tyrannical' way towards a young boy. The young boy is like one of the prisoners in Zimbardo's study and, because of Mike's behaviour towards him, he has taken on the role as a member of the crowd. He has become depressed and passive, and he feels helpless. His crying is similar to the extreme reactions seen amongst the prisoners in Zimbardo's study. Although the boy wants to leave, Mike will not allow him to do that, even though the boy is perfectly within his rights to leave the football ground whenever he wants to. During the second half of the game, as a result of Mike's 'increasingly cruel and sadistic' behaviour during the first half, the boy has become 'increasingly passive' and 'accepting of his plight', just as the prisoners in Zimbardo's study did.

Research methods: (a) The aim of the study was to see if awareness of what happened in Zimbardo's prison study would change the way prisoner officers treated prisoners in British prisons.
(b) Watching a film of what happened in Zimbardo's prison study changes the way prison officers treat prisoners in British prisons.
(c) The IV is exposure to a film of Zimbardo's prison study. The DV is prison officers' interactions with prisoners over the next month.
(d) It is possible that the two prisons in which prisoners were placed differed greatly in terms of the physical and organisational environment and the nature of the inmates. This could mean that, if those officers who had seen the Zimbardo film were placed into a well organised prison with non-violent prisoners, their interactions with prisoners would be more positive. If those who watched the documentary were placed in a poorly-organised prison with violent prisoners, their interactions may be more confrontational. This means that subsequent interactions might be due to aspects of the prison itself, rather than the effects of watching Zimbardo's film.

Situational variables affecting obedience p.10–11

One for you to try: Mike's bright yellow high-visibility jacket acts as a symbol of legitimate authority given the situation's context. It functions like the laboratory coat in Milgram's study. When Mike removes his jacket, the crowd do not see his authority as legitimate. This is equivalent to the variation in Milgram's study in which the experimenter did not wear his laboratory coat. Milgram found that obedience was significantly reduced when the experimenter became 'an ordinary man giving orders'. The same thing possibly happens when Mike removes his jacket.

Research methods: Finding 1: These include the finding that obedience levels drop from 40% to 30% when the teacher has to have physical contact with the learner when delivering shocks. Conclusion 1: This shows that victim proximity is an important factor when determining obedience, with greater proximity being associated with less obedience.
Finding 2: When the experimenter is no longer in the same room as the teacher, obedience levels drop from 65% to 21%. Conclusion 2: This shows that authority proximity is an important factor in determining obedience, with greater proximity being associated with greater obedience.

Agentic state and legitimacy of authority p.12–13

One for you to try: Milgram's agency theory says that when we undergo agentic shift, we move from an autonomous state (in which we see ourselves as being responsible for our behaviour) to an agentic state (in which we see ourselves as an agent for carrying out another person's wishes). Susan does not see herself as responsible for the instruction to wear uniform. Instead, she sees the head teacher as being responsible. As a result, she is in the agentic state, and simply the 'messenger' who is responsible for another person's wishes, hence she says 'don't blame me'.

Research methods: A Random. *Strength:* All members of the population have an equal chance of being selected, thus reducing any bias in selection of the sample. *Limitation:* Some potential members of the sample may not want to take part, creating a biased sample limited to those who do want to. B Stratified. *Strength:* Because the sample proportionally represents males and females on the course, this is potentially the least biased sampling method for this study. *Limitation:* Because subgroups of males and females on the course must be identified and then randomly selected from these subgroups, this is a time-consuming process. C Systematic. *Strength:* This is a cost and time efficient way of obtaining a sample of social psychology students as researchers would already have a list of all potential participants. *Limitation:* If the first member of the student sample is not selected randomly, then the overall sample becomes biased. D Volunteer. *Strength:* Advertising on the departmental noticeboard overcomes the problem of selecting students who may then not want to take part. *Limitation:* Participants may be highly motivated to take part, and therefore differ from a typical student from this population.

The Authoritarian Personality p.14–15

One for you to try: One way of explaining their differences of opinion is in terms of the authoritarian personality. Authoritarian personalities agree with California F scale statements such as 'Rules are there for people to follow not change'. It is possible that Guy is an authoritarian personality and sees things in 'black and white', whereas Tony may be better educated or to the political left, hence their difference of opinion about the officer on trial.

Research methods: (a) The scattergram shows a positive correlation.
(b) A high score on the California F scale is associated with a high score on the obedience measure, or as scores on the F scale increase, they tend to increase on the obedience measure.
(c) The main limitation is that causality cannot be inferred on the basis of a correlation alone. Just because a high score on the F scale is associated with a high score on the obedience measure, it does not necessarily mean that changes in one variable are causing changes in the other variable.
(d) Counterbalancing prevents order effects. Hopefully, any effect there is of doing the F scale questionnaire followed by the obedience measure questionnaire will be 'counterbalanced' by any effect there is of doing the obedience measure questionnaire followed by the F scale questionnaire.

Resistance to social influence p.16–17

One for you to try: Liz is displaying an internal locus of control (LOC). She has no time for people who don't help themselves, which is consistent with the internal LOC belief that what happens to people is a product of their own ability and effort. As such she would be more resistant to social influence than Jane, who shows an external LOC. Such people believe that what happens to them is determined by external factors such as the influence of others. The fact that she relies on her husband for her opinions means she would be more susceptible to social influence.

Research methods: One finding is that internals (89%) are more likely than externals (14%) to question the caretaker when no reason is given for his instructions. This shows that internals are more likely to resist social influence when told to behave in a certain way. Another finding is that when a reason is given, internals (15%) are just as likely as externals (14%) to follow instructions. This shows that personality does not influence our resistance to social influence provided that a reason is given for us to follow an instruction.

Minority influence p.18–19

One for you to try: Sylvia is trying to convert the majority (who do not eat sushi) to her own minority position (of eating sushi every day). Research shows that Sylvia will be more likely to be influential if she behaves consistently and demonstrates commitment in her behaviour. Unfortunately, Sylvia's friends have seen her eating a super deluxe beef burger. If Sylvia behaved consistently, and showed commitment, her friends might have considered her position more carefully. Unfortunately, she didn't, and as a result her friends are unlikely to be persuaded by her.

Research methods: (a) A control condition provides us with a 'baseline' against which we can compare experimental conditions. In Moscovici et al's study, the researchers needed to know how many of the blue slides were judged to be green when no form of social influence was applied. Moscovici et al found that in the control condition no participant referred to the slides as green whereas in the consistent condition 8% of people were influenced to say the slide was green and only 1% in the inconsistent condition.
(b) An IV is something that is directly manipulated by a researcher in order to measure any resulting change in behaviour (the DV).
(c) The IV is whether the minority behaved consistently or inconsistently in their judgements. The DV is the percentage of trials in which the majority gave the same wrong answer as the minority.
(d) The position of the minority in the group when giving their answers (e.g. first, second, last).
(e) An extraneous variable (EV) is anything (other than the IV) which could potentially affect the DV whereas a confounding variable is any EV which is left uncontrolled and so is likely to have affected the DV.

Social influence processes in social change p.20–21

One for you to try: One approach Mike could use is a social norms intervention. There seems to be a misperception between how many supporters actually do put their litter in a bin, and how many supporters are believed to put their litter in a bin. Mike needs to correct this misperception. Perhaps one thing he could do is put up a sign with a statement such as 'Most supporters don't throw their litter on the ground' or 'Most supporters put their litter in bins'. Research shows that when peoples' misperceptions about the frequency of a behaviour are corrected, their behaviour tends to change. Hopefully, when the supporters had their misperceptions corrected their behaviour would change, making Mike's life a lot easier.

Research methods: (a) In a stratified sample, participants are randomly selected from each subgroup in proportion to their occurrence in the population. A stratified sample in this study might divide the overall population into different genders and age groups. This would give a sample of drivers that would ensure an appropriately representative sample (e.g. there may be a higher number of male participants between the ages of 30–45 if this is the largest subgroup of drivers identified).
(b) A pilot study is a small-scale trial run of a research design, to check all aspects of the procedure (for example whether participants understood the instructions) and change these if necessary. If a social

norms intervention was used, the researchers could check that those in this group noticed the message and also understood what it was saying. If not, they could make the message clearer and more prominent.
(c) A study such as this might have a number of implications for the economy. By reducing the number of cars on the road, this could reduce the likelihood of car-related accidents and have cleaner air in cities, which would reduce the impact on the NHS. Likewise, by making fewer journeys by car, this would save people money, which they could plough back into the economy in other ways (e.g. by spending more), which would have a positive financial impact on local traders, restaurants and so on.

Chapter 2 Memory
Short- and long-term memory p.22–23

One for you to try: Yasmin has difficulty in remembering her new mobile phone number as the capacity of STM is between 5-9 items. Her mobile number is 11 digits long so exceeds the capacity of STM. She can remember her holiday to Disneyland, however, as the duration of LTM is up to a lifetime.

Research methods: (a) There is a negative correlation between chronological age and short-term memory capacity as measured by digit span.

(b)
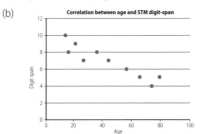

(c) −0.82
How do I answer: The correct statement is C.

The multi-store model of memory p.24–25

One for you to try: The multi-store model (MSM) is an explanation of memory based on three separate memory stores, sensory memory, short-term memory and long-term memory and how information is transferred from one store to another. STM has a limited duration of approximately 18 seconds and a limited capacity. Radha's grandfather struggles to remember recent events, which suggests that these are not being transferred to his long-term memory and so are lost from STM. LTM is potentially unlimited in duration and capacity. This is consistent with the fact that Radha's grandfather can remember events that happened years ago, before his memory problem developed.

Research methods: (a) The aim was to test whether using mind maps helps to consolidate memory for new material in long-term memory.
(b) The IV was the use of visual mind maps. The DV was the number of correct answers to questions on the article about St Lucia.
(c) The use of a mind-map during the learning phase increases recall of information one week later.
(d) This is a directional hypothesis.
(e) There could be a difference (e.g. in age or academic ability) between the two classes. These differences could impact on their memory ability and make any conclusions about the effect of using mind-maps less valid. Differences between the two classes could also be significant if one class regularly uses mind-maps as a learning aid and so would be more used to them. The researchers may not have tested the two classes for their knowledge of St Lucia before the study begins, so the difference between them may have less to do with mind-maps and more to do with prior knowledge.
(f) Variables are controlled, so researchers can be confident that any change in the DV is due to the IV. Researchers can monitor how long groups spent reading the article, so can be sure differences in test

scores between groups can be attributed to the use of mind maps, rather than overall time spent on the task. A problem is that participants may know they are in a study, so may show demand characteristics. Participants in the mind map group may make more of an effort to remember material because they recognize this is what the researcher expects to happen.

The working memory model p.26–27

One for you to try: The working memory model proposes one store for visual processing and a separate store for processing sounds. Carly was using her visual-spatial sketchpad to browse through deals on her laptop and her phonological loop when talking to her mother on the phone. The model suggests that if the same components are used during dual-task performance, one task interferes with the processing of the other. As talking to her mother and listening to her son both used the same component, the phonological loop, this meant that Carly could not fully process her son's verbal request.

Research methods: (a) The researcher would have used a pilot study to check whether the presentation on the computer screen worked and whether participants fully understood the instructions. If there were any problems she could put these issues right for the main study.
(b) Younger participants (aged 18–25) show better working memory performance than do older participants (aged 60–75).
(c) The researcher would have chosen a directional hypothesis on the basis that previous research had suggested that working memory tends to decline with age. As a result, she predicted that younger participants would perform better than older participants.
(d) One limitation of using a volunteer sample, is that volunteers may differ in some way from those who do not volunteer. This would pose problems for any conclusions that might be drawn because personality differences between volunteers and non-volunteers rather than age might be the cause of the working memory deficits found in the study.
(e) The researcher has chosen from a group of university students and the other group from the local community. As working memory and intelligence are related, educational level may be a confounding variable in the study. Students in the 18–25 group would also be more used to using computers on a regular basis, therefore the mode of presentation may impact on performance.

Types of long-term memory p.28–29

One for you to try: Clive is still able to play the piano and sing; therefore it would appear that he has retained his procedural knowledge, however he is unable to remember a holiday to Australia and therefore it would appear that his episodic memory is no longer intact.

Research methods: (a) Investigator effects are any cues from an investigator that lead to certain behaviours in the participant, causing them to act in accordance with the investigator's expectations.
(b) Because the researcher expects his AD patients to show more significant episodic deficits, he may interact with them differently than the group of control participants.
(c) This could be overcome by having an independent experimenter carrying out the assessments and by using a double-blind procedure where the experimenter does not know whether participants are AD or controls.
(d) An ethical issue is that some of the AD patients may not be able to give their informed consent because they are unable to understand the nature of the study or any risks involved. The researcher could deal with this issue by having a relative or medical professional for each AD patient who can act 'in loco parentis', giving or withholding consent on behalf of that patient.
(e) The purpose of a peer review is to ensure that published research is of high quality, to prevent incorrect data entering the public domain via

publication and to ensure that research funding by government and charitable bodies is allocated responsibly.

Explanations for forgetting – Interference p.30–31

One for you to try: Vanessa is experiencing retroactive interference. This is where learning something new interferes with previously learned material. After moving to Spain and learning Spanish, this interfered with the German she had previously learned, with the result that she mixes up German words with their Spanish equivalent. Likewise, since moving from Spain to the UK and learning English, she finds that this interferes with her previously learned Spanish, as she now has trouble remembering Spanish words.

Research methods: (a) Group A = 5+6+8+7+4+4+5+6+10+4+5 = 60
60/10 = 6
Group B = 11+15+12+13+19+11+12+15+16+16 = 140. 140/10 = 14
(b) The standard deviation suggests that there is a greater dispersion (variability) of scores for Group B, in comparison to Group A. The larger the standard deviation the more spread a set of scores is about the mean, and therefore it is less representative than a set of scores with a smaller standard deviation. As a result, this may be less useful for the experimenter.

Explanations for forgetting – Retrieval failure p.32–33

One for you to try: The results of Godden and Baddeley suggest that information is best recalled when it is learned in the same context, or environment, as where it is later recalled. Therefore, the teacher's advice is likely to improve Emmanuel's memory, as learning the information in the room where he is going to be tested, will provide Emmanuel with environmental cues that are likely to help him remember the information.

Research methods: (a) Independent groups
(b) A matched pairs design could have been used. This would have been more suitable because participants could have been matched on their previous performance on research methods. This would have ensured that any difference in performance between the two groups could be attributed to the room they were tested in, and not their previous research methods ability.
(c) It is likely that Group 1 would have better recall of the content of the lesson. This is because Group 2 would experience context-dependent forgetting because the recall environment does not match the initial context of learning.
(d) These results would support retrieval failure because they demonstrate that memory is most effective if information that was present at encoding (e.g. the context of learning) is also available at time of retrieval (e.g. the recall environment). The closer the cue to the original, the more useful it is. Cues were closer for Group 1 than they were for Group 2.

Accuracy of eyewitness testimony: Misleading information p.34–35

One for you to try: The memory of the event may have been altered as a result of post-event discussion. Research by Gabbert et al. (2003) found that participants who discussed an event went on to mistakenly recall information that they had not witnessed, in a video of a theft. These results suggests that the people who witnessed the Space Shuttle Challenger explode, may have incorporate information from other people who had witnessed the disaster. Consequently, their eyewitness accounts may have been distorted and become inaccurate as a result of post-event discussion.
Research methods: (a) Loftus and Palmer (1974)
(b) IV = the verb used in the question about how fast the cars were going. DV = Estimates of speed of the cars in mph.
(c)(i) Independent and dependent variables should be defined in a way that they can easily be measured or

tested. (ii) Participants who hear the word `smashed' in a question about the speed of cars prior to an accident estimate higher speeds in mph than do those who hear the word 'contacted'.
(d) A possible extraneous variable is that some participants might not be drivers, and so less accurate in estimating speed. This could be controlled by ensuring equal numbers of drivers and non-drivers in the two conditions, or restricting the sample to only people who were drivers.
(e)They should explain exactly what will happen in the experiment, what the participants' role will be, and any potential risks of participation. They should also explain what steps they will take to ensure confidentiality of participants' data.

Accuracy of eyewitness testimony: Anxiety p.36–37

One for you to try: The sergeant's claim appears to be based on Deffenbacher et al.'s conclusion that laboratory studies show that anxiety reduces accuracy, and that real-life studies tend to find an even greater loss in accuracy. However, Becky could point out that the majority of these studies were laboratory studies and that research by Christianson and Hubinette (1993) found that, for real witnesses to bank robberies, those who were most anxious (the victims) had the best recall. Becky can also tell her colleague about more recent research. For example, Halford and Milne (2005) found that victims of violent crimes were more accurate in their recall of crime scene information compared to victims of non-violent crimes. Becky's sergeant claimed that he usually gave less credibility to witness statements from people who had been threatened with a weapon, yet Halford and Milnes's research seems to contradict his claim.

Research methods: (a) A – Scattergram , B – Bar chart

(b)

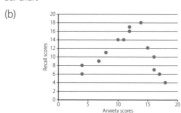

(c)

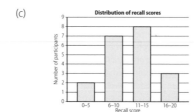

Improving the accuracy of eyewitness testimony: The cognitive interview p.38–39

One for you to try: Any two techniques are appropriate. However, the key to this question is that you apply the answer to the extract, for example: Changed perspective – try to recall the incident from the perspective of the teacher. What do you think she would have seen? Mental reinstatement of the original context – I would like you to think back to the day the man burst into the psychology room. What topic were you studying? What time of day was the lesson? Who were you sitting next to? Etc.

Research methods: (a) There is a curvilinear relationship between anxiety level and accuracy of eye-witness recall. At very low and very high anxiety levels, recall accuracy is relatively poor. Optimum recall accuracy occurs at moderate levels of anxiety.
(b) Low anxiety condition: Median = 11, Mode = 11; Moderate anxiety condition: Median = 15, Mode = 14; High anxiety condition: Median = 10, Mode = 10

(c)

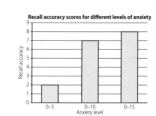

Chapter 3 Attachment

Caregiver–infant interactions p.40–41

One for you to try: This demonstrates interactional synchrony. When infant and caregiver interact, the infant tends to mirror what the caregiver is doing. This is evident in Darren and Rebecca's behaviour. Rebecca smiles when Darren smiles, and moves her head in time with his head movements.

Research methods: (a) Controlled observations enable control of the environment so observers can focus on specific behaviours. In this research, by controlling the environment it was possible to film infants without outside interference that might otherwise affect their behaviour.
(b) Controlled observations may lack ecological validity as the situation may feel unnatural to the infants. As a result, they may not act in a completely natural way.
(c) Confidentiality is a legal right of all participants in that there should be no way that anybody reading the data could connect it to a particular participant. In this case data and recordings for each infant should be coded using numbers instead of names. The data and the video recording files should then be in a password protected file on a secure computer.

The development of attachment p.42–43

One for you to try: Research by Schaffer and Emerson found that fathers such as Gary were less likely to be primary attachment figures than mothers. There are biological reasons for this. The female hormone oestrogen underlies caring behaviour. This might explain why Adam has formed closer attachments with his mother and his grandmother. Other research (e.g. Heermann et al., 1994) has found that men are less sensitive to infant cues. If Gary is less sensitive to Adam's needs (e.g. feeding him when he is hungry, soothing him when he is upset), then it is unlikely that he will become a primary attachment figure.

Research methods: (a) The IV is naturally occurring rather than being manipulated by the researcher, i.e. the IV in this study is whether the individuals had secure or insecure attachments as infants.
(b) Adolescents who completed the attachment type questionnaires may not be representative of the population as many would not have had the time or the motivation to answer all the questions.

(c)

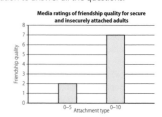

Animal studies of attachment p.44–45

One for you to try: Lorenz claimed that if goslings were exposed to a moving object during a sensitive period, they become imprinted on that object. This is irreversible and has an effect on later mate preferences (sexual imprinting). Keepers use a condor shaped hand puppet to prevent the chicks imprinting on the humans that feed it. This means that when they are released into the wild, they will seek a mate that is a member of their own species.

Research methods: (a) The aim of this study was to see whether cats were more attached to their owners than they were to a random human.

(b) Cats display different attachment behaviour toward their owners than they do toward a random human.

Explanations of attachment: Learning theory p.46–47

One for you to try: According to learning theory, Nathan may become attached to his father Jon, if Jon is providing food. Food is an unconditioned stimulus that procedures and unconditioned response of pleasure. If Jon, who is the neutral stimulus, continually feeds his son Nathan, then Nathan will form an association between his father and the pleasure from being fed. Eventually Jon will become a conditioned stimulus which produces a conditioned response, feelings of pleasure in Nathan, which results in the formation of an attachment.

Research methods: (a) Two ethical issues are confidentiality (e.g. not linking names with data) and protection from psychological harm (e.g. not arousing guilt in the working mothers).
(b) Confidentiality – the researcher could use numbers instead of names, and ensure that all data is kept secure using a password protected computer. Protection from psychological harm – debriefing can return mothers to their pre-study psychological state and reassurances given about the positive aspects of having a working mother.
(c) It gives guidelines as to which behaviours are acceptable when carrying out a research study, and what behaviours are not acceptable and offers guidelines on how to deal with ethical dilemmas. If a psychologist conducts unacceptable research, the BPS may bar them from the Society and from practising psychology or carrying out research.
(d) The mean is a measure of central tendency, calculated by adding up all the scores and dividing by the number of participants or items. The standard deviation is a measure of dispersion and is a calculation of the average distance of each data item from the mean.
(e) The table shows a difference in the mean attachment scores between those infants whose mothers work and those whose mothers stay at home. The 'stay at home mother' infants scored higher on average on the attachment measure than the working mother infants. However, the much larger standard deviation scores for the working mother infants showed that their attachment scores were much more widely dispersed than the other group. This suggests more evidence of wide individual differences in this group.

Explanations of attachment: Bowlby's theory p.48–49

One for you to try: (a) Victor (b) Toby (c) Lola

Research methods: (a) The IV is naturally occurring rather than being manipulated by the researcher, i.e. the IV in this study is whether the individuals had secure or insecure attachments as infants.
(b) The main ethical issues include: privacy and confidentiality, although other considerations such as right to withdraw are also creditworthy. The researcher would need to ensure that the participants' information was kept confidential. This means that the responses cannot be matched to the individual participants. To do this the research could assign each participant a unique number which only the psychologist is aware of. The questionnaires and results would then be analysed in relation to this unique number and not the participant's real name.
(c) An extraneous variable could be temperament. As people with a 'difficult' temperament may find it less easy to both develop secure attachments in infancy and to have successful adult relationships, researchers should use personality tests to match participants in each group for temperament.

Ainsworth's Strange Situation: Types of attachment p.50–51

One for you to try: Ashley is likely to be classified as insecure-avoidant. She is willing to explore the environment, however she is indifferent to separation and avoids contact upon reunion with her caregiver. Alex on the other hand is likely to be classified as insecure-resistant. She shows low levels of exploration and is distressed when separated from her caregiver. Finally, she angrily resists being picked up upon reunion with her caregiver.

Research methods: (a) Time sampling: Noting what a target individual is doing every 30 seconds (or an appropriate time interval), by ticking behavioural categories on a checklist. A limitation is that observers miss important behaviours that occur outside the 10 second frequency so have a limited overview of attachment behaviours between the dogs and their owners.
(b) Behaviours were videotaped so that researchers could analyse the behaviours afterwards rather than trying to do it at the time.
(c) Two observers were used to establish inter-observer reliability and so avoid subjective bias.

Cultural variations in attachment p.52–53

One for you to try: Like the Strange Situation, intervention programmes are based on Western ideas of childcare and attachment behaviours. In the USA, parents tend to encourage independence, but this is not the case in Japan, where children are more likely to be classified as insecurely attached using the Strange Situation than in the US. In Japan, infants rarely experience separation from their mothers, and mothers are more likely to encourage dependency in their infants. As a result, infants in Japan display lower levels of independence and exploration compared to the US, therefore these intervention programmes might be seen as inappropriate.

Research methods: (a) A meta-analysis assesses trends in data across a number of studies and evaluates the overall effect size using statistical analysis.
(b) van IJzendoorn and Kroonenberg were trying to assess general patterns of attachment across eight cultures, so a meta-analysis of studies carried out in those cultures was the most appropriate technique for establishing this.
(c) Strength – Conclusions are based on a much wider sample of participants, so conclusions can still be drawn, even if some of the studies produced contradictory results.
Limitation – As the research methodology of some of the studies may vary considerably, this means that the studies that make up the meta-analysis may not be truly comparable.

Bowlby's theory of maternal deprivation p.54–55

One for you to try: Bowlby claimed that a child who has a prolonged separation may become emotionally disturbed if this happens before the age of two-and-a-half and if there is no substitute mother-person available. As Max is still under the age of two-and-a-half, he remains vulnerable to separation so Sally needs to minimise the impact of the separation. Children need a 'warm, intimate and continuous relationship' with a mother figure to ensure good mental health. As a result of the Robertsons' research, parents such as Sally are encouraged to maintain a continuous relationship with their children by visiting their children often while in hospital.

Research methods: One issue with the use of interviews is interviewer bias which is a form of investigator effect (1 mark). Interviewer bias may be unconscious, with expectations communicated non-verbally through tone of voice, length of pause etc (1 mark). To avoid interviewer bias, interviewers must be trained to ask the questions in a neutral and consistent way (1 mark).

Romanian orphan studies: Effects of institutionalisation p.56–57

One for you to try: Rutter and Sonuga-Barke's study of Romanian orphans found that children adopted before the age of six months old develop 'normally' by the age of four. As Alin was adopted by 18 months old, but Rutter and Sonuga-Barke claimed that the earlier children are adopted, the more likely it is they will catch up with their non-institutionalised peers. Le Mare and Audet's study found that the effects of institutionalisation tended to disappear over time and any physical underdevelopment found in institutionalised children had improved by the age of 11. This explains why Alin had made significant gains after adoption, and was able to overcome any issues of physical underdevelopment.

Research methods: One strength of using case studies is that they provide rich and interesting information on a particular topic, which is difficult to examine using other methods. Therefore the researchers would generate lots of information about the effects of institutionalisation on Alin, which have high levels of ecological validity. However, one limitation of using case studies is that they are difficult, if not impossible to replicate. As Alin is a unique example, it would be difficult to find another 'case' which is exactly the same as Alin and therefore psychologists are unable to replicate the findings to see if the same effects appear in other children.

The influence of early attachment p.58–59

One for you to try: The most likely findings are that respondents who were securely attached as infants would have more successful romantic relationships as adults. Those who were insecurely attached as infants would have developed a less positive internal working model of relationships, therefore it is likely that these respondents would report less successful romantic relationships in adulthood.

Research methods: (a) It would be preferable to use an interview because it allows the researcher to ask more searching questions about attachment and relationship experiences, and to obtain valuable qualitative data.
(b) It might be preferable to use a questionnaire because of the sensitive nature of the subject matter. Respondents might be more likely to take part because of the relative anonymity of their responses.
(c) An ethical issue using the interview is that respondents might become upset or embarrassed because of the sensitivity of the questions. An ethical issue using a questionnaire is informed consent. The researcher would have no way of knowing whether the respondent truly understood the risks of participation prior to completing the questionnaire.
(d) The first issue could be dealt with by using a pilot study where a representative sample could feed back about whether they found any of the questions difficult and then these could be changed. The second issue could be dealt with by delivering the questionnaire online, and where respondents must read an information sheet and answer a few simple questions based on this before they can start on the questionnaire.
(e) 1. Other possible reasons for relationship failure (e.g. mental health issues, aggression). 2. Negative recall bias – people in unsuccessful relationships more likely to recall insecure attachments.

Chapter 4 Psychopathology
Definitions of abnormality p.60–61

One for you to try: Cheryl's behaviour fits the 'deviation from social norms' definition. The norm is to be sad or sombre at a funeral, and she laughed and made phone calls, which would appear abnormal. Also, she stands very close and makes people uncomfortable, violating the social norm about keeping a certain distance from people.

Research methods: (a) 2.28% (b) 2.28/100 x 66,000,000 = 1,504,800

Definitions of abnormality (continued) p.62–63

Two for you to try: 1. Anna's behaviour is most likely to be defined in terms of a 'failure to function adequately'. This is because her behaviour interferes with her ability to carry on with her daily routine, in this case being able to leave the house without undue anxiety, and making her late for work.

2. (a) Sandra is using the 'failure to function adequately' definition as this involves the individual feeling distressed about their feelings or behaviour.
(b) Not being able to get out of the house and see friends would cause distress.
(c) Some people may not be distressed by their own behaviour, for example if they have schizophrenia they may not realise anything is wrong, but their behaviour may cause distress to other people; it depends who is judging.

Research methods: (a) People with mental disorders had more difficulties in everyday life than people with physical disorders, as shown by the higher mean WHODAS score for people with mental disorders than physical disorders. The standard deviations for the two groups were quite similar, however, meaning there is a similar variation in ability to cope with daily life in these two groups (slightly greater spread for people with mental disorders). (b) The researchers wanted to represent all age groups and genders proportionally to the Australian population, to ensure the results represent the population and can be generalised.

How do I answer: Q1 B and E. Q2 C and D.

Mental disorders p.64–65

One for you to try: A cognitive characteristic shown by Hughes was his belief that because everybody carries germs the only way he could live longer was by avoiding germs. A behavioural characteristic shown by Hughes was dictating the same phrases over and over again. An emotional characteristic was the distress he felt about being contaminated by germs.

Research methods: (a) Country C (b) Country A (c) Country A (d) Depression (2.1)

The behavioural approach to explaining phobias p.66–67

One for you to try: (a) Mowrer would say that Stuart has acquired a phobia through classical conditioning. Pain is an unconditioned stimulus that produces an unconditioned response of fear. When the dog was associated with pain (it bit Stuart) it became a conditioned stimulus, and the fear became a conditioned response. Mowrer would explain avoidance behaviour in terms of operant conditioning. By avoiding dog, Stuart's fear is reduced, and is therefore reinforced. This is an example of negative reinforcement.
(b) Watson and Rayner found that Little Albert generalised his fear of the white rat to other objects that were similar to it, such as a fur coat and even Watson wearing a Santa Claus mask. Even though Dave was bitten by a Dalmatian, he is generalising his fear to at least one other breed of dog (Dave's Great Dane).
Research methods: (a) Fear of snakes (b) 6.5 (30.8 − 24.3) (c) 10.5 (34.8 − 24.3) (d) Nominal (data are in separate categories)

The behavioural approach to treating phobias p.68–69

One for you to try: The therapist could begin by teaching Celine how to relax her muscles completely. Celine could be taken to a building similar in height to the Eiffel Tower in order to confront her fear. Over a session of several hours, Celine's adrenalin levels would initially rise but at some point they would decrease. This would allow a new stimulus-response link to be learned, which would be between the feared stimulus and relaxation. When Celine reported no anxiety at the top of the building, she would no longer be phobic and would be free to enjoy her weekend. Hopefully, Celine would not experience so much anxiety that

she was prevented from confronting her fear, but this is an issue with flooding. As with the previous question, a maximum of 2 marks would be awarded for a reasonable description of flooding without any engagement.

Research methods: (a) The results suggest that flooding (76%) is nearly twice as effective as systematic desensitisation (41%) in the treatment of aviophobia.
(b) Since flooding does not use a hierarchy whereas systematic desensitisation does, and given that flooding is much more effective, this suggests that it is not necessary for a hierarchy to be used.
(c) Because flooding involves exposure to an extreme form of the threatening situation, it can be a highly traumatic procedure. People are told of this before the therapy begins, and the findings in the table suggest that more people are put off by the procedures involved in flooding than those involved in systematic desensitisation.

The cognitive approach to explaining depression p.70–71

One for you to try: The activating event (A) in the passage is Becky telling Boris she can't go to the concert with him. The belief (B), which in this case is probably irrational, is that Becky must really hate Boris. The consequence (C) of the irrational belief is Boris being too upset to go to concert himself.

Research methods: (a) One advantage of gaining qualitative data is that it offers the researcher the chance to gain in-depth information that would not be possible with a simple rating scale. For example, the patients receiving CBT could give information about the specific areas in which they felt the greatest improvement.
(b) Factor 1: The different therapies would have been delivered by different therapists. Research has shown that the qualities of the individual therapist are every bit as important as the qualities of the therapies in the study. Therefore these would have a strong effect on any potential outcomes for the patient. Factor 2: Patients may well have been referred to the different types of therapies based on the severity of their symptoms or other factors that would make one type of therapy more suitable than the others. This would also influence the speed at which they would improve, or even the amount of improvement that might be reasonably expected.
(c) One finding is that the level of self-reported improvement of patients with depression who received REBT was greater than for the other two therapies. This suggests that REBT is a more effective treatment for depression than either psychoanalysis or counselling. A second finding is that the level of self-reported improvement of patients with anxiety who received REBT was approximately the same as that reported for the other two therapies. This suggests that all three therapies are moderately and equally effective in the treatment of anxiety.

The cognitive approach to treating depression p.72–73

One for you to try: Irrational belief 1. Sophie believes that she needs to prove her competence all the time. This could be disputed by telling Sophie that she will be happier if she achieves at a realistic level rather than strives for perfection. Irrational belief; 2. Sophie believes that it is a disaster if things don't go the way she wants them to. This could be disputed by telling Sophie that although it is unfortunate when things don't go the way she wants them to it is certainly not catastrophic, and that she can make plans for her life to be as enjoyable as possible. Irrational belief; 3. Sophie believes that she has to be approved by everyone all the time. This could be disputed by telling Sophie that whilst we would all like to be approved by others we do not need such approval.

Research methods: (a) One advantage of gaining qualitative data is that it offers the researcher the chance to gain in-depth information that would not

be possible with a simple rating scale. For example, the patients receiving CBT could give information about the specific areas in which they felt the greatest improvement.
(b) Factor 1: The different therapies would have been delivered by different therapists. Research has shown that the qualities of the individual therapist are every bit as important as the qualities of the therapies in the study. Therefore these would have a strong effect on any potential outcomes for the patient. Factor 2: Patients may well have been referred to the different types of therapies based on the severity of their symptoms or other factors that would make one type of therapy more suitable than the others. This would also influence the speed at which they would improve, or even the amount of improvement that might be reasonably expected.
(c) One finding is that the level of self-reported improvement of patients with depression who received REBT was greater than for the other two therapies. This suggests that REBT is a more effective treatment for depression than either psychoanalysis or counselling. A second finding is that the level of self-reported improvement of patients with anxiety who received REBT was approximately the same as that reported for the other two therapies. This suggests that all three therapies are moderately and equally effective in the treatment of anxiety.

The biological approach to explaining OCD p.74–75

One for you to try: Although people with a first-degree relative with OCD are more likely to develop the disorder than people who do not have a family history of the condition, Leon seems to have forgotten about the role of environmental influences. As well as sharing genes, families also share environments, and it could be that it is the shared family environment which is responsible for other family members developing OCD. Likewise, Andy also seems to have forgotten that as well as sharing their genes, identical twins also typically share environments as well. A further point Allegra could make concerns the concordance rate, which Andy says is 'really high'. It may be, but the concordance rate is not 100%, which means that environmental factors must be playing some role in the cause of OCD.

Research methods: One finding is that there was a greater reduction in the severity of symptoms for participants who took tricyclic drugs compared with those who took SSRI drugs. One conclusion that could be drawn from this finding is that tricyclic drugs are more effective than SSRIs in the treatment of OCD. A second finding is that the reduction in symptoms for participants who took SSRIs was less than for those who were given the placebo. A conclusion that could be drawn from this finding is that any improvement over the three months for those who took SSRIs could be solely due to a placebo effect rather than any effect due to the drug.

The biological approach to treating OCD p.76–77

One for you to try: (a) First, Paul might have told Linda that research shows that drugs are effective in reducing the symptoms of OCD compared with placebos, at least in the short-term. Second, he might have told her that drug therapy requires little effort and time on her part compared with psychological therapies, where she might have to attend regular meetings and put considerable thought into dealing with her problem. Third, Paul could have pointed out the economic benefits of drugs compared with psychological therapies. If Linda was prescribed her drugs, the cost would be much less than if she was referred for psychological therapy.
(b) Caroline might have pointed out to Linda that whilst Paul was right about the short-term benefits of drug therapy, there is little evidence about the long-term benefits of drug therapy. She could also point out that all therapeutic drugs have side effects associated with them,

and that these might be sufficiently unpleasant to cause Linda to stop taking the drugs. Finally, she might make the point that Linda may become physically dependent on the drugs (or addicted to them) and that even if she didn't, the drugs were only masking her condition and not actually curing it.

Research methods: First, the participants were not able to give fully informed consent as they weren't told which group they were in – this is deception. Second, if one treatment was better than another, some of the participants were disadvantaged as they weren't given the best treatment to reduce their OCD symptoms. Third, some drugs have side effects and these could have harmed participants, which is a problem when they were not aware which drug they were taking, as they might not have realised that the side effects were caused by the treatment.

Chapter 5 Approaches in psychology
The origins of psychology p.78–79
Two for you to try: 1. (a) Wundt's methods were inconsistent because he relied on unobservable responses. Participants had to report on their own thought processes, and they might not be honest, or might not be able to identify all the stages of perception as some of it is unconscious.
(b) The behaviourists focused on observable behaviours and did not try to investigate internal mental processes. This meant procedures were replicable and measurement of responses was objective, giving more reliable results.
2. a and b

Research methods: (a) This is a self-report method, and people's responses will be affected by social desirability bias – they may not want to admit their judgemental thoughts as it would make them look bad. Also, being asked to count judgemental thoughts will affect the thoughts they have by prompting them to think in this way, so this will change the number of judgemental thoughts and also affect the reliability.
(b) This procedure could actually increase participants' sexist or judgemental thoughts, which would then cause potential harm to them or to other people they interact with, by leading to discrimination or prejudice. Also the data collected by the student would have issues of confidentiality, as the student would know which of their participants had most judgemental thoughts.

The behaviourist approach p.80–81
One for you to try: When the pigeon pecked the red sign saying 'exit' it was positively reinforced by being rewarded for its behaviour, which meant that it was more likely to repeat this behaviour in the future. When the pigeon pecked the green sign saying 'Do NOT press' it was punished, so the pigeon was unlikely to repeat the behaviour in the future. It would learn to avoid the punishing (harmful) effect of the electric shock.

Research methods: (a) The mean is an appropriate measure of central tendency because it takes into account all of the data, while avoiding extreme scores. In this case there are no extreme scores as the researcher would expect the time to decrease with each trial. (b) Mean = 27 (c) Range = 48 seconds

Social learning theory p.82–83
One for you to try: Mrs Watkins can positively reinforce desired behaviour by praising those children who raise their hands, in front of everyone else. This means that the other children may learn vicariously and also want to receive praise and start acting appropriately, by also raising their hands. She could also use punishment, by giving the children who call out a detention, in front of everyone else. This means that the other children may learn vicariously and want to avoid the punishment of a detention and therefore stop calling out answers.

Research methods: (a) 18
Research methods: (a) 18

(b)

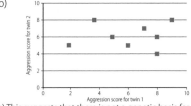

(c) This suggests that there is not a genetic basis for aggression, as there is no clear correlation between the aggression scores of pairs of twins.

The cognitive approach p.84–85
One for you to try: Because of her schemas, Maisie expects things to happen in a particular way in a restaurant. For example she may imagine that she saw the people ordering drinks, then food, then eating, then asking for the bill, even if she hadn't really seen this.
Research methods: (a) 11 and 6 (b) Useful to show the distribution (spread of the score). Indicates the participants in condition 1 are more variable than the participants in condition 2. (c) Independent groups (d) Mann-Whitney: A test of difference, independent groups (unrelated), ordinal level (words may differ in their familiarity or memorability). OR Unrelated t-test: A test of difference, independent groups, interval level (if words have been pre-tested to be equally difficult).

The biological approach p.86–87
One for you to try: Samuel and Daniel have an identical genotype as they are MZ twins. Although, they have the predisposition to develop the same personalities as each other, environment factors will result in the differences found. Their phenotypes are different, possibly because Samuel has engaged with sociable and lively people.

Research methods: As 22 twin pairs had received the same number of detentions, the twins may have had genes which led to poor behaviour. However, 28 twin pairs received different numbers of detentions, indicating that, even if they had the same genotype (sequence of genes) their experiences would be unique and the environment affected their phenotype (observable characteristics) so their behaviour was not identical.

The psychodynamic approach – A Level only zone p.88–89
One for you to try: Sadie's trauma has been repressed into her unconscious but still affects her emotion and behaviour, such as anxiety and difficulty going out. Thinking about and understanding her trauma might help her to develop insight and find better ways to deal with her conflicting emotions, so she can enjoy life more.

Research methods: Finding 1: The graph shows that there was less improvement in terms of symptom reduction for patients undergoing psychoanalysis for the first six months compared to CBT, but at one year psychoanalysis was superior.
Conclusion 1: This suggests that psychoanalysis is more effective in the long term as a treatment for depression, whereas CBT is more effective in the short term. Finding 2: Both psychoanalysis and CBT show more improvement at all three points compared to a placebo group.
Conclusion 2: This shows that there is a real therapeutic benefit to both therapies, as both have been shown to reduce depressive symptoms more effectively than a placebo condition.

Humanistic psychology – A Level only zone p.90–91
One for you to try: The counsellor should take a holistic approach, facilitate Jasmine in solving her own problems – supporting her in moving upwards in Maslow's hierarchy towards self-esteem and self-actualisation – and provide empathy, acceptance and unconditional positive regard to help her to overcome the conditions of worth from parents / broken

relationship.
Research methods: (a) This was a single-blind design, so that the expectations of the researchers didn't affect the participants (demand characteristics). (b) The 'agency' group felt happier than the other group, because they felt more in control of their lives, which fits with Rogers' view that we need to feel self-worth. The control group declined because they felt unable to seek their own self-actualisation and probably felt their self-esteem reduced too (two top levels of Maslow's hierarchy of needs).

Comparison of approaches – A Level only zone p.92–93
One for you to try: (a) Behaviourist: Alex has learned by operant conditioning and been reinforced previously for carrying out experiments successfully, so he wants to repeat this.
Social learning: Alex has observed someone else carrying out successful experiments and being rewarded for this. Vicarious reinforcement has occurred and he want to imitate this.
Cognitive: Alex has a schema about 'science' involving experiments, and as he wants to be a scientist, he must carry out an experiment.
Biological: Alex has a particular biological disposition to carrying out experimental research as it fits his neural pathways which have been built up by extensive experience in his other studies. Maybe he studies science subjects.
Psychodynamic: Alex has experienced some trauma and his unconscious mind is protecting him from anxiety by ensuring that he does not explore any areas of psychology which might bring up emotional memories or conflicts.
Humanistic: Alex has conditions of worth from his parents who he feels approve him based on their view of masculine scientific behaviour, and he needs to prove to them that psychology is a proper science subject by researching experimentally.

Research methods: (a) Similarity: Both consider identification and imitation. Difference: In psychodynamic approach, the unconscious is a main focus whereas in SLT there is emphasis on conscious thought (mediational processes). (b) Similarity: Interactions with the environment or other people affect future behaviour. Difference: Behaviourist approach is deterministic whereas humanistic psychology emphasises free will. (c) Similarity: Both consider stages of development (foetus/child/adult in biological, psychosexual stages in psychodynamic). Difference: Biological is based on scientific evidence and experimental research, whereas psychodynamic is based on untestable claims and interpretation of case studies.

Chapter 6 Biopsychology
The nervous system p.94–95
One for you to try: Sophie becomes very tense when she sees the spider because her brain has identified a threat and sends signals via her sympathetic nervous system (SNS) to her muscles, tensing them up ready for a fight or flight response. Her SNS also stimulates her heart to beat faster and her breathing rate to increase, so she can get more oxygen to her muscles ready for this emergency response. She feels sick because her blood is diverted away from her digestive system. When Charlotte has removed the spider Sophie calms down because her parasympathetic nervous system is activated and restores her to a normal physiological state (rest and digest).

Research methods: (a) Adrenaline levels were a way of operationalising stress, as adrenaline is part of the stress response. (b) To be able to compare, to see if high workload caused stress, or just the working environment at the sawmill, which both groups experienced. (c) As the finishers had higher adrenaline at work than at home, this indicates that their work was making them stressed. The control group was also more stressed at work than at home, so there was an effect of the workplace. But as the finishers' adrenaline was higher than the control group, the higher workload seems to be more stressful than the cleaning or maintenance.

Neurons and synaptic transmission p.96–97

One for you to try: For example, if the researchers stimulated several neurons which all caused an EPSP in the post-synaptic neuron, then spatial or temporal summation mean that an action potential is produced. On the other hand, if they stimulated a combination of neurons some of which caused IPSPs, then the post-synaptic neuron would not fire.

Research methods: (a) For example, One finding: Students who failed maths GCSE used a lot more oxygen in condition 2 than condition 1. This suggests that: They were anxious in condition 2 and therefore their sympathetic nervous system was activated by a stress response, so they used more oxygen. Second finding: Students taking maths A level also used more oxygen in condition 2 than condition 1, but not as much more as the students who failed maths. This suggests that the extra mental effort of performing calculations used more oxygen anyway.
(b) So that they did not have tense muscles which use extra oxygen, so the difference in oxygen use is due to brain activity.
(c) Opportunity sample: visit A level Maths classes and GCSE retake classes in a college and recruit some participants from each.

The endocrine system p.98–99

One for you to try: For example, Sandra's pituitary tumour may be producing excess ACTH. This stimulates production of cortisol in the adrenal cortex, a stress hormone which may increase her blood pressure and make her feel fatigued and anxious when it is present in her blood stream over a long period. This will also slow down healing processes, making her cuts take longer to heal, as it affects the immune system.

Research methods: (a) Conflict causes stress, so the adrenaline and noradrenaline would be released by the adrenal medulla as part of the fight-or-flight response.
(b) An argument in a laboratory is likely to be different from at home, as it may be a stressful environment and the couples would be aware of being observed, so would behave differently from in private, maybe feeling stressed about having a conflict when they were being observed, rather than about the topic being discussed. This means that the results may lack ecological validity.
(c) The couples may have had other strategies to deal with stress at home, such as going for a run, or doing something fun together to defuse the stress. Alternatively, they may have been less self-controlled when they were not being observed, and had a full-out argument, which would have been even more stressful and led to higher stress hormone levels.

The fight-or-flight response p.100–101

One for you to try: For example, Karl seems to have a male aggressive response, which may be due to the SRY gene on his Y chromosome. This causes him to release a lot of adrenaline in response to stress, and he faces up to the group of teenagers. In contrast, Karla freezes, which is a common initial response to a threat. She still has an acute stress response to the threatening group, and the adrenaline in her blood stream cause her to become pale (as blood moves away from her skin) and shake (as her muscles tense up ready to run away).

Research methods: (a) People who volunteer may not be typical of soldiers, for example they may be more interested in talking about their feelings than the average soldier.
(b) A fight response is most common, and the vast majority of veterans had this response at some time. Playing dead is least common, and only a very small number of veterans responded in this way, or admitted to it. Flight is less common than a freeze response.

(c) There is an ethical issue of confidentiality: admitting they had run away (flight) could cause problems for soldiers, as this could be a punishable offence. The researcher would need to promise confidentiality and anonymity. There is another issue of potential harm when veterans remember very stressful and traumatic incidents which could trigger post-traumatic stress. They should be offered therapy to help them deal with their experiences and memories.

Localisation of function p.102–103

One for you to try: For example, the patient may have damage to Broca's area which is where speech production is localised. This means that the stroke has affected the posterior part of the left frontal lobe. His Wernicke's area seems to be unaffected, as he is still able to understand speech.

Research methods: For example, the patient may not be able to give fully informed consent due to the stroke, which may have affected other cognitive functions as well as speech. The researcher should try to obtain consent as far as possible from the patient, but also from his family and should keep all details anonymous.

Lateralisation and split-brain research p.104–105

One for you to try: For example, B.L. sees the cat with her left visual field, and the information from here is processed in the right visual cortex. This information is then restricted to the right hemisphere, so can't be processed into speech as the speech production areas (Broca's area) are in the left hemisphere. However, B.L. can still pick the correct card with her left hand as this is controlled by her right hemisphere. As her right visual field sees the lion, this is processed by her left visual cortex and can be transferred to her speech areas, so she says she's seen a lion.

Research methods: (a) Participants remember different numbers of words heard by their left ear than by their right ear.
(b) Repeated measures. As participants are tested by hearing different word lists with their right and left ear, they may experience interference between the two word lists. This would mean that they may be less accurate in their recall of the second set of words.
(c) 60%
(d) (0, 2, 3, 3, 5, 6, 7, 8, 9, 10) Median = 5.5
(e) ((7+2+4+0+1+7+6+1+2+4)/10) Mean = 3.4

Plasticity and functional recovery of the brain p.106–107

One for you to try: Nick's grandfather is probably at least 60, but even 60-year-olds have some brain plasticity, so he could recover some function. Exercise or physiotherapy could help him develop new neural connections or unmask dormant synapses so that different areas can take over the function of brain areas that were damaged by his stroke, for example the motor cortex regions which are needed for walking.

Research methods: (a) 27.8% (b) Bar chart. (c) Patients with TBI who had more years of education were more likely to achieve DFR.

Ways of studying the brain p.108–109

Two for you to try: 1. (a) EEG would be appropriate for Flora because she has been experiencing seizures, which may be caused by epilepsy, and EEG is very useful for recognising the abnormal brain waves during an epileptic seizure. If the neurologist finds these typical patterns, Flora will have a diagnosis of epilepsy and can be given appropriate drug treatment.
(b) EEG does not pinpoint the exact source of the abnormality, as the electrodes pick up signals from a fairly wide area, so EEG would not enable Flora to have specific surgical treatment on the focus of the seizures, without further investigations. Also, Flora would have to experience a seizure while she is being monitored, which means that if she doesn't have this typical EEG pattern, epilepsy is still not ruled out.
2. 1C, 2D, 3A, 4B

Research methods: For example, HM may not have been able to give fully informed consent to this, as he kept forgetting that he was involved in research. This was dealt with by asking interested parties and family members to give consent, and he did seem to be very enthusiastic about helping people by participating in experiments throughout his lifetime.

Circadian rhythms p.110–111

One for you to try: For example, Katie seems to be a 'morning person' whereas Jack is an 'evening person'. These individual differences may be innate or learnt, and they could try to adjust their sleep patterns by making sure they get out in the light together during the day so their sleep-wake cycles are affected by the light in the same way. They could also try keeping their bedroom cool as temperature also affects the body clock.

Research methods: (a) A line graph. (b) The findings show that the body temperature is lowest at 4 am and highest at 6 pm. There is more variation in temperatures (shown by the higher standard deviation) at 8am and around 8pm, which could be caused by different activity levels of participants at those times.

Ultradian and infradian rhythms p.112–113

One for you to try: Mr Walker could make sure that the timetable allows students to take a break every 90 minutes, to fit in with their 90-minute ultradian cycle of alertness and fatigue. He could also consider shorter college days in the winter as many people are affected by the seasons in annual rhythms.

Research methods: (a) There is less than 5% chance of this difference representing a real difference in the data between births during a full moon or a new moon. This is very unlikely, so the belief of the midwives is not supported by the evidence.
(b) The peer review would examine the research to see if it is original and worthwhile for publication. The reviewers would check the validity of methodology and statistical analysis to ensure only valid conclusions are published. This makes sure that published research can be relied on by the public or other researchers.

Endogenous pacemakers and exogenous zeitgebers p.114–115

One for you to try: Jade should make use of the exogenous zeitgebers of light and social cues to reset her biological clock. She could do this before she flies east from Chicago by making sure she is exposed to bright light during the day to shift her sleep-wake cycle a bit. When she gets back home she should go outside early in the day, to be exposed to warm daylight so that her retinal melanopsin-containing cells send signals to the suprachiasmatic nucleus that it is now daytime. She should also socialise during the day and not at night time, so that the social cues help to reset her endogenous pacemakers.

Research methods: (a) This is a field experiment because the children are being tested in their own homes, rather than being brought into a sleep lab. The children will be in their own beds with their normal bedtime routine. This is much less disruptive to their lives.
(b) A strength is that a field experiment tests the effect of changing the IV (light) in the children's own homes so there is good mundane realism, and therefore the experiment has ecological validity and applies to children's normal lives. A limitation is that other variables are not controlled, such as whether the children changed their routine in other ways because of the light difference, such as reading more or playing more on screens.
(c) The children's sleep may be affected by different light levels, which could cause harm. The researcher should ensure that parents know that if their children are being adversely affected by lack of sleep, they can withdraw them from the study and replace their normal curtains.

(d) The design is independent groups, which means that different children are experiencing the two conditions. Individual differences, such as normal sleep patterns or insomnia, could affect the results. A repeated measures design could deal with this as each child would take part in both conditions, doing the second one three months later, and the order of conditions could be counterbalanced so that half had blackout blinds first and the other half had thin curtains first.

Chapter 7 Research methods
The experimental method p.116
One for you to try: For example, (a) The aim is to see whether rewards affect performance. (b) IV = receiving £1 or not for doing the test, DV = score on the test. (c) Children who are offered £1 achieve higher scores on the test than those who receive nothing. (d) Directional hypothesis. (e) The children who got the reward might be smarter anyway. Therefore they would do better on the test, not because they got the reward but because they were smarter and this would confound the results. (f) One strength is the experimenter could repeat this study if he had controlled all the variables carefully such as using the same test and the same reward to see if the results were reliable. One limitation is that the situation was contrived so the children might have behaved differently to how they would behave when tested at school – they probably wouldn't be offered money so it isn't very realistic.
Research methods: Kerry's answer: 1 + 1 mark (neither variable is operationalised).
Megan's answer: 1 + 0 marks (second answer is not a variable).
Rohan's answer: 2 + 2 marks (both variables are operationalised)

Control of variables p.117
One for you to try: 1D, 2C, 3A, 4B

Return to hypotheses and other things p.118–119
Five for you to try: 1. a. The strategy used to learn words (A or B) affects the number of words recalled. b. Because no previous research is mentioned. c. The experiment was only carried out on children, so the findings cannot be generalised to adult learners – this would be a problem of population validity. The children may already learn French, or some may be native French speakers, so their learning of French words may relate to other skills and strategies that they already possess, there is no guarantee that they were actually using strategy A and B – this is a problem of internal validity.

2. A and C

3. 1C, 2B, 3A, 4E, 5D, 6F

4. D

5. A: 0 marks – this is not a pilot study as the researchers have used all the participants. B: 1 mark – correct but not applied to this investigation. C: 2 marks – good suggestion of a reason for carrying out a pilot study in this investigation.

Experimental design p.120–121
Three for you to try: 1. a) There are different people in each condition of the experiment, (e.g., left-handed in one condition and right-handed in the other condition) so each participant carries out the creativity test once. b) Because people are either righthanded or left-handed; they can't be in both groups. Right-handed and left-handed people are being compared: this is the IV. c) A strength is that there are no order effects, so participants do not get bored and perform worse in the creativity test, or improve through practice. A weakness is that participant effects act as a confounding variable, so there may happen to be people in one group who are more experienced in these type of creativity test and will perform better for that reason rather than because of their right- or left-handedness. This makes it difficult to draw valid conclusions about the effect of the IV on the DV. d) There will be a difference in the performance of right-handed and left-handed people in a creativity test.

2. 1E, 2A, 3B, 4F, 5D, 6C

3. The repeated measures design removes participant effects, which would be a problem with an independent groups design, and could be caused by different individuals having different tolerances for caffeine. It means that each participant's results are compared before and after drinking coffee, so they act as their own control in the experiment, rather than being compared with different participants.

Laboratory and field experiments p.122
Two for you to try: 1. C
2. (a) (b) (c)

Natural and quasi-experiments p.123
One for you to try: 1. (a) IV – watch TV more than five hours a day or not. DV – aggression ratings. (b) natural experiment. (c) People have chosen whether to watch a lot of TV or not, they have not been put into groups, so the IV was not manipulated by the researcher. It was a study of their behaviour in a natural environment. (d) It is likely to have low validity as the groups were self-selecting, so people who watch more TV may already be more aggressive; or people who watch a lot of TV don't have time to be aggressive. This means other variables are confounding the findings.

More problems with experiments p.124–125
Three for you to try:

1. (a)

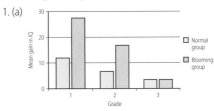

(b) The teachers' expectations made a huge difference to children's progress in grade 1, as they made more than twice as much gains in IQ when teachers believed they had high scores for intellectual blooming. In grade 2 the 'high score' group also did much better than normal children. However, by grade 3 the teachers' expectations didn't make any difference. Overall, children made most progress when they were younger anyway.

2. For example, the individuals who were asked to take part in an experiment thought there must be some scientific purpose to the request, so they were willing to cooperate without knowing more – maybe they knew that researchers can't always tell you the purpose before the experiment takes place. People who were just asked to perform press-ups without being told it was for an experiment, but just for a favour, didn't see the purpose and were amazed. This shows how demand characteristics might arise in an experimental setting, as people are generally willing to cooperate with the project of Science.

3. C

Sampling p.126–127
Three for you to try: 1. For example, (a) Could be any of the 3 methods plus an explanation of how, e.g. one method would be an opportunity sample. You could just go up to people in the street and ask them how many calls they make per day and also rate their friendliness. (b) Strength as appropriate to part (a) but should include some context related to the stem as the question says '… in this study', e.g. this is the easiest method you could do because you can straight away go get your 30 people in the street rather than waiting for volunteers or contacting a random sample. (c) Independent groups. (d) Mobile phone use (1 mark), number of calls per day (1 mark for operationalisation). (e) It is a natural experiment because the IV has not been controlled by the experimenter. People are put in categories according to their existing behaviour.

2. Dylan's answer = 3 out of 3 marks (Dylan has provided one strength and one criticism, each with some elaboration). Carrie's answer = 2 out of 3 marks (first sentence not really an evaluation, second sentence is a criticism with some elaboration). Charlotte's answer = 1 out of 3 marks (mention of 'bias' gains one mark, the rest is not relevant).

3. Opportunity sample: C D
Volunteer sample: B E
Random sample: A F

Ethical issues p.128
Two for you to try: 1. Participants could have had more accurate briefing so they knew what to expect; to avoid harm, an objective observer could have stopped the study or given the participants the option of withdrawing when they appeared distressed; closed circuit tv could have been used to monitor the participants; they could have been given a means of recording their feelings so that their level of distress could be assessed on a daily basis.
2. B

Dealing with ethical issues p.129
One for you to try: 1. For example, (a) It is a laboratory experiment because the IV is age and this has not been manipulated by the researcher. (b) If you used repeated measures you would have to use the same participants as children and adults and have to wait a long time. (c) One issue is deception and another issue is informed consent. She could deal with deception by debriefing participants at which time she would tell them the real aims and might offer that they could withhold their data. She would discuss any concerns they had. A second issue is informed consent. She would deal with this by seeking some outline consent before the study began, especially to gain consent from the children's parents. She would give an outline of what will be involved (e.g. tell them they would be watching a film of a robbery and answering a questionnaire). (Other options: confidentiality, or psychological harm)

Observational techniques p.130
One for you to try: Study A (a) controlled (b) overt (c) nonparticipant (d) yes, because parents gave consent and the study was stopped if children became unduly distressed. Study B (a) naturalistic (b) overt (c) non-participant (d) yes, as participants gave consent and were in normal everyday situation. Study C (a) naturalistic (b) covert (c) non-participant (d) Yes, as long as consent was obtained from parents, as children were in their normal situation. Study D (a) naturalistic (b) covert (c) non-participant (d) maybe not, as privacy was being invaded and he could not get any retrospective consent for using data. Study E (a) naturalistic (b) covert (c) participant (d) yes, as long as they gained consent retrospectively to use the data. Or no, as they were deliberately deceiving psychiatrists and other staff.

Observational design p.131
Three for you to try: 1. For example, (a) Avoiding a stranger (stranger anxiety), closeness to mother on her return (reunion behaviour). (b) The observations may not be reliable because the observer may misinterpret a behaviour and think a child was avoiding someone when they might have been playing a game. (c) It means you can arrange the setting to be able to test what you are interested in, such as arranging for the stranger to come and go.

2. D

3. The conversations may contain private details, and the young people would not expect their conversations to be recorded, so there is an issue of privacy. He could ask for retrospective consent, and promise confidentiality and anonymity.

Self-report techniques p.132
Two for you to try: 1. For example, (a) The psychologist might want to check whether the questions for the children were easy to understand and

could also check the standardised instructions are clear. (b) The psychologist can give the questionnaire out to a lot of children so you get a lot of replies to analyse. If you were conducting interviews each would take a lot more time than questionnaires which would reduce the number of participants that could be involved. (c) It might be better to use an interview so you could encourage the children to elaborate and explain their answers about their experiences of day care. Children also might find it difficult to write their answers down so an interview would be better.

2. B

Self-report design p.133
One for you to try: (a) For example: For how many years have you smoked? – 0 1 2 3 4 5 6 more than 6. (closed question). What do you dislike about smoking? (open question). (b) (P)The interviewer should be careful to be neutral, (E) not showing any response which might increase social desirability effects, (E) such as seeming to disapprove of smoking. They must be careful with their tone of voice and facial expression, (L) so that their behaviour does not affect the responses that the interviewee gives. (c) 'Do you think smoking is really disgusting?'

Correlations p.134–135
Three for you to try: 1. For example, (a) Ask teachers to rate each child on a scale of 1 to 10 where 10 is very aggressive. (b) There is a correlation between hours spent in day care per week and aggressiveness rating. (c) A correlational analysis only demonstrates a relationship, it cannot tell us whether one variable caused the change in the other. In this case whether day care caused aggressiveness.

2. For example, it would be appropriate to use a pilot study to check that key aspects of the design worked. For example, to check the standardised instructions are clear enough for the participants (the parents or teachers who are rating the children's aggressiveness) to understand what they are required to do. Also to check the method of assessing how many hours a week children were in nursery to see if the method was reliable

3. 1A, 2E, 3D, 4B, 5F, 6C

Other research methods p.136–137
Three for you to try: 1. For example, (a) They might use psychological tests to assess the emotional development of some of the children who had been there. (b) They might use a volunteer sample where they advertise for an institution who would be willing to take part.

2. For example, (a) One technique would be interviewing. The psychologists would interview people arrested for rioting and also people who had been affected. (b) One limitation would be that people don't tell the truth, especially the people who had committed crimes, who would try to put themselves in a good light (social desirability bias). The people affected might also not tell the truth, they might exaggerate the effect the riots had had. Another limitation would be that it is retrospective recall and people don't always remember past events accurately. (c) One strength is the rich detail that could be collected, which might give new insights into rioting behaviour and change our views about the causes and effects of rioting.

3. 1E, 2C, 3I, 4A, 5F, 6B, 7K, 8D, 9G, 10J, 11H

Mathematical skills p.138–139
Three for you to try: 1. (a) 8/40 = 0.2 = 20%
b) 16/40 = 0.4 = 40%
c) 20 observations of each adult in 10 minutes = 30 second intervals.

---

2. (a) 37.5% = 38% to 2sf (b) There are fewer girls than boys. (c) 2/100 = 1/50 (d) For example: 4200 ÷ 42 = 100 (e) 9 (f) 0.25 ×(72 + 72) = 36 (g) 0.1 × (96 × 3) = 28.8 = 29 to 2sf

3. 1/10 = 0.1 = 10%, 1/25 = 0.04 = 4%, 3/16 = 0.1875 = 18.75%, 1/8 = 0.125 = 12.5%, ½ = 0.5 = 50%, 83/150 = 0.55 (to 2sf) = 55% (to 2sf)

Measures of central tendency and dispersion p.140–141
Two for you to try: 1. (a) (72 + 67 + 61 + 55 + 56 + 34 + 39 + 43) ÷ 8 = 53.4% to 3sf (b) For example, standard deviation as it takes into account all of the data but is not affected by extreme values. (c) A line graph.

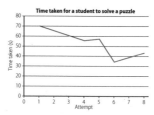

Time taken for a student to solve a puzzle

Horizontal axis = attempt, vertical axis = time taken. (d) The student got faster up to the 6th attempt, which was probably due to learning, as the puzzles are similar. The student then got slower for the last two attempts, which may have been due to tiredness or boredom.

2. The mean number of words recalled in condition 1 is higher than in condition 2, so participants recall more words in the same room than a different room. The standard deviation is also higher for condition 1 than condition 2, which shows the spread of data is greater in condition 1, so there is more variability between participants recalling in the same room than those recalling in a different room.

Display of quantitative data and data distributions p.142–143
Two for you to try: 1. A

2. A: bar chart B: histogram or frequency polygon C: scattergram D: bar chart E: frequency polygon or grouped bar chart

Types of data p.144–145
Three for you to try: 1. B, C

2. (a) (i) Describe behaviour, use photos or video clips to demonstrate different examples of aggressive behaviour, for example pushing, or aggressive facial expressions. (ii) Make a tally chart of behavioural categories, for example hitting, pushing, and use time sampling to tally each behaviour. (b) Qualitative data gives a rich description of behaviours, and allows for the recording of unexpected behaviours, but it does not give a representation of how frequent they were. Quantitative data is useful for comparing frequencies of different behaviours in individual children but does not indicate how important they were, what led up to them, or how other children responded. Also any unexpected behaviours which do not fit into an existing category will be missed out of the analysis. Quantitative data is more suitable to address the hypothesis about boys playing more aggressively, as 'more' suggests a quantitative comparison. (It would also be valid to argue for qualitative data, with a suitable reason.)

3. (e) Primary data from his 40 thieves research, and secondary data from other psychologists' studies of disturbed children.

Introduction to statistical testing p.146–147
One for you to try: (a) Hypothesis: People will lose weight in three months on this slimming programme.
(b) - - + - - 0 - + - -
(c) S=2
(d) N=9
(e) critical value of S = 1.
(f) This is not significant.
(g) Yes, as most people lost weight
(h) The hypothesis cannot be accepted as S was not significant.

The scientific process and peer review p.148–149
Three for you to try: 1 a. For example: 1 Poor methodology; 2 controversial findings; 3 a replication study.

b. 1 Improves its validity; 2 Reduces its validity; 3 May not affect its conclusions but weaker statistical analysis as sample size is smaller than it would be.

2. D

3. There may have been demand characteristics, as Zimbardo was in the role of prison superintendent, so 'guards' would have behaved in the way they thought he expected them to. Also, the sample was restricted to young, white males and may not represent other members of the population. Zimbardo should have stayed out of the situation and used independent observers to monitor it. He should have used a broader range of participants, to represent females, different ethnic groups and older people too.

Psychology and the economy p.150–151
Two for you to try: 1. For example: citizens are not aware that they are being influenced by the Nudge Unit, so this could be said to be an invasion of privacy or autonomy of individuals, with a lack of consent. They are unelected and people may not like the idea that they are being influenced without their knowledge by psychologists and economists. On the other hand, people are constantly influenced by advertisers without realising, and the Nudge Unit was appointed by an elected government in order to improve society as a whole. There is substantial evidence of positive outcomes which benefit individuals via improving the economy. There should be safeguards in place, and the Nudge Unit should be accountable to a disinterested Ethics Committee for their actions.

2. (a)

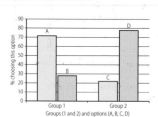

(b) Conclusion: The way that the statements were framed (positive or negative) affected people's choice of treatments, so positive framing persuaded people to choose treatment A rather than B, and negative framing caused them to choose D rather than C, even though the outcomes were exactly the same.